Blockchain for Business

T0292971

This book discusses the up-and-coming blockchain technology in a structured way from the conceptual, technological, and business perspectives, thereby providing the integrated insight that is essential for truly understanding blockchain applications and their impact. While most people may know about blockchain from Bitcoin and news about its price in the financial markets, blockchain is a technology that increasingly permeates the way in which modern businesses operate. However, its dynamics and functioning remain obscure for most people. This book gives readers the tools to understand the full extent to which blockchain technology is or can be used in business. First, the book focuses on the functioning of blockchain systems, introducing basic concepts such as transactions, consensus mechanisms, and smart contracts, as well as giving a smooth introduction to the basic features of cryptography that underpin blockchain technology, e.g., digital signatures and hashing. Then, the book focuses on specific blockchain platforms (Bitcoin, Ethereum, private blockchain platforms) currently used for the implementation of cryptocurrencies and other blockchain systems. Finally, it introduces a set of tools to understand and analyze the suitability of blockchain technology in different business scenarios from the business model, and business operation perspectives. Examples and case studies of blockchain applications currently in production are discussed extensively across the book. This book targets students and educators with an interest in blockchain technology providing a one-stop shop to obtain a deep and complete insight in blockchain technology and its applicability in different business scenarios. The textbook is designed primarily for third and fourth year undergraduate students in industrial engineering, business and management, and information systems. However, it can be adopted also in the computer science majors, since it does not strictly require any specific pre-requisite knowledge. At the graduate level, this book can be used in courses for industrial engineering, information systems, and management students. Finally, the book is also of interest to practitioners, like business analysts, process analysts, and information system architects, to understand the enabling and transformative potential of blockchain in a given business scenario.

Marco Comuzzi is Associate Professor and Director of the Blockchain Research Center at the Ulsan National Institute of Science and Technology in Korea since 2016.

Paul Grefen is Senior Full Professor at Eindhoven University of Technology in the Netherlands since 2003 and Principal Architect at Eviden Digital Transformation Consulting since 2020.

Giovanni Meroni is Assistant Professor at Technical University of Denmark (DTU) since 2022.

Blockchain for Business

IT Principles into Practice

Marco Comuzzi, Paul Grefen, and Giovanni Meroni

LONDON AND NEW YORK

Designed cover image: © Getty Images

First published 2023
by Routledge
4 Park Square, Milton Park, Abingdon, Oxon OX14 4RN

and by Routledge
605 Third Avenue, New York, NY 10158

Routledge is an imprint of the Taylor & Francis Group, an informa business

British Library Cataloguing-in-Publication Data
A catalogue record for this book is available from the British Library

Library of Congress Cataloging-in-Publication Data
Names: Comuzzi, Marco, author. | Grefen, Paul, author. |
Meroni, Giovanni, author.
Title: Blockchain for business : it principles into practice /
Marco Comuzzi, Paul Grefen and Giovanni Meroni.
Description: 1 Edition. | New York, NY : Routledge, 2023. |
Includes bibliographical references and index. |
Identifiers: LCCN 2022061444 (print) | LCCN 2022061445 (ebook) |
ISBN 9781032342481 (hardback) | ISBN 9781032342467 (paperback) |
ISBN 9781003321187 (ebook)
Subjects: LCSH: Business—Data processing. | Blockchains (Databases)—
Industrial applications. | Database management.
Classification: LCC HF5548.2 .C596 2023 (print) | LCC HF5548.2 (ebook) |
DDC 650.0285—dc23/eng/20221222
LC record available at https://lccn.loc.gov/2022061444
LC ebook record available at https://lccn.loc.gov/2022061445

ISBN: 9781032342481 (hbk)
ISBN: 9781032342467 (pbk)
ISBN: 9781003321187 (ebk)

DOI: 10.4324/9781003321187

Typeset in Bembo
by codeMantra

Contents

Preface

The book that you are holding fulfils a primary need of the authors: finding an appropriate textbook for our courses on digital transformation using blockchain. While there are excellent books focusing on the technical implementation aspects of specific blockchains, such as Bitcoin or Ethereum, or looking at blockchain from a software engineering or financial engineering perspective, we have struggled to find a book taking a 'design science' standpoint on blockchain: providing sufficient explanation of the technical details in order to understand how blockchain can be used to address specific business needs in the real world. This is exactly the objective of this book.

For students, we hope that this book serves a twofold objective. First, helping you to shed some light on the inner functioning of a new technology like blockchain, in its different forms. Second, allowing you to critically assess whether blockchain is an appropriate solution for a (new or existing) business scenario.

For professionals, depending on your background, this book will also serve diverse needs. If you come from a business-oriented background, then this book helps you to understand the technical details behind a technology that is increasingly adopted in the corporate world. If your background concerns more the software design and implementation, this book helps you find suitable business applications for a technology that you may know deeply only from a technical standpoint, but for which you have struggled to grasp the usefulness in the practical world.

No matter what your background is, our objective is to give you the tools to evaluate the potential of blockchain critically and fairly. In fact, while the world is populated by many blockchain 'maximalists', who think blockchain is the solution to everything, and blockchain 'minimalists', who think blockchain is only cryptocurrency, and cryptocurrency is only a global scam, in this book we take a balanced and critical perspective on the impact of blockchain on modern, digitally supported and digitally enabled business. Our Latin ancestors, unsurprisingly, used to say that 'in medio stat virtus', or more precisely, 'virtus est medium vitiorum et utrimque reductum' ('virtue is the middle between two vices, and is equally removed from either extreme', Horace, Epistole, I, 18, 9).

Finally, for educators, we are sure that many of you have also felt the lack of books addressing blockchain technology from a design science perspective. This lack prompted us to write this book in the first place. Hence, we hope you find this book useful, primarily as a one-stop shop for everything related to blockchain in your teaching. We also hope that you can appreciate our effort to strike a balance between academic depth and practical applicability while discussing different aspects of blockchain.

Marco Comuzzi, Paul Grefen, and Giovanni Meroni

Acknowledgments

Many people in academia and industry as well as many of our students have contributed, often unknowingly, to shaping the content of this book through numerous conversations during lectures, or at conferences and project meetings. Baris Ozkan of Eindhoven University of Technology and Pierluigi Plebani of Politecnico di Milano are thanked for their helpful feedback on the manuscript. The anonymous reviewers of the proposal for this book are also thanked for their feedback and suggestions. The publishing team at Routledge is thanked for the pleasant and reliable cooperation, even during 'Covid19-ridden' times. Finally, we are thankful to our partners, families, and friends for their support during the development of this book.

Marco Comuzzi, Paul Grefen, and Giovanni Meroni

Part I

Blockchain basics – the mechanisms that make blockchain work

The first part of this book faces the challenge of introducing the concept of blockchain. Because of its novelty and multidisciplinary aspects, introducing blockchain to students is challenging, irrespective of their background, whether more technical or more business-oriented. In this book, we decided to tackle this challenge by (i) first presenting blockchain as a general mechanism, abstracting from any specific implementation of it, and (ii) separating the presentation of the blockchain mechanism from the technical details of the core technology enabling it, i.e., cryptographic tools. As a result, in the first part, you find three chapters (Chapters 1, 3, and 4) that introduce the blockchain mechanism in an abstract way, and a separate one (Chapter 2) that focuses on the cryptographic tools underpinning blockchain.

More elaborately, Chapter 1 introduces the basic concepts of blockchain using an example drawn from the world of e-sports. It is then concluded by a discussion on how this book is structured and how it should be used. After having introduced the cryptographic tools of blockchain in Chapter 2, Chapter 3 gives a more detailed and formal characterization of the blockchain mechanism. Finally, Chapter 4 extends the definition of blockchain given in Chapter 3 by introducing the concept of blockchain smart contracts.

DOI: 10.4324/9781003321187-1

1 A gentle introduction to the world of blockchain

Learning goals

1.A The reader can discuss the notion of trust as a basic premise of asset and information exchange.

1.B The reader can explain the fundamental elements of a blockchain and how these establish trust among business actors who do not trust each other.

1.C The reader can demonstrate how blockchain can be used to support information exchange in a simple e-sport scenario.

1.D The reader can explain the structure of this book and understands how it can be used by readers with different backgrounds and learning objectives.

1.1 What is blockchain?

One of hardest questions that students ask to a teacher is actually a very simple one: 'What is blockchain?' In this initial chapter of this book, we answer this question in two steps.

The first step (see Section 1.2) concerns understanding the concept of trust and how it underpins the exchange of assets among economic agents. The mechanisms supporting asset exchange can be designed in different ways to support varying levels of trust. Assets can be anything like money, goods, or valuable information. In a digital world, an asset is represented by data in a digital format that prove the characteristics of that asset. There are many kinds of characteristics, but ownership of an asset is obviously a very important one. The exchange of this kind of data represents business transactions, which require a basis for trust. The issue of trust and, more specifically, how it can be created and maintained, is one of the fundamental drivers of blockchain technology. It is also the reason why this technology has been considered revolutionary. To understand the concept of trust and how mechanisms can be designed to enable it, we use the example of different forms that money has assumed throughout history.

In the second step (see Section 1.3), we move from the concept of trust to the mechanism to create and support it. To do so, we introduce a simple example system that is constructed using the basic functionality associated with blockchain. This is a fictitious online system for e-sports (online gaming). Online gaming is a booming industry attracting the interest of people of all ages and investors alike. The increasing economic interests around this industry call for mechanisms to improve the trust regarding the

DOI: 10.4324/9781003321187-2

execution of games among the stakeholders, like gaming platforms, players, advertisers, and the audience. To keep the example understandable, we consider the game of chess, i.e., a game that everybody has played or at least has heard of at least once in their life. We call this system BC4C (Blockchain for Chess). Using this example, we show in depth what it means to build a blockchain or, in better terms, to design an application based on blockchain that addresses a specific (business) goal. This example also helps us to realize that blockchain implementation relies on several specific technologies, like networking and distributed systems, databases, and, most importantly, cryptography.

1.2 Money, trust, and design choices

Markets, as the locus of economic exchange of goods or services, existed well before the emergence of what we call money today (see Figure 1.1). In fact, in ancient times, but still even today in many niche scenarios, economic exchange took the form of bartering. A fisherman and a butcher, for instance, would meet on a Sunday morning on the market square of their village to exchange goods: the fisherman would bring fish, the butcher would bring meat. If they wanted and they agreed, they could exchange a fish for a steak. In this way, the butcher's family could have fish stew on Sunday night, while the fisherman could enjoy a steak before the start of yet another week of hard work at sea.

The essence of such an exchange is the reciprocal trust in the value of the fish and the steak that are exchanged: both the fisherman and the butcher can inspect the fish and the steak that they are about to exchange (for instance, the weight, appearance, and freshness) to establish that the fish and the steak have the same value and, therefore, can be exchanged for one another. Obviously, bartering only works well if two parties want each other's goods and if these goods have the same value. If the butcher wants vegetables instead of a fish, the exchange is much harder: he must assume that he can find a farmer that wants to exchange the fish in return for vegetable produce (which puts the butcher in a bad negotiation position, as he obviously doesn't want the fish).

To solve this issue, a more flexible way to regulate the exchange of goods and services emerged very early on in ancient times. It involved the invention of 'money'. Money can be defined as any item or verifiable record generally acceptable as a form of payment [Dav02]. The initial common form of money is the so-called commodity money. The value of this money comes from the commodity – usually a precious metal – of which it is made. Typical examples of commodity money are the golden and silver coins

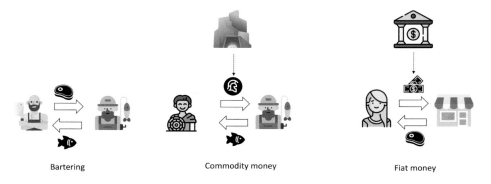

Bartering   Commodity money   Fiat money

Figure 1.1 Different forms of means to regulate value exchange across history.

coined by the Roman empire or sought by pirates across the seven seas. Also in this case, trust is what makes the commodity money a viable mechanism to regulate economic exchanges: the commodity of which money is made is universally trusted to be scarce and durable and, therefore, of a high value to whoever owns it. Hence, golden or silver coins can be used to regulate an economic exchange of goods or services deemed of the same value. As everybody wants these coins, we do not have the problem discussed before of a butcher stuck with a fish that he does not want.

Finally, we get to modern times, in which we need even more flexibility to make economic exchanges. We are not used to carrying around physical goods (like fish or steaks) to be exchanged for other ones, nor golden or silver coins. Rather, we carry with us paper notes that have an almost null intrinsic value (indeed, what is the actual value of the paper and ink used to print a US dollar note?), but that can still be used in economic exchanges. Or even more extreme, we carry with us cheap plastic cards with a small electronic chip that we do not exchange at all. We simply use these to provide evidence that we own the money required to purchase the goods or services in some bank account. These are the currently well-known debit and credit cards (which would highly confuse the fisherman and the butcher of our first example). While these cards are more convenient and safer to use, they introduce a problem that we do not have with fish, steaks, golden coins, or banknotes: the authentication of the owner. Identifying the owner of a fish or a banknote is trivial: the owner is simply the one that has these assets with them when the economic exchange takes place (obviously these may have been stolen by their current owner, but hey, no system is perfect!). In the case of debit/credit cards, the challenge of authenticating the owner is however deeper. Since the cards are linked to a bank account, every time they are used there must be a mechanism in place to securely and reliably verify that the identity of the owner of the card matches the one of the owners of the bank account to which the card is linked. This obviously requires authentication by the carrier of a card and safe storage of the account details by a bank.

What gives value to this modern form of money? Also in this case, it is the establishment of a trust mechanism. This modern form of money, in fact, is called 'fiat' money. Fiat is a Latin word that we can roughly translate into 'let it be': money has value because some entity that is trusted by all people 'lets this exist'. The entity that usually gives value to fiat money is a nation-state (or a union thereof in the case of the European Union and the Euro currency). The state prints the notes and mints the coins via its central bank and establishes that these are so-called 'legal tender', i.e., they are accepted legally to regulate economic exchanges. In other words, money as legal tender means that a nation-state always accepts this money from its citizen for paying taxes. This creates the circle of trust that is required for the circulation of this form of money. People accept to be paid for their labor by their employer using this money because they are able to use it to pay taxes; shops accept it from their customers because, again, they are able to use it to pay taxes; and so forth. Obviously, this mechanism can work only if the nation-state issuing the money can be trusted. No one, in fact, is eager to own money issued by countries that are, for instance, politically unstable or engaged in long-standing wars with their neighbors.

A similar trust-establishing mechanism is behind many other forms of 'private' currencies that we commonly use, possibly even on a daily basis. One such example is the use of meal vouchers for a student cafeteria on a university campus. Meal vouchers have value as long as they are exchanged among actors who trust their value. A student may use a meal voucher to have lunch, but also to repay a debt that he has with a friend attending the same university. This works because this friend also trusts that it will be possible to buy lunch with that voucher at the university's cafeteria. However, the same voucher is of no value if used outside the university context. No restaurant outside the university campus accepts the voucher. Consequently, nobody trusts the voucher to have any value outside the university campus. In other words, the university is the 'third party' or the 'central authority' that, similarly to nation- states in the case of fiat money, issues and guarantees the value of the meal vouchers.

The newest incarnation of money is that of cryptocurrencies, like Bitcoin. This kind of money does not need to be regulated by a third party, like a nation-state or a university. Its value is instead established by the users of the money and by the technological platform that they use to exchange the money. To really understand this kind of money (e.g., its creation, ownership, and exchange), we need to understand more about blockchain. Hence, we will return to this kind of money later in this book. Blockchain is in fact the mechanism behind cryptocurrencies.

To summarize, what have we learned from this brief analysis of different forms of money?

1   That economic exchange depends on trust. Therefore, the value of the means used to regulate an economic exchange is established through a trust-based mechanism.
2   That different design choices can be made regarding the design of different forms of money to establish trust.

We have discussed above four different ways through which people can trust the value of money:

a   The trust in the goods that are physically exchanged in a barter trade (the goods are the money themselves).
b   The trust in the value of the commodity of which the money is made in the case of commodity money.
c   The trust in the institution that issues the fiat money, such as nation-states in the case of world currencies or the university in the case of meal vouchers.
d   The trust in the blockchain mechanism through which cryptocurrencies are implemented.

In Table 1.1 we show the development of the exchange mechanisms discussed above. It starts with (1) the physical exchange of valuable objects (like meat or fish) which does not need to be regulated by an authority. The development continues with (2) precious coins, which do have an intrinsic value (like the gold used to make them) but are often issued by an authority (like the Roman emperor) that vows for their status or quality, which we call semi-regulation here. The next step is that of (3) physical exchange of fiat money, which requires full regulation by a central authority. When we remove the physical exchange, we get to (4) exchange by credit/debit cards, which also requires full regulation. A development that we have not discussed before is that of (5) community virtual currencies (like currencies in virtual gaming worlds), which we characterize as semi-regulated: there is a regulator, but this is not a formal authority. The final step in the development is that of (6) cryptocurrencies, which do not need a regulation by a central authority nor any physical exchange.

Table 1.1 Development of different forms of money through time

	Non-regulated by central authority	Semi-regulated by central authority	Regulated by central authority
Physical exchange	(1) Valuable objects	(2) Precious coins	(3) Non-precious coins paper bills
Non-physical exchange	(6) Crypto currencies	(5) Community virtual currencies	(4) Debit cards, credit cards

In the next section, we generalize the issue of trust in regulating economic exchanges to the case of information exchanges. In the modern age, data and information are extremely valuable assets [BWW+07], increasingly available natively in digital form. Because of its value, citizens and organizations strive to protect their personal information. At the same time, the ownership of data and information can accrue immense profits to any organization (for instance for marketing, or generally to gain a competitive advantage). To be effective and efficient, a mechanism for information exchange should address the same issues that we have identified above for money, such as value determination, ownership, or ownership authentication. That is, business actors exchanging information should be supported by a trust mechanism. The most straightforward way to implement trust is again to rely on a central authority. However, the blockchain mechanism can help us to support business actors while exchanging information without relying on a central authority.

As an example, the next section considers the scenario of e-sports, i.e., (professional) competitions using video games. E-sports can be abstracted as scenarios where a number of actors (the players) need to exchange valuable information (the moves that they want to play in a game) to achieve a business goal (winning a game).

1.3 Defining blockchain by example: playing chess with blockchain

E-sports are a (professional) form of competition using video games. They normally involve online multi-player video games often played at a global level. The global market of e-sports was valued slightly above 1 billion USD in 2021 and it is poised to grow above 2.8 billion in 2025 at a CAGR (Compound Aggregate Growth Rate) of more than 20% [NXW+22]. The value of this market derives first from marketing activities and game sales. This is due to the sheer amount of interest that e-sports generates in the public, especially in the younger audience. However, a large share of this market also can be generated by gambling, i.e., placing bets on the outcome of games and competitions.

As introduced before, for the objectives of this book, an e-sport online game can be abstracted into the following simple settings: a number of business actors competing with each other to win a game. Playing the game means exchanging information regarding the moves that the players are willing to execute in a game. Regulating this information exchange can be fairly complex, depending on the rules of the game. The rules of an online game in fact are usually more complex than the rules regulating an economic exchange using money. When using money, basically we simply must produce reliable evidence that we have enough money for our purpose (i.e., buying a product or sending some money to a friend). When playing a game, there is normally a (possibly complex) set of rules defining what we are allowed to do in a game.

To continue our discussion, we now need to consider a concrete example. In the interest of clarity, in the remainder we consider the game of chess. We assume in fact that everybody has at least some familiarity with it. Moreover, chess is a game that is regularly played on many online platforms. Note, however, that what we discuss next can be in principle applied to any online game.

The problem that we are facing is regarding supporting players across the world with an Internet connection to play chess online against each other. The players also want to be able to pause a game that they are playing, reconnecting at a later time at their will to resume it. From a trust standpoint, there are two main challenges to be addressed in this scenario:

- To play games, the players must be authenticated: similarly to the problem of money ownership discussed above, there must be a mechanism in place ensuring that one player could not impersonate another player. This creates a basic feeling of trust, with users becoming confident that nobody else except them is allowed to play their own games.
- The state of each game currently played should be stored safely. In this way, it could be possible for the players to pause and resume an existing game. At the same time, it should also be impossible for anybody to modify the state of the games that are being played, except for the two players involved in a game (provided that a player cannot modify the state of a game without the approval of the other one). This creates the trust required by users to pause and resume games at any time. Safely storing the state of the games is similar to safely storing records of money ownership at a bank. In the same way in which we need to trust banks to keep our money safe, players would like that the state of the games that they are playing is stored somewhere safely.

Now, an online gaming platform obviously addresses these two challenges. The platform can authenticate the players in some way, for instance by creating a unique username and password for each of them. The platform can also store the status of each game being played, so that players can disconnect from a game and resume playing at any time. The platform can also ensure that nobody except the two players involved can modify the state of a game, e.g., proposing and executing new moves.

This solution relies on a fundamental assumption: the players must trust the platform. Specifically, they must trust that:

- The platform is always available.
- The platform does not allow the players to cheat, for instance by allowing them to change their moves while other players are disconnected.
- The platform itself does not cheat, for instance modifying the status of an existing game (for instance for the benefit of a malicious gambling cartel!) when the players are disconnected.

Instead of the online gaming platform, can we devise a different implementation of this mechanism to address the trust issues identified above? In the context of this book, the answer is obviously 'yes' and it relies, not surprisingly, on implementing a blockchain mechanism. In the remainder, we refer to this mechanism as BC4C (Blockchain for Chess).

The mechanism that we are looking for cannot rely on a 'central authority'. In this context, we use blockchain to create, by design, the trust that is needed among the players, without the need to create it using a central authority, like the online gaming platform. More in detail, the blockchain mechanism to play chess that we want to design relies on the following fundamental principles:

- Ensuring that the players can agree on the initial state of a game.
- Enabling the recording of the moves played in any game in an immutable database by every player.
- Defining rules to let the players determine which moves are valid, and can therefore be recorded in the database, and which are not.
- Enabling the authentication of the players.

These principles are discussed in detail next.

1.3.1 Defining an initial state of a game

When starting a new game, the players must agree on an initial state of it. In a game of chess, or generally in any online game, any decently knowledgeable player knows what the initial state is. In the game of chess, the initial state is determined by the correct positions of each piece on the chess table. Therefore, the implementation of this step is trivial: we can simply assume that the initial state of the game is always the 'standard' one of a game of chess and that players always agree on it. The importance of this step will emerge later, when we discuss how the players could reconstruct the state of games at any point in time.

1.3.2 Defining rules do determine valid moves

The players need a set of shared rules to determine which moves must be considered valid and which others not. Also in this case, the importance of this step will emerge later when discussing the mechanism through which the state of every game can be reconstructed. The implementation of this step is also trivial. Again, chess players with a decent knowledge of the game are likely to know what type of moves are allowed for each type of piece on the board and when a checkmate can be declared. Hence, we can establish the following simple protocol to assess the validity of moves in a game:

- first, a move in an ongoing game is submitted by a player, and
- second, a move must be approved by the other player before it is considered valid and, therefore, recorded.

Every player stores each approved move in a local database. This database has some special properties. First, new data can be added to this database, but existing data can neither be deleted from it, nor modified. Second, the local copies of this database maintained by each player are consistent, that is, they store exactly the same data.

The simple protocol for determining the validity of moves presented above avoids the common issues that could arise in the absence of a central authority. In particular, an invalid move submitted by one player, for instance to gain an unfair advantage, would not be accepted by the other player and never stored by any player in their database.[1]

1.3.3 An immutable database to record moves

One important principle of the mechanism governing BC4C is that the database where each player stores the approved moves is immutable. As briefly mentioned above, 'immutable' refers to the property of this database to be append-only. We can only add new content to this database. What is already stored in it can neither be deleted nor modified.

Why is such a database required? First, the database stores the moves of every game. In this way, every player can reconstruct the current state of any game simply by replaying the recorded moves starting from the initial state. Second, being immutable, all players can trust that any other player, including the ones against which they are playing games, can reconstruct exactly the same state for any game. Players, in fact, are not able to modify any move stored in the database.

The combination of the three features presented so far (a shared initial state of each game, rules to determine valid moves, and an immutable database to record them replicated by each player) removes the need for a central authority. These features create in fact the trust among players, who can feel free to disconnect and reconnect from an ongoing game. The simple protocol for establishing valid moves, in fact, guarantees (in a reasonable way) that every game is played following the rules of chess. Then, players disconnecting from a game can always reconnect and recreate the current state of any game simply by replaying all the moves stored in the immutable database starting from the initial state. Finally, the immutability of the database guarantees that players cannot modify the moves of any game, including theirs. This for instance removes the risk of players cheating by modifying their previous moves in a game.

Note that, until now, we have not worried about how we can technically build an immutable database, but we simply assume that it is possible to do so. Building an immutable database requires the knowledge of cryptographic tools, which we discuss in Chapter 2. In this chapter, however, it is important to recognize that immutability must be a design property of the database: it is not enough to establish a database usage policy that prevents its users to update or delete existing content. Such a policy, in fact, may be overruled at any time by an administrator. An administrator that could modify any data stored in the database would be an intermediary that the players cannot trust. Instead, the database must physically prevent anybody, not even an administrator, to delete or update existing data in it because of the way in which it is designed and implemented.

1.3.4 Authenticating the players

One final principle of BC4C concerns how to authenticate the players when playing a game. A problem that we have not solved until now, in fact, is how to guarantee that players participating in a game are indeed who they claim to be. An online platform can implement an authentication mechanism easily with usernames and passwords.

How can we authenticate players without a central authority? We do not provide the full-fledged solution to this problem now. As we did above for the immutable database, we simply assume that such a way of authenticating players is technically possible. Conceptually, the solution to this problem lies in switching perspective. The online gaming platform authenticates the players for 'sessions', in which players can possibly play multiple games submitting and/or approving many moves. In BC4C, players are authenticated with 'every single move'. We require in fact to authenticate every single interaction that a player has with another player, that is, authenticating every move submitted in a game. Technically, as discussed in Chapter 2, this means that every message submitted by a player to other players must be 'digitally signed'. For now, it is sufficient to know that digitally signing an electronic message means to add to it a little amount of data (i.e., a digital signature) that, similarly to a handwritten signature, allows any other player to identify the sender of the message univocally and undoubtedly.

The BC4C mechanism that we discussed in this chapter can be considered a blockchain. Hence, even though we have not yet given a proper definition of blockchain, based on the discussion made thus far we can highlight some of the principal characteristics of a system based on blockchain (see Figure 1.2):

- It is a system in which there is no central authority, i.e., all participants have the same role, i.e., rights and duties. In BC4C, the only users that exist are the players: they must agree on the initial state when a new game is started, they can submit moves and they must validate the moves submitted by the other players against whom they are playing. A computer scientist calls these kind of participants 'peers'

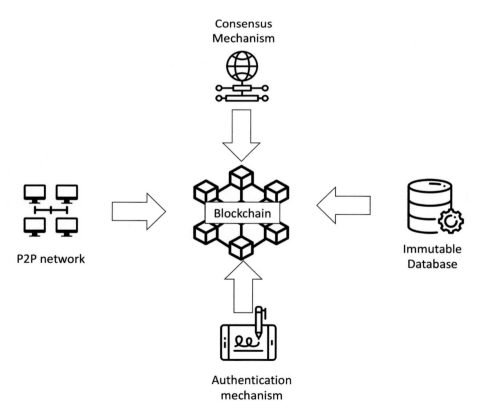

Figure 1.2 Basic ingredients of the blockchain recipe.

and says that this system relies on a 'peer-to-peer' (P2P) network of users. So, a blockchain involves a peer-to-peer network.

- The system has a set of rules (or a 'protocol', as a computer scientist would say) that are known to all players. These rules guarantee that the players can trust each other when using the system. In other words, the players may not trust each other in principle, but they trust the rules of the system and, through this common trust in the protocol, they are assured to play the game in a fair way. In the remainder of this book, we will learn to call these rules a 'consensus mechanism'. So, a blockchain involves the definition of a consensus mechanism that guarantees that all participants can reconstruct the state of the system at any point in time.
- The blockchain mechanism is enabled by specific technology. More in detail, we have identified two distinguishing technological features of blockchain systems: immutable databases and digitally signed messages. The former allows every player to reconstruct the state of the games. The latter guarantees that players are authenticated when interacting with other players. More precisely, every interaction that they have with other players is digitally signed.

Now, if we call a message that the peers of a blockchain exchange a 'transaction', then, from a technical standpoint, we can say that *a blockchain involves a network of peers who exchange digitally signed transactions and store them in a replicated immutable database.*

Sounds like we are already blockchain experts, doesn't it?

1.4 Exploring the potential of blockchain

Before we present the content of this book in more detail and the way it can be used in different learning contexts, in this section we briefly discuss the potential of applying blockchain in real-world business scenarios that are more meaningful than the one considered in the BC4C example considered until now.

First, even though the BC4C example is simply illustrative, it already shows that, in principle, blockchain technology can be used to build trustless online gaming systems (e-sports). The term 'trustless' here means that preexisting trust between the participants is not required to exchange value – the blockchain mechanism creates the trust. Supporting 'real' online games using blockchain may introduce challenges more complex to overcome. For instance, defining an initial state and a set of rules to let the players agree on the validity of the moves may be far from trivial. Nevertheless, we have a feeling that blockchain can enable interesting future scenarios. Online gaming is a multi-billion-dollar industry and, particularly with the recent emergence of competitive e-sports, issues such as trust among players, fairness of gaming platforms, and generally the transparency of the industry are becoming fundamental. Blockchain can help to establish the required level of trust among the players to make the industry more transparent.

Another application of blockchain that we have already mentioned in this chapter and that most readers of this book probably are aware of is cryptocurrency. The idea of a cryptocurrency is to create 'value tokens', i.e., a new form of money, that is not backed by any nation-state through their central bank, but that instead assumes its value from the trust that the users put in the technology that enables its exchange, i.e., blockchain. Many issues related to the design of a cryptocurrency are even less challenging that the ones of supporting online gaming using blockchain. For instance, the messages exchanged by the users of a cryptocurrency are simple transfers of value tokens. The entire state of the system can be captured simply by the number of tokens owned by every user. The rules to validate the transfers of tokens also appear to be straightforward: basically, we must ensure that users can only transfer tokens that they own to other users. Other aspects, however, make the design of cryptocurrencies challenging. One fundamental aspect is guaranteeing that the users cannot transfer, i.e., spend, the tokens that they own more than once. This issue is discussed more in detail in Chapter 3, while more details about real-world cryptocurrency systems – Bitcoin and Ethereum – are given in Chapters 5 and 6, respectively.

Blockchain technology is also used to address more traditional information exchange needs in different business scenarios. One such scenario is the monitoring of supply chains. A supply chain is a typical scenario where business entities that do not necessarily trust each other work together to create value (by making sure to deliver the goods ordered by the customers on time). Several of the challenges of designing BC4C also apply to a supply chain scenario. In fact, it is often impossible to identify a 'central authority' that can oversee an entire supply chain guaranteeing the veracity and quality of the information exchanged. This problem exists because of both a technical reason (it is hard to find an organization that has the technical knowledge to monitor all the phases of a complex supply chain) and a business-oriented one (the actors along the supply chain may not trust the central authority and never share critical data regarding their own business with it for reasons of market competition). Blockchain technology can be the solution in this context. Blockchain allows the actors along the supply chain to securely share at least the data necessary for effectively coordinating the different actors along the supply chain. The design of blockchain systems for supply chain monitoring has also different requirements compared to online gaming or cryptocurrencies. For instance, the users are likely to be a closed community of business partners. Hence, there is no need to give the opportunity to anybody outside the business ecosystem to join the system. Additionally, complex data access policies may be necessary: instead of being shared by all the participants in the system, the information exchanged may be shared only by a subset of the actors. For instance, retail supermarkets may be willing to share information regarding their warehouse replenishment policies only with their logistics provider in charge of the last mile, but not with every possible partner along the supply chain. The application of blockchain in supply chains is discussed in Part 2 after having introduced private blockchain systems (Chapters 6 and 7), and also revisited in Part 3.

Finally, let us conclude this discussion considering an application of blockchain that emerged together with the rise of big data and the data economy in the past decade, i.e., the secure and reliable management of IoT data. Complex networks of sensors are increasingly equipping different types of products and services. For instance, elevators or other heavy machinery installed at client sites can constantly feed the headquarters with monitoring data, enabling predictive maintenance; or industrial-grade waste drums and the trucks transporting them can be equipped with GPS and other types of sensors to enable their monitoring in real time. More generally, the Internet-of-Things (IoT) is touted to soon enable equipping our living environments (homes, cars, cities) with sensors constantly feeding data that can be exploited to improve our quality of living, optimizing traffic management, energy consumption, or shared resource utilization. Often, the management of sensor data is characterized by privacy and reliability issues. For instance, when a disaster is investigated, sensor data may provide important evidence regarding its root causes. However, how can we ensure that the sensor data, for instance, have not been corrupted after storage and that it is still possible to link them to the actual sensor from which they originated? Blockchain can help address these issues, by creating reliable distributed and immutable records of sensor data. The management of IoT data using blockchain introduces new challenges when compared to cryptocurrencies, online gaming, or supply chain monitoring. For example, given the sheer amount of data to be handled, data processing performance and storage space become fundamental. The challenges introduced by the application of blockchain to IoT data are discussed in Chapter 8.

1.5 Overview of this book

This book is divided into three parts.

Part 1 aims at introducing an 'implementation-agnostic' definition of blockchain concepts, mechanisms and technology. The objective is to define these in general terms, without being specifically tied to a particular implementation, like Bitcoin, Ethereum, or any other framework to implement blockchain-based systems. To this aim, Chapter 3 discusses the basic concepts necessary to understand the functioning of blockchain technology, such as blockchain networks (public or private), blockchain protocols, blockchain data structures (blocks, transactions, and immutable ledgers), and consensus mechanisms. In Chapter 4, we extend these basic concepts introducing the concept of smart contracts. Smart contracts represent the key to turn blockchain systems into general-purpose systems that can process any type of information exchanged by a network of users. To fully grasp this implementation-agnostic definition of blockchain, a basic background in cryptography is required. Cryptographic techniques, such as digital signatures and cryptographic hashing, in fact, are fundamental enablers of blockchain. As such, they cannot be left out of the picture when introducing blockchain. Chapter 2 fills this gap by discussing basic cryptographic tools enabling blockchain technology. We acknowledge that cryptography may be tough to digest for readers lacking a background in computer science. Therefore, these concepts are introduced in Chapter 2 at a conceptual level, abstracting whenever possible from the more technical details, but also providing plenty of examples and references to online resources through which interested readers can experience more details first-hand.

Part 2 of the book deals with the concrete implementations of blockchain. These include concrete blockchain systems that have been operating successfully for many years and concrete frameworks that can be used to create blockchain systems in specific business scenarios. Chapter 5 introduces Bitcoin as the most prominent example of a blockchain enabling the creation of a cryptocurrency that is used worldwide. Chapter 6 introduces Ethereum. The Ethereum blockchain also provides a world-renowned cryptocurrency. However, most importantly Ethereum is the first blockchain that introduced the feature of smart contracts. Chapter 7 focuses on the so-called private blockchain systems. We discuss in detail two frameworks to develop blockchain systems supporting business scenarios involving a network of private partners: Hyperledger and Corda. Hyperledger is an umbrella project for different blockchain frameworks. In this book, we focus mainly on Hyperledger Fabric, which is the technology behind the most successful private blockchain systems currently in production. Corda is a blockchain framework that recently has gained extensive traction, particularly in the financial sector. Finally, Chapter 8 focuses on the impact that blockchain technology can have on the IoT. We discuss different examples of how blockchain can be used to create systems where information captured by sensor networks can be managed in a trustless environment.

Part 3 of the book gives readers the tools to understand the suitability of blockchain technology for a business scenario or, switching the perspective, to identify which business scenarios can benefit from using blockchain. The objective of this part of the book is to debunk the myth that blockchain technology is so revolutionary that it will change forever any industry in the future. This has been often claimed particularly since 2019, when the price of Bitcoin had its first dramatic upward run. We argue in this book that blockchain is a technology that, as any other one that emerged in the past, should be carefully appraised for its suitability to a particular business application. Obviously, blockchain has already shown its potential to create cryptocurrencies, solving the problem of developing digital currencies that do not rely on a central bank to realize their value. However, we will understand that cryptocurrency is a rather simple application of blockchain technology and that blockchain can enable novel applications in many other business scenarios with more complex and critical information-sharing requirements. Chapter 9 provides a model to understand the suitability of blockchain for a specific (given) business scenario. Chapter 10 focuses on blockchain and business models, discussing how blockchain can extend existing business models and enable new ones. Finally, Chapter 11 discusses the impact of blockchain on so-called outcome-based business model. This refers to a novel and emerging class of business scenarios where the remuneration of a service provider is defined by the value that a service provider creates for its customers, rather than using a measure of the number of resources employed to provide a service. In such scenarios, blockchain becomes a means enabling the reliable and trustless assessment of the value accrued by customers when using a service.

Each chapter is equipped with a set of questions and/or exercises. Each chapter of Part 1 and Part 2 is also equipped with a case study. In Part 1, the case studies give a historical perspective of the evolution of the collection of technologies from which blockchain emerged, spanning from the role of cryptography in revolutionizing digital communications, to alternative forms of digital cash systems that preceded Bitcoin. In Part 2, the case studies discuss concrete applications of blockchain technology. These range from systems currently in production in different industries, such as blockchain to enable traceability in the diamond trade to proof-of-concept systems developed within academic projects in which the authors have been involved, such as blockchain for monitoring IoT-supported business processes. The chapters of Part 3 do not have a specific case study, but they are instead infused with the discussion of several real-world applications of blockchain.

1.6 How to use this book

We have written the three parts of this book to be as much as possible self-contained and, therefore, to be tackled independently and combined by readers to satisfy their personal learning goals. Following a traditional approach in human–computer interaction [Nie19], we present below how this book can be used by four different personas, who exemplify the main profiles that we expect as the readers of this book.

1.6.1 Zoe (22 yo, last year business undergraduate student)

Zoe has an interest in finance and has recently been particularly attracted by crypto-currencies and non-fungible tokens (NFTs). However, while she has been able to form a rough picture of the market dynamics behind, for instance, the value of Bitcoin, she feels that her lack of understanding of the technology underlying crypto-assets is preventing her to fully grasp the importance of these markets and their future trends. Being completely new to cryptography and blockchain technology, Zoe will focus on Part 1 and Part 2 of this book, to understand what blockchain technology is and what applications of it currently exist in the real world.

1.6.2 Yang (20 yo, second year undergraduate student in industrial engineering)

Yang has a strong background in data science and optimization. Blockchain is completely new to him, but he has some background in computer science, having taken some CS courses about information system design and implementation. Yang's dream is to land a job in one of the university startups, developing new applications based on blockchain. Yang feels that, while machine learning and data science may soon become a completely automated task in most organizations, the careful design of systems to support information and value exchange in a business context will always require advanced human expertise. He has heard of blockchain in one of the CS courses and he has been looking forward to understanding this technology more in depth. Like Zoe, Yang will focus on Part 1 and Part 2 of this book. Specifically, the model of blockchain systems introduced in Part 1 will give him a solid basis to understand other blockchain systems used by university startups that are not covered in this book.

1.6.3 Xenia (31 yo, IT consultant)

Xenia is an IT professional. She has a bachelor's degree in computer science obtained long ago. She has been working in IT consultancy for eight years and she is currently attending a professional master's program in IT management to improve her career advancement chances. She is working on a dissertation regarding the new business models that can be enabled by blockchain and she is looking for more resources to extend her knowledge about blockchain. Xenia will focus on Part 1 and Part 3 of this book. Part 1 will help her developing a deep understanding of blockchain technology in an implementation–agnostic way. Part 3 will allow her to understand different business scenarios in which blockchain can be effective. The case studies discussed in the book will also help her to understand how blockchain technology is applied in many real-world contexts.

1.6.4 William (23 yo, Master in business systems design)

William has an undergraduate degree in computer science and has recently started a master's program in business systems design. He has chosen to specialize in information systems because he has always been interested in how IT can help businesses. He studied blockchain technology in a cryptography course, learning the more technical aspects related to digital signatures and cryptographic hashing. As part of this course, he has also completed a project regarding the generation of blocks and transaction hashes in a toy blockchain system. William will focus mainly on Part 2 and Part 3 of this book. Part 2 will help him understand the details about the specific implementations of block-chain, such as smart contracts in Ethereum. Part 3 will help him understand the business applications of blockchain. He is, in fact, planning to complete a final project on the feasibility of blockchain to produce secure and reliable records of academic achievements, which will also include the development of a small proof-of-concept prototype using Ethereum.

1.7 Overview of blockchain applications discussed in this book

1.7.1 Part 1

Chapter 2. *How cryptography has changed the world*: To give a historical perspective on the role of cryptography in society (and hence on blockchain developments), we revisit the milestones in the development of cryptographic techniques, discussing in particular the main applications of cryptography tools, from protecting military communications, to securing communications between computers, to the threat posed to modern cryptography by quantum computing.

Chapter 3. *The Predecessors of Bitcoin*: We revisit the history of digital currencies and virtual coins, such as Hashcash, before the advent of Bitcoin. The objective is to understand their main design features and the reasons, mainly technical, why they failed to become a global phenomenon like Bitcoin.

Chapter 4. *The original definition of Smart Contract*: Similar to the treatment of digital currencies and virtual coins in the previous chapter, in this chapter we revisit the history of smart contracts. Specifically, we start from the definition given by the cryptographer Nick Szabo in the late 1990s, discussing how the concept of smart contracts has evolved until the recent developments in blockchain technology.

1.7.2 Part 2

Chapter 5. *Bitcoin in the real world*: We discuss the applications of Bitcoin in the real world, both as an investment asset and a form of payment. We discuss how the value of Bitcoin in fiat currencies has evolved since its inception and the factors that affect the value of Bitcoins. We then look at the countries that have made Bitcoin legal tender as a form of payment, to understand the reasons for this choice and the main problems encountered in making Bitcoin a widespread form of payment.

Chapter 6. *Everledger*: Everledger is a digital transparency company, providing Ethereum-based technology solutions to increase transparency in global supply chains. One of the first industries targeted by Everledger has been the trade of luxury goods, in particular the secure tracking of the provenance of diamonds.

Chapter 7. *Real-world applications of private blockchain: the Spunta Banca project and IBM's FoodTrust*. We present two private blockchain applications created using the frameworks discussed in Chapter 7. Spunta Banca, implemented using Corda, provides a blockchain-based solution for the reconciliation of interbank transactions exploiting Corda. It is currently used by more than 100 Italian banks in production. FoodTrust, powered by Hyperledger Fabric, is IBM's solution for blockchain-based monitoring of food provenance toward consumers. The first pilot of the solution has been developed in collaboration with Walmart, the largest retailer in the US.

Chapter 8. *Trusted Artifact-Driven Process Monitoring using Blockchain*: We discuss the development of a solution based on Ethereum to exploit IoT devices in the monitoring of multi-party business processes. This is an academic project, which has led to the development of a prototype demonstrated in real-world use cases in Northern Italy.

1.7.3 Part 3

The last part of the book focuses specifically on understanding the usage of blockchain in real-world applications. As such, you will not find only one case study for each chapter. Instead, the chapters of Part 3 are infused with the discussion of several classes of real-world applications that could benefit from blockchain.

1.8 Questions and exercises

1 In this chapter we have identified national currencies and university meal vouchers as examples of fiat money. Based on your personal experience and/or knowledge, are you able to identify another form of fiat money? Who are the users of this form of money? Who/what is the 'central authority' that gives values to this money? What are the boundaries within which this money has value for its users?

2 In this chapter, we have introduced the idea of blockchain considering the example of the game of chess. Consider now a different type of (simple) game and show how the basic elements of a blockchain (like consensus mechanism and content of the immutable database) should be customized to fit the rules of the game that you have chosen.

3 For each of the following business scenarios, discuss why or why not blockchain could be a good mechanism. In particular, think about whether you can identify a central authority, whether it is desirable to substitute it with a blockchain system and whether the immutability of the data over time is a desirable property:
   i Handling information regarding spare parts and work in progress in a large manufacturing company, e.g., shipbuilding.
   ii Managing information to demonstrate the provenance and veracity of academic transcripts worldwide.
   iii Managing information of a national court of law (cases, trials, convictions, etc.).

Note

1 Note that malicious players may in principle refuse to accept checkmate or other moves that cause the other player to win. We do not consider this problem in this simple example. In principle, however, this can be solved by allowing players other than the ones involved in a game to certify the validity of the moves. The validity of the moves may even be checked by a computer program in which the rules are simply codified, without the need of any manual approval by the players.

2 Cryptographic tools for blockchain

Learning goals

2.A The reader can explain how digital messages can be encoded into bit sequences.

2.B The reader can represent numbers using different number systems (bases).

2.C The reader can list and discuss the properties of cryptographic hashing functions.

2.D The reader can explain the mechanisms of public key encryption and digital signatures.

2.E The reader can discuss the applications of cryptographic hashing functions and digital signatures.

2.1 Computer-readable representation of digital messages

Computers simply can be thought of as big and extremely powerful calculators. In fact, they can only process numbers. Even the most complex operations executed by a computer, like AI-based self-driving of a car, boil down to crunching numbers. Every digital message, like a message on a chat, a post on social media, or a photo, must be encoded into numbers in order to be processed by a computer.

The cryptographic tools that we present in this chapter are specific types of processing operations that computers can execute. They also require that any input to them must be a number. Therefore, before presenting them, first, we need to understand how a digital message processed by a computer can become a number. This requires the understanding of two concepts: character encoding and base-2 representation of numbers.

2.1.1 Character encoding

Encoding of user input into a computer-readable format concerns translating this input into numbers that a computer can process. Decoding refers to translating in the opposite direction: from numbers processed by a computer to intelligible user input. Given a user input message, there are obviously infinite ways in which this can be encoded into numbers. For this reason, computer scientists have defined different standard encoding/decoding 'schemes' for different types of user input, like text, photos, or video. An encoding/decoding scheme describes the way in which user input is translated into numbers (and vice versa).

Most of the content processed by a computer is provided as text input from a keyboard. Computers obviously also handle other forms of multimedia digital content,

DOI: 10.4324/9781003321187-3

such as photos or videos, but text is by far the most common type of input used. Hence, in this chapter, as an example, we focus on the encoding/decoding of text input. Text input is usually provided to a computer as a sequence of characters. Text encoding/ decoding schemes usually map each character of an input text into a number. Hence, they are referred to as 'character encoding' schemes. In the remainder, we focus on the encoding phase, i.e., from user input text to numbers. Knowing the encoding scheme, in fact, the decoding is straightforward.

The best way to understand a character encoding scheme is to present a concrete one. We present in this section the ASCII (American Standard Code for Information Interchange) encoding [ASC69]. It was proposed in the 1960s and most modern character encoding schemes are still based on it nowadays.

The ASCII encoding scheme, in a nutshell, is specified by two tables. One table concerns the mapping of printable characters to numbers (Figure 2.1). The second one shows the mapping of control (non-printable) characters (Figure 2.2). Not all input from a keyboard, in fact, results in characters that can be printed on a screen. Pressing the 'enter' or 'shift' keys, for instance, usually executes some control not linked to a printed character (e.g., making a new line or enabling capital letters on the keyboard).

Dec	Char	Dec	Char	Dec	Char
32	SPACE	64	@	96	`
33	!	65	A	97	a
34	"	66	B	98	b
35	#	67	C	99	c
36	$	68	D	100	d
37	%	69	E	101	e
38	&	70	F	102	f
39	'	71	G	103	g
40	(	72	H	104	h
41	)	73	I	105	i
42	*	74	J	106	j
43	+	75	K	107	k
44	,	76	L	108	l
45	-	77	M	109	m
46	.	78	N	110	n
47	/	79	O	111	o
48	0	80	P	112	p
49	1	81	Q	113	q
50	2	82	R	114	r
51	3	83	S	115	s
52	4	84	T	116	t
53	5	85	U	117	u
54	6	86	V	118	v
55	7	87	W	119	w
56	8	88	X	120	x
57	9	89	Y	121	y
58	:	90	Z	122	z
59	;	91	[	123	{
60	<	92	\	124		
61	=	93	]	125	}
62	>	94	^	126	~
63	?	95	_	127	DEL

Figure 2.1 Printable characters mapping in ASCII ('Dec' represents the encoding in Base-10 of the printable character 'Char').

```
Dec  Char
----------
   0  NUL (null)
   1  SOH (start of heading)
   2  STX (start of text)
   3  ETX (end of text)
   4  EOT (end of transmission)
   5  ENQ (enquiry)
   6  ACK (acknowledge)
   7  BEL (bell)
   8  BS  (backspace)
   9  TAB (horizontal tab)
  10  LF  (NL line feed, new line)
  11  VT  (vertical tab)
  12  FF  (NP form feed, new page)
  13  CR  (carriage return)
  14  SO  (shift out)
  15  SI  (shift in)
  16  DLE (data link escape)
  17  DC1 (device control 1)
  18  DC2 (device control 2)
  19  DC3 (device control 3)
  20  DC4 (device control 4)
  21  NAK (negative acknowledge)
  22  SYN (synchronous idle)
  23  ETB (end of trans. block)
  24  CAN (cancel)
  25  EM  (end of medium)
  26  SUB (substitute)
  27  ESC (escape)
  28  FS  (file separator)
  29  GS  (group separator)
  30  RS  (record separator)
  31  US  (unit separator)
```

Figure 2.2 Control characters mapping in ASCII ('Dec' represents the encoding in Base-10 of the control character 'Char').

Using the mapping of Figures 2.1 and 2.2, any keyboard input can be translated into a sequence of numbers, and vice versa. For instance, the word 'blockchain' is translated into the sequence of numbers '98 108 111 99 107 104 97 105 110', whereas 'Blockchain' becomes '66 108 111 99 107 104 97 105 110'.

2.1.2 Base-2 number representation

We said above that computers can only process numbers. More precisely, they can process only two digits: 0 and 1. The digit '0' usually is associated with a low voltage electric signal; the digit '1' with a high voltage electric signal. The same concept applies also to storage. That is, a hard disk or a memory unit of a computer can only store two digits: 0 and 1. Therefore, after (or during the) encoding, it is fundamental to translate the user input into numbers expressed using only 0s and 1s. We are used to working with numbers expressed in the so-called 'Base-10', which uses the common 10 digits (0, 1, …, 9). Using only 0s and 1s means to express numbers using the so-called 'Base-2'. You may already know that the basic unit of storage/processing in a computer, i.e., a single '1' or '0', is called a 'bit'. Hence, expressing an encoded user input using Base-2 can also be seen as expressing it as a 'sequence of bits'.

The translation of numbers from Base-10 and Base-2 (and vice versa) is exemplified in Figure 2.3. Obviously, relying only on two digits, the number of digits required in Base-2 is on average much higher than Base-10. With only 2 digits, in fact, a number can be expressed only as the sum of the powers of 2.

There are more compact ways to express sequences of bits than Base-2 (or Base-10). Practically, any base that is a power of 2 can serve as a more compact way. Two bases that are often used to represent sequences of bits in printed material in a compact way are the Base-16 and Base-64 (see Figure 2.4). The Base-16 uses the standard 10 digits and the first 6 letters of the alphabet ('a' to 'f', either small or capital letters can be used)

Base 10	Base 2
$26_{10} = 20 + 6 = (2 * 10^1) + (6 * 10^0)$	$26_2 = 11010 = 16 + 8 + 2 = (1 * 2^4) + (1 * 2^3) + (0 * 2^2) + (1 * 2^1) + (0 * 2^0)$
$11_{10} = 10 + 1 = (10 * 10^1) + (1 * 10^0)$	$11_2 = 1011 = 8 + 2 + 1 = (1 * 2^3) + (0 * 2^2) + (1 * 2^1) + (1 * 2^0)$
$345_{10} = 300 + 40 + 5 = (3 * 10^2) +$ $+ (4 * 10^1) + (5 * 10^0)$	$345_2 = 101011001 = 256 + 64 + 16 + 8 + 1 = (1 * 2^8) + (0 * 2^7) +$ $(1 * 2^6) + (0 * 2^5) +$ $(1 * 2^4) + (1 * 2^3) +$ $(0 * 2^2) + (0 * 2^1) +$ $(1 * 2^0)$

Figure 2.3 From Base-10 to Base-2 (and vice versa): examples. Note that the subscripts indicate the base in which a number is expressed.

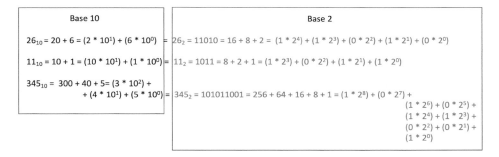

$7_{16} = 7 * 16^0 = 7_{10} = (0)111_2$

$d_{16} = 13 * 16^0 = 12_{10} = 1100_2$

$b6_{16} = (11 * 16^1) + (6 * 16^0) = 182_{10} = 1011\ 0110_2$

<base16 table>

Value	Char	Value	Char
0	0	8	8
1	1	9	9
2	2	10	a
3	3	11	b
4	4	12	c
5	5	13	d
6	6	14	e
7	7	15	f

< base64 table >

Value	Character	Value	Character	Value	Character	Value	Character
0	A	16	Q	32	g	48	w
1	B	17	R	33	h	49	x
2	C	18	S	34	i	50	y
3	D	19	T	35	j	51	z
4	E	20	U	36	k	52	0
5	F	21	V	37	l	53	1
6	G	22	W	38	m	54	2
7	H	23	X	39	n	55	3
8	I	24	Y	40	o	56	4
9	J	25	Z	41	p	57	5
10	K	26	a	42	q	58	6
11	L	27	b	43	r	59	7
12	M	28	c	44	s	60	8
13	N	29	d	45	t	61	9
14	O	30	e	46	u	62	+
15	P	31	f	47	v	63	/

$m_{64} = 38 * 64^0 = 38_{10} = 100110_2$

$p6zP_{64} = (41 * 64^3) + (58 * 64^2) + (59 * 64^1) + (15 * 64^0) = 10988751_{10} =$ $101001\ 111010\ 110011\ 001111_2$

Figure 2.4 Base-16 and Base-64 number representation examples (in the tables, 'Value' represents the Base-10 digit and 'Char' the corresponding Base-16 or Base-64 one).

$182_{10} = 49_{58} = (3 * 58^1) + (8 * 58^0)$
$10988751_{10} = yKaE_{58} = (56 * 58^3) + (18 * 58^2) + (33 * 58^1) + (13 * 58^0)$

Value	Character	Value	Character	Value	Character	Value	Character
0	1	1	2	2	3	3	4
4	5	5	6	6	7	7	8
8	9	9	A	10	B	11	C
12	D	13	E	14	F	15	G
16	H	17	J	18	K	19	L
20	M	21	N	22	P	23	Q
24	R	25	S	26	T	27	U
28	V	29	W	30	X	31	Y
32	Z	33	a	34	b	35	c
36	d	37	e	38	f	39	g
40	h	41	i	42	j	43	k
44	m	45	n	46	o	47	p
48	q	49	r	50	s	51	t
52	u	53	v	54	w	55	x
56	y	57	z				

Figure 2.5 Examples of Bitcoin's Base-58 number representation.

as digits. The Base-64 uses the standard 10 digits, the 52 letters of the alphabet (both small and capital face; so 'a' is a different digit than 'A'), and the two special symbols '+' and '/'. Note that, using the Base-16 format, every digit represents 4 bits of information. Using the Base-64 format, every digit represents 6 bits of information.

An alternative format is Base-58. This is the encoding used to represent Bitcoin accounts in a readable format. Figure 2.5 shows the Base-58 digits for representing in printed form the Bitcoin account numbers. Bitcoin's Base-58 encoding uses the following digits: '123456789ABCDEFGHJKLMNPQRSTUVWXYZabcdefghijkmnopqrstuvwxyz'. This type of encoding has been conceived to improve readability by human readers compared, mainly, to Base-64. Compared to Base-64, the Bitcoin's Base-58 excludes the two special symbols and other digits that can easily be mistaken for each other by a human reader (i.e., the number '0' and the letter 'O', and the letter 'l' [small 'L'] and 'I' [capital 'i']).

2.2 Cryptographic hashing

After having discussed how to represent digital messages as sequences of bits, we are ready to introduce the cryptographic tools used by blockchain. These are the cryptographic hashing functions and the digital signature mechanisms. The former is presented in this section. The latter is presented in Section 2.4. Section 2.3 presents the general issue of message encryption. Understanding message encryption is a prerequisite for understanding the digital signature mechanism.

To discuss cryptographic hashing, we first introduce a simple 'mathematical' definition of the cryptographic hash function. Then, we discuss the practical meaning of cryptographic hash functions and their applications.

2.2.1 Cryptographic hash functions: definition

A cryptographic hash function H is a mathematical function that converts a digital message M into a hash value h of fixed length (see Figure 2.6). Usually, the hash value h is short. Conversely, the message M can be any digital message, such as a short username or an entire book in digital format. Because the size of the input M is unbound, the hash value h can also be seen as a 'digest' of M. A cryptographic hash function that

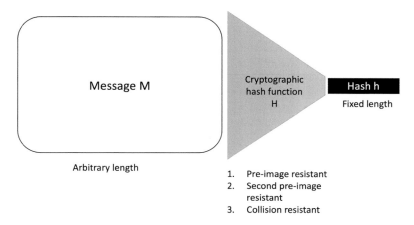

Figure 2.6 Cryptographic hash function.

returns a hash of size 'n' bits is referred to as an n–bit hash function. For popular hashing functions, n is usually comprised between 128 and 512 bits.

A cryptographic hash function H has three properties:

1 *Pre-image resistance*: It must be computationally hard to invert the function H, that is, to find M given the hash h.
2 *Second pre-image resistance*: Given the message M and the hash h, it must be computationally hard to find a different message N such that $H(M) = H(N) = h$.
3 *Collision resistance*: It must be computationally hard to find two different messages, M and N, that map onto the same hash value h, that is, for which $H(M) = H(N)$.

Note that 'computationally hard' in the definitions above means impossible in practical scenarios in the real world. In other words, it must take such a large amount of computational power to, for instance, invert a cryptographic hashing function, that this can be considered impossible to be achieved by anybody in the real world.

The first property establishes that the content of the message M cannot be reconstructed from its hash h. Hence, the hash h is a digest of the message M, but it is not a compressed version of M. A compressing function, like the zipped version of a file, must be in fact invertible: given the compressed version, it should be possible to re–obtain the original, non-compressed version. This is not the case with cryptographic hashes: given the hash h, it must be impossible to obtain the message M that generated h.

To understand the second property, let us consider the case in which the hash h is required to establish the legitimacy of a certain message M. In this context, the second property states that an attacker that obtains both M and h cannot substitute M with a different message N using the same hash h as a proof of legitimacy.

The third property defines the practical uniqueness of a hash (a.k.a. 'collision avoidance'). In other words, the function H maps a message M to a unique hash value h. Combining the second and third property, a hash h can be seen as a unique identifier of a message M. No two messages M and N should in fact map to the same hash h. Even if only one bit in the message M changes, then the hash h of M also changes.

Regarding specifically the third property, it must be noted that it is impossible to design a cryptographic hash function H that guarantees complete 'collision avoidance'. Demonstrating this is trivial, even for readers who are not computer science experts. This property derives from the fact that the size of the input M is unbounded and, consequently, infinite. Since the domain of the function H is unbounded, it is impossible to guarantee that, for any cryptographic function H, collisions (i.e., two messages mapping to the same hash) may never ever be found. When designing H, the best we can do is to make such collisions 'highly unlikely' or, as said above, virtually impossible in practical scenarios.

2.2.2 *Applications and implementations*

Cryptographic hash functions are widely adopted in the blockchain. At this stage in the book, however, we do not know enough about blockchain to discuss this kind of applications. Nevertheless, we can discuss other well-known applications of cryptographic hash functions in the context of proof of file integrity and encrypted passwords. Applications of this kind have been in place for many years. They underpin the functionality of the Internet as we use it every day.

One problem that cryptographic hash functions can solve is that of proving the integrity of a file that we download from the Internet (see Figure 2.7). This is particularly relevant while downloading and installing software applications on a computer. A program installing a software on a computer usually requires high-level privileges, like the ability to write on the hard disk and to modify the configuration settings of the operating system. A 'man-in-the-middle' may then have the incentive to modify the content of what we are downloading to achieve some malicious objective. For instance, it may modify the content of the download such that, instead of downloading and installing a

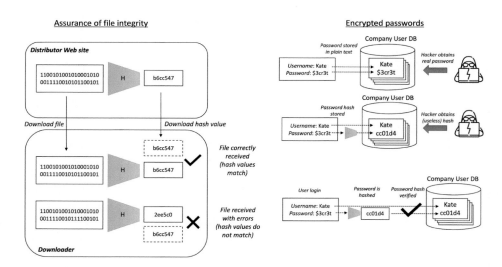

Figure 2.7 Applications of cryptographic hash functions. On the left, the mechanism for assurance of file integrity using hash functions; on the right, the mechanism for encrypting user password using hash functions.

simple editor for our photos, we would instead install a computer virus. The virus may then take control of the files on our computer, asking for a ransom in Bitcoins (!).

How can we avoid this situation using cryptographic hashing functions? The key lies in distributing also the hash of the content that has been downloaded. The software distributor would make available, besides the file to download, also its hash *h*, calculated using a (well-designed) hashing function *H*. The downloader, after finishing the download, runs the same function *H* on the file downloaded. In this way, they can verify whether the hash obtained matches the one published by the distributor. If that is the case, then the downloader can rest assured that the file downloaded is exactly the one published by the distributor. If, in fact, even only 1 bit of the file was maliciously modified during the transmission, the hash obtained by the downloader will not match the one published by the distributor. If not, then the downloader should not install the software downloaded (and probably also notify the distributor that something is wrong!). Note that while the attacker in the middle could modify the file during the download, the hash can simply be published by the software distributor on a Web page for the downloader to verify. The hash is in fact a relatively short sequence of bits.

A second problem that is addressed by cryptographic hash functions is encrypting user passwords (see Figure 2.7). We maintain accounts (usernames and passwords) on dozens of Web sites. These sites obviously need to store our password in some database in order to verify it whenever we log in. However, does this mean that, for instance, a database administrator of a Web site on which we have an account can actually see our password? Malicious administrators may obviously exploit this privilege. For instance, they may collect all users' passwords, sell them to hackers or use them directly for some illicit activities. Thanks to cryptographic hashing functions, the answer to this question is obviously 'no'.

A Web site in fact stores our password in an 'encrypted' format. This means that (i) the password is not stored in its original format (the 'plaintext'), but (ii) it can still be verified whenever needed. In practice, this is done by storing the hash of a password obtained using a cryptographic hash function instead of the actual password. The hash of the password cannot be inverted to obtain the actual password (thanks to the 'pre-image resistance' property mentioned above). Whenever a user inputs the password, this can be verified by calculating its hash and checking whether this matches the one in the Web site database.

To conclude the discussion about cryptographic hash function, the Computer Science Focus below briefly presents three families of hashing functions currently used widely in the real world.

Computer science focus: cryptographic hashing functions in the real world

MD5

The MD5 (Message Digest vs. 5) is a cryptographic function proposed in 1991 by Ronald Rivest at MIT [Riv92]. It is a block cypher algorithm. The input message is broken down into chunks of 512 bits and then several transformations are applied until a hash of 128 bits (i.e., 32 digits in Base-16) is generated. Since its inception, it has been widely used. In 2008, however, after several vulnerabilities in it were found, it was declared to be cryptographically broken and unsuitable for further use. Most importantly, it was demonstrated that collisions could have been found using a desktop computer in a few seconds. Despite this, it is still in use nowadays, mainly as a means to verify data integrity, but only from unintentional corruption of the data.

SHA

The Secure Hash Algorithms (SHA) [Pre10] is a family of cryptographic hash functions published by the National Institute of Standards and Technology (NIST). The SHA-1 function returns a 160-bits hash. It is similar to the MD5 function and it has also been found to have significant weaknesses. The SHA-2 is a family of two similar hash functions returning hashes of 256 and 512 bits, respectively. These improve SHA-1 and are currently considered secure hashing functions. The SHA-3 is intended as a replacement for the SHA-2 algorithms with increased security. The SHA-2 and SHA-3 hashing functions are widely used in secure Internet communications and, as discussed later in this book, also in the implementation of blockchain systems.

RIPEMD

The RIPE Message Digest [RIA01] is a family of cryptographic functions developed between 1992 and 1996. It comprises functions returning hashes of 128, 160, 256, and 320 bits. The RIPEMD-128 is not considered secure. Several vulnerabilities have been found in it. While these functions are less popular than the SHA hashing functions, they are used in the design of Bitcoin and other cryptocurrencies. This is because calculating RIPEMD hash is usually quicker than SHA hashes.

2.3 Message encryption: symmetric and asymmetric

Encryption is the discipline within cryptography focusing on securing digital communications (see Figure 2.8). The principal objective of encryption is to avoid eavesdropping during the communications by a malicious 'man-in-the-middle' attacker. When eavesdropping, an attacker aims at obtaining a digital message sent by a receiver to a sender and, most importantly, understanding it. Note that digital communication in this context should be intended in a broad sense. As shown in Figure 2.8, encrypting the content of a hard disk is also a form of digital communication. Alice is in fact communicating with her future self, who wants to retrieve a file from the disk in the future. While the file is stored, she would like that the file is not obtained by anybody else and that, even if that happens, the content of the disk will not be understandable to the attacker.

Algorithms to encrypt the content of digital communications, i.e., digital messages, are called cyphers. The original message is usually called the 'plaintext' message. Its

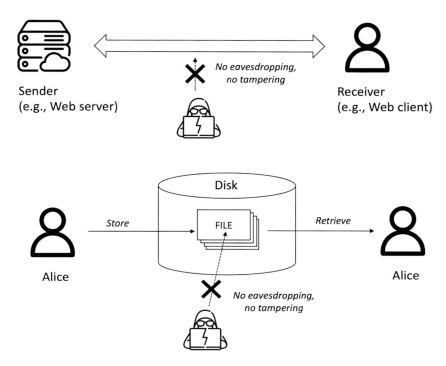

Figure 2.8 Securing digital communications.

encrypted version after using a cypher is called 'cyphertext'. A cyphertext should not be understandable by a human or a computer, unless a mechanism to decrypt it (i.e., turning it into its original plaintext) is provided. Encryption and decryption through a cypher require a piece of auxiliary information, usually called the 'key'. Symmetric encryption refers to cyphers using the same key for encrypting and decrypting. Asymmetric encryption refers to cyphers where different keys are used for each operation. In this section, we provide an example of a concrete (and very simple) symmetric encryption cypher: the 'Caesar cypher'. Later, we present asymmetric encryption only at a conceptual level, mentioning popular implementations of this encryption mechanism commonly used in real-world applications.

2.3.1 Symmetric encryption: the Caesar cypher

The Caesar cypher is a simple cypher invented by the Roman general and later emperor Julius Caesar to secure the communications (not digital at the time!) between him and his legions during wars. This cypher accepts as input a message expressed in any alphabet. For simplicity, we refer here to the traditional Roman alphabet. The Caesar cypher is a 'substitution' cypher, where each letter of an alphabet is mapped onto a different one. The 'key' to this mapping is the number of positions in the alphabet of which each letter should be shifted forward to obtain the cyphertext version of it. Figure 2.9 shows an example. The 'key' used in this example is 3.

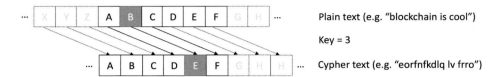

Figure 2.9 The Caesar Cypher exemplified.

Therefore, each letter is shifted forward of three positions in the alphabet to obtain the cyphertext. Note that the alphabet is treated as a 'closed circle' (for instance the letter 'z' maps to the letter 'c' in the example). Messages are decrypted simply by shifting backward each letter in the alphabet of a number of positions equal to the value of the key.

The Caesar Cypher is a symmetric one. Both the sender and the receiver must know the value of the key to communicate effectively. Unfortunately, it is also easy to crack, particularly if one could use a computer. If we know that a Caesar Cypher has been used, then we can simply try all the possible keys on a cyphertext (26 positions if we are using the standard English alphabet). One of these 26 keys will return a plaintext that we could understand. Even if we do not know that a Caesar Cypher has been used, substitution cyphers can be cracked by studying the frequency of individual letters, bigram, etc. in the cyphertext. In written text, in fact, individual letters and their combinations tend to appear at well-known frequencies in different languages. If we have enough cyphertext to work with, we could start studying the frequency of occurrence of individual letters, bigrams, etc. in it until we could make an educated guess about the language in which the plaintext is written and the value of the key.

The example of the Caesar cypher shows that substitution cyphers are, generally, not particularly secure. This is why modern symmetric cyphers are 'block' cyphers. In a block cypher algorithm, messages are encrypted by blocks, i.e., groups, of characters (or blocks of bits), instead of single characters. This increases their security. However, since for blockchain we are mainly interested in cryptographic tools enabled by asymmetric encryption, we do not discuss these cyphers further in this book.

2.3.2 Asymmetric encryption

Asymmetric encryption is implemented by cyphers in which different keys are used for encrypting and decrypting a message. Given the complexity of this kind of cyphers, it is not possible to provide a concrete example of them in this book. References to concrete asymmetric systems are given at the end of this section. The objective of this section is to present asymmetric encryption conceptually. Specifically, we want to highlight how it can support more complex cryptographic applications than symmetric encryption.

The basic mechanism of asymmetric encryption is depicted in Figure 2.10. It involves two keys. These two keys are mathematically related so that one is used for encrypting messages and the other one for decrypting them. The keys are also

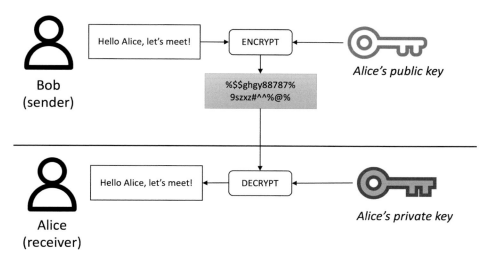

Figure 2.10 Asymmetric encryption (public key encryption).

assigned another property, i.e., whether they are 'public' or 'private'. A private key is such that it should not be distributed by its owner. It must be always kept secret by the owner. A public key can be distributed by its owner to anyone who needs it. Note that in symmetric encryption a key is always private. For instance, neither Caesar nor his lieutenants and soldiers should ever make the value of the key public when using a Caesar cypher. If an enemy gets hold of the value of the key, in fact, they could decrypt any message exchanged by them, or even encrypt fake commands as if they were issued by their general.

In asymmetric encryption, a user (Alice in Figure 2.10), who wants the world to be able to communicate with her, makes her public key available. Now, Bob can use Alice's public key to encrypt a message that he wants to send to her. Attackers in the middle may eavesdrop Bob's message. However, they will obtain only an encrypted message that they are not able to decrypt. Alice is the only one who can decrypt the messages encrypted using her public key, thanks to her private key. As mentioned before, secure communications between Alice and the world (including Bob) are guaranteed as long as nobody except Alice knows her private key.

Asymmetric encryption improves the symmetric one by reducing the number of actors required to know a private (secret) key. With a symmetric cypher, everyone involved in the communication must know the value of the key, which must remain secret to attackers. In asymmetric encryption, only the private key of the receiver must remain secret to the attackers. If Julius Caesar knew about asymmetric encryption, he could have written his public key on every road milestone across Europe!

As we did for cryptographic hashing, we conclude this section by briefly presenting two of the most prominent asymmetric encryption mechanism used today in the Computer Science Focus below.

Computer Science focus: modern asymmetric encryption systems

RSA cryptosystem

The Rivest Shamir and Adleman (RSA) [RSA78] is a system that can be used to generate pairs of public and private keys for asymmetric encryption. It is one of the oldest system invented and its acronym derives from the surnames of Ronald Rivest, Adli Shamir, and Leonard Adleman, who published the algorithm in 1977. The RSA system relies on the practical difficulty of factoring the product of two large prime numbers and of inverting the modulo function (i.e., the function returning the remainder of the division of two numbers). RSA is a relatively slow algorithm. Because of this reason, rather than encrypting the actual messages, it is often used to transmit securely the keys of symmetric cyphers that are then used to encrypt/decrypt messages.

Elliptic curve cryptosystem

The Elliptic-curve cryptography (ECC) [Bro09] is a system for generating pairs of public and private keys for asymmetric encryption based on the algebraic structure of elliptic curves over finite fields. More practically, the generation of the keys exploits the complexity of solving the so-called 'discrete logarithm problem'. ECC cryptography is generally faster than RSA (in key generation, message signing, decrypting of cypher text, and signatures, etc.), mainly because it achieves equivalent security using keys of smaller sizes. For this reason, it is used by modern cryptocurrency systems such as Bitcoin and Ethereum.

2.4 Digital signatures

The last cryptographic tool that we must introduce to understand blockchain is the digital signature mechanism. The problem addressed by digital signatures is the one of authenticating the digital messages between a sender and a receiver. Authentication is defined by the following two properties:

- The receiver must be able to verify undoubtedly the identity of the sender of a message.
- The sender must not be able to repudiate a message that they sent to a receiver.

These two properties are the same we expect from other authentication mechanisms that we use in the real world. We sign a private letter (when we still send it instead of an email!) to make sure that the receiver knows undoubtedly that we (and not somebody else) wrote it. Similarly, our signature is required on important documents often for a matter of non-repudiation: by signing a document, we acknowledge that we read it and we cannot repudiate that we know what is written in it in the future. Authentication also exploits other means than signatures. A pin number for a debit or credit card is a typical example of a private key. We must keep it secret, and it identifies us undoubtedly as the owner of the card associated with it.

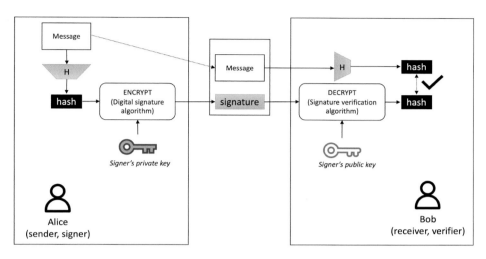

Figure 2.11 The digital signature mechanism.

Digital signatures implement an authentication mechanism similar to unique pin numbers in the case of digital communications. Figure 2.11 presents the digital signature mechanism. It combines asymmetric encryption and cryptographic hashing. Alice (the sender or, more generally, the 'signer' of a message) wants to send a message to Bob (the receiver, but also the 'verifier' of the signature in this context). Alice wants her message to be digitally signed. In this way, upon receiving the message, Bob will know for sure that Alice is indeed the sender of it. First, Alice calculates a cryptographic hash of the message that she wants to send (step 1). Then (step 2), this hash is encrypted by Alice using her private key. The hash of the message is its digital signature. Thanks to the properties of cryptographic hashing, it is in fact practically unique and it can only be generated from this particular message sent by Alice. Any other message, which differs for at least 1 bit from the one sent by Alice, has in fact a different hash. Moreover, it could only have been generated by Alice using her private key. In Step 3, the message and its digital signature are sent to Bob. After receiving the data, Bob does two things. First (Step 4), he calculates the cryptographic hash of the message. Then (Step 5), he decrypts the digital signature using Alice's public key. Finally (Step 6), he verifies that the hash of the message matches the decrypted digital signature.

The mechanism described above ensures that:

1 The message has not been modified while in transit. If it had, in fact, the hash calculated by Bob would not match the digital signature attached by Alice to her message.
2 Bob can establish undoubtedly that Alice is the sender of the message. The digital signature, in fact, could have been produced only by Alice, using her private key.
3 Alice cannot repudiate the fact that she sent the message received by Bob. The digital signature, in fact, could have been generated only by her.

Note that, when compared to the asymmetric encryption discussed in the previous section, in the digital signature mechanism the roles of the private and public keys are switched. The sender uses the private key to generate a part of the message (the digital signature). The receiver uses the public key of the sender to verify the authenticity of the digital signature.

It is also important to understand that the digital signature mechanism is orthogonal to message encryption. In Figure 2.11, the message is digitally signed, but not encrypted. This means that Bob can verify that Alice is the sender of the message, but a malicious attacker can eavesdrop on the message in plaintext while in transit. The digital signature mechanism of Figure 2.11 can be extended to include the encryption of the message. Depending on the application scenario there are two options:

- 'Encrypt and sign', in which the digital signature is generated using the cyphertext version of the message, i.e., after it is encrypted. This is the most straightforward option.
- 'Sign and encrypt', in which the digital signature is first generated before both the message and the signature are encrypted and sent. This option is often preferred because an attacker would have to first break the outer encryption before getting access to the digital signature.

In practice, digital signatures in the digital world work very similarly to wax seals in the (ancient) real world. High authorities, such as queens and kings, or the pope, used to send around the world their communications enclosed in envelopes sealed using a wax seal. A wax seal was supposed to be unique to the sender and hard to forge. For instance, it could be generated by imprinting a royal or papal ring, which was virtually impossible to forge, into warm wax. For the receiver, the wax seal was a guarantee of the identity of the sender. The message enclosed in a wax-sealed envelope, however, may or may not have been encrypted using some secret code.

2.5 Case study: a brief history of cryptography

The need for people to communicate securely secrets and messages of high importance has been around for thousands of years. Obviously, 'classic' cryptography relies only on pen and paper, rudimental mechanical aids, and plenty of imagination and inventiveness. In the world of fiction, for instance, the *Da Vinci Code*, a global bestseller written by American author Dan Brown in 2003, revolves around a mysterious mechanical device protecting a secret code allegedly revealing the location of the Holy Grail.

The establishment of cryptography as a discipline of intellectual endeavor is usually positioned in the 19th century. This is for two main reasons. On the one hand, the emergence of more complex cyphers and encryption methods to secure war communications. On the other , the emergence of more structured efforts to deal with cryptoanalysis, i.e., the systematic process of analyzing cryptographic systems with the aim of breaking them.

Since the 19th century, cryptography has been confined to military communications and, as such, has remained a concern of the military, governments, and secret services. One of the most prominent examples is the Enigma machine, a cypher device to protect commercial, diplomatic, and military communications widely used in the early 20th century. It has an electromechanical rotor mechanism that scrambles the 26 letters of the alphabet to implement a cipher. The rotor is connected to a set of lights to communicate with the user. Most prominently, this machine was used by Nazi Germany to protect their military communications. The cracking of the Enigma machine by Polish mathematicians in the early 30s was a breakthrough that facilitated the deciphering of German military communications by the Allied forces during World War II.

The role of cryptography in society has changed with the invention of public-key encryption and public data encryption standards. With public key encryption, the keys to secure communications need no longer be kept secret. The key to encrypt the message, specifically, could become public and distributed to anyone. This has allowed cryptography to cross the boundaries of military and diplomatic communications, enabling it to protect virtually any digital communication. The emergence of the Internet in the 1990s obviously provided plenty of opportunities and needs for the application of cryptographic tools. Nowadays, a large part of communications over the Internet, like access to Web pages, emails, or instant messaging, is protected by some kind of encryption protocol.

In the future, the most important development for cryptography is the one of quantum computing. Quantum computing [RP00] concerns the development of a new class of computing systems that exploit the principles of quantum mechanics, such as superposition and entanglement of quantum particles. Quantum computers may be able to achieve computational speeds orders of magnitude higher than even the most powerful current traditional computers. As such, they threaten the effectiveness of the most widely used cryptographic tools. For instance, digital signature mechanisms rely on the computational intractability of discrete mathematic problems, such as inverting modulo functions or solving discrete logarithms. While these problems cannot be solved in an acceptable time by even the most powerful traditional computers, quantum computers may be able to solve these problems relatively quickly. Thus, they endanger in principle the security of all systems where digital signatures are used, including blockchain.

The threat posed by quantum computers to cryptography is mitigated by two contingent factors. First, the development of quantum computers has been a bumpy road and we are still far away from having powerful and reliable quantum computers available on a large scale. Second, the scientific community has been aware of the quantum computing threat for a long time, and 'post-quantum' cryptographic tools are currently being designed and implemented by many researchers around the world [BL17].

2.6 Conclusions

This chapter did not talk about blockchain. Instead, it has introduced the basic cryptographic tools that are needed by blockchain to function. These are the cryptographic hash functions and the mechanism of digital signatures. Starting from the next chapter, we will see that hash functions enable the immutability of the data in a blockchain. Digital signatures enable the authentication of the participants in a blockchain.

Starting from the next chapter, we can finally talk about blockchain. The next chapter in fact introduces a definition of the blockchain mechanism that is general and abstract, i.e., which does not depend on any specific implementation of blockchain technology.

2.7 Questions and exercises

1 Given the Base-16 number 0x86d, answer the following questions: What number is it in Base-10? Is 1000 0110 1101 its correct representation in Base-2?

2   Convert the Base–10 number 678 in Base–16 and Base–2.

3   Can 0xabb67ad99 be the Base–16 representation of a 40–bit sequence?

4   Consider the Caesar cypher and a meaningful message m in English that has been encrypted using it; the obtained cyphertext c is 'isvjrjohpu pz mhuahzapj'.

   Which key (n) was used? What is the message?

   [consider only small letters in the 26–letter English alphabet]

5   In this chapter we have studied the application of cryptographic hashing for securing Internet downloads, encrypted password storage, and as part of the digital signature mechanism. Can you identify another application in which cryptographic hashing can be useful?

6   Extend the Figure 2.11 to depict the 'Sign and encrypt' and 'Encrypt and sign' mechanisms in digital signatures.

3 An implementation–agnostic definition of blockchain

Learning goals

3.A   The reader can explain the difference between public and private block-chain networks.

3.B   The reader can explain the concept of blockchain transaction and the gossiping of transactions in a network.

3.C   The reader can describe the typical structure of a block and understands how a chain of blocks can become immutable.

3.D   The reader can explain the need for a consensus mechanism in a blockchain and the problems that it addresses.

3.E   The reader can use the specification of the example system BC4C.

3.1 What is blockchain?

In this chapter we can finally answer the question that opened this book in Chapter 1: 'What is blockchain?' Blockchain is a mechanism, implemented through several technologies, to build systems that enable their users to exchange digital information (representing assets, like money, physical services and products, or valuable information) in a 'trustless' way. Trustless means that the users of a blockchain system may not trust each other (and we should never assume that they do, unless explicitly specified). Trust among the users is guaranteed instead by the blockchain mechanism, which underpins the system that they use to exchange assets. It is fundamental to understand that the trust of the users in the blockchain technology derives from its design features, such as the immutability of the data stored in it or the consensus mechanism. In other words, the trust is created by intrinsic features of the blockchain technology that the users cannot change or adapt to their specific needs.

From a technical standpoint, blockchain combines several technologies. Some of these, like digital signatures and cryptographic hashing, belong to the discipline of cryptography and have been introduced in Chapter 2. Other technologies, such as peer-to-peer networking and immutable databases, are introduced in detail later in this chapter.

Through the use of technology, the blockchain mechanism enables the implementation of blockchain systems. These are distributed information systems that use blockchain at their core to create trust among their users. Blockchain systems are the foundation of cryptocurrencies, which means that all cryptocurrencies have a blockchain system

DOI: 10.4324/9781003321187-4

at their core that users must use to exchange the cryptocurrency tokens. However, blockchain systems are not limited to cryptocurrencies. They support the implementation of information systems in several different scenarios, ranging from shipping containers management, to monitoring the food provenance or the diamond trade, or energy exchange in private microgrids.

3.2 Blockchain as a P2P network

A blockchain system involves a peer-to-peer (P2P) network of computational nodes connected through the Internet. A P2P network is such when all its nodes are the same, that is, they have the same rights and they get access to the same functionality. File-sharing networks, such as the BitTorrent protocol, are typical examples of P2P networks. Users of a file-sharing application can download files hosted by other users of the network and can host files to be downloaded by others. A P2P network assigns the same rights to every node, but it does not enforce the exercise of any of such rights from any of its users. For instance, in a file-sharing network every user has the right to host files that others can download, but many users do not use this right. They simply connect to the network to download files, but they do not host files that others can download. Other users act mainly as content providers, i.e., they provide files for others to download but they do not use the network to download files. Other users do both. Similarly, the nodes of a blockchain system are usually granted the same rights, but it is up to them to exercise these rights. In a blockchain system implementing a cryptocurrency, most nodes use the system to exchange the cryptocurrency tokens, but only few of them, for various reasons that are discussed in Part 2 of the book, implement specific functionality required to execute the consensus protocol.

Users connect to a blockchain network using a computer connected to the Internet and by running a specific software application. The functionality of this software is specified by a consortium, foundation, or other organization(s) that oversee the development and management of a blockchain network. As in any P2P network, when connecting to a blockchain network, a user normally does not directly connect to all the nodes that are already connected to the network. In other words, a computer connected

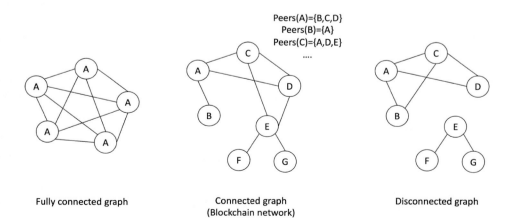

| Fully connected graph | Connected graph (Blockchain network) | Disconnected graph |

Figure 3.1 Connectivity in graphs and peer-to-peer networks.

to a blockchain network does not know an Internet address for all the other computers connected. Instead, a new user connects to a limited set of other users. These are normally chosen based on geographical proximity. The blockchain network, however, is built in such a way that there is always a path, starting from a given user, to reach any other user. Therefore, the nodes of a blockchain network form a connected graph, but a blockchain network is not a 'fully' connected graph (see Figure 3.1). In the remainder, we refer to the set of nodes to which a node is connected in a blockchain network as its 'peers'.

3.2.1 What is a user of a blockchain network?

The objective of this section is to shed light on the terminology to describe the users of a blockchain network and their internal computational functionality. First, we distinguish between users, clients, nodes, and accounts, which are terms often mentioned when describing specific implementations of blockchain systems. For instance, in the previous section we used the words 'user' and 'node' at different stages to refer to the participants in a blockchain network.

User: A user is a physical or organizational entity who uses a blockchain network. It can be Alice, Bob, Mrs. White, or Mr. Black, or any private or government-related organization. In many cases, the identity of a user may not be even known. For instance, Bitcoin and other cryptocurrencies users are identified by the address of their account (see below), but their actual identity is normally unknown.

Client: We usually refer to the client as the software application through which a user interacts with a blockchain system. The client can be a Web site, a mobile app, or a cryptocurrency ATM (which is basically a public computer where users can manage their Bitcoin accounts).

Node: Inside a client, a node is the software that implements the application logic required to interact with a blockchain network. In a cryptocurrency system, for instance, a node implements the logic to create the transactions transferring tokens to other users.

Account: In a blockchain system, an account is a unique identifier of a user interacting with a blockchain network. An account is usually the entity authenticating the messages that are issued by nodes on a blockchain network. Therefore, an account is usually associated with a private and public key to sign (authenticate) such messages and to verify the ones issued by other users of the network, respectively.

After having defined the users of a blockchain network and the software that they use to connect to the network, we can now introduce the concept of blockchain protocol:

Blockchain protocol: It is the set of rules that specify how a node can interact with other nodes in a blockchain network. These rules concern many aspects, ranging from the valid format of the messages (transactions) that nodes can issue in a blockchain network, to the rules of the consensus protocol. These rules constitute the specification of the software run by a node of a blockchain system. In other words, a node is a software implementation of the rules of the protocol of a blockchain system.

A blockchain system can be seen as the combination of the users in a blockchain network and the clients, nodes, and accounts that they use to interact with other users of the network.

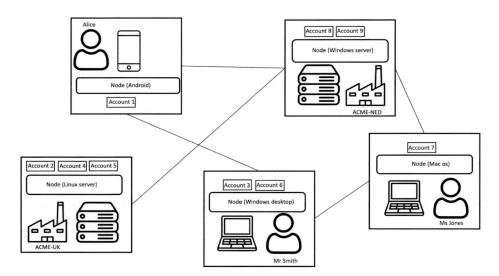

Figure 3.2 Users, clients, nodes, and accounts in a blockchain network. Each different type of node (server, desktop, mobile) may run a different software 'client' to connect to the blockchain network.

In real-world settings (see Figure 3.2), a user may interact with a blockchain system using one or more clients and through one or more nodes. Each node may then manage one or more accounts. For instance, a user of the Bitcoin network may send and receive bitcoins using an app on a mobile phone or a Web application. Both clients would include a node, i.e., a standard implementation of the Bitcoin protocol. A node can control one or more accounts, each of them identified by a different Bitcoin address through which a user can send or receive bitcoins.

In most cases, considering multiple clients, nodes, and/or accounts for a single user of a blockchain system introduces additional layers of complexity that hinder the understanding of the basic functioning of a blockchain system. Therefore, in the remainder of this book, without lacking generality and unless explicitly needed, we always refer to a standard configuration of one user, using one client containing one node, which controls one account. Since, in this simplified configuration, the concept of user, client, node, and account basically coincide, we often use them interchangeably. Specifically, we use in most cases the concept of 'node' of a blockchain network. According to the definition given above, in fact, a node is the part of a user's client implementing the application logic specific to the interaction with a blockchain network.

Before discussing in depth the functionality of a node of a blockchain system, we introduce here one more definition, the 'wallet'. You may have often heard about this concept, particularly in the context of Bitcoin and other cryptocurrencies.

Wallet: In the context of cryptocurrencies, a wallet is a software application that allows users to access and manage their digital assets (tokens), e.g., bitcoins. A wallet is normally owned by one user. Even if under-the-hood it may be using multiple accounts to interact with a blockchain network, a wallet usually allows digital asset management on a per-user basis. For instance, a Bitcoin wallet, normally owned by one specific user, may use different Bitcoin accounts to send and receive bitcoins. The details of these different accounts are usually hidden from a user. When using a wallet, users simply see the bitcoins that they own (i.e., the sum of all bitcoins in the accounts controlled by the wallet). The wallet allows users to send/receive Bitcoins to/from other users, who may be identified in different ways, e.g., by an email address or a specific Bitcoin account address.

Based on this definition, a wallet is a combination of a client, a node, and (possibly) several accounts controlled by one user of a blockchain system. Given this spurious characterization, in the remainder of the book we avoid referring to wallets as first-class citizens of a blockchain system.

3.2.2 Public and private blockchain networks

One important way to characterize blockchain systems is whether they rely on a public or private blockchain network.

A *public blockchain network* is one in which anybody can become a user. In these blockchain networks, a consortium, a foundation, an organization, or a group thereof maintains and updates when deemed necessary the specifications of the protocol used by the nodes of the network. The blockchain protocol in this case is usually made public, in the form of white papers and open-source standard client implementations. In this way, anybody can inspect the protocol and the software applications implementing it, if needed. Several implementations of the protocol can be available. These are software programs (written in different languages and for different platforms) that anybody can download and install on a computer to be able to run a node of the blockchain network. The Bitcoin network is probably the most prominent example of a public blockchain network. At https://bitcoin.org, several implementations of the software required to run a node of the Bitcoin blockchain network (referred to perhaps improperly as the 'wallet') are available, e.g., for Android/Ios mobile phones and for Windows/Mac/Linux desktops. Anyone can download this software and run a node of the Bitcoin network. A node obviously has an initial balance equal to 0 bitcoins, but it can receive bitcoins from other nodes.

A public blockchain network should be carefully designed to ensure its scalability. If successful, in fact, the number of nodes in the network may rapidly increase. For instance, the Bitcoin network was initially constituted by a few nodes and now it entails millions of nodes across the entire world.

A *private blockchain network* is one in which the access to the network is vetted. There is a mechanism in place to grant the right to participate into the blockchain network to a new node. The rights to access the blockchain network are granted by a consortium, foundation, organization, or group thereof that created the network in the first place. This type of blockchain systems are normally deployed in specific business scenarios. In such scenarios, a well-defined set of business partners, such as the organizations involved along a supply chain, decide to support at least part of their business using a blockchain system. First, they agree on the protocol used by the system. Then, they also decide which nodes and under which conditions these can be admitted into the system. The blockchain protocol and its implementations, in this case, are likely to be private. In many cases, in fact, being admitted to the system may represent a source of competitive advantage for an organization. Therefore, the system users may have a strong incentive in maintaining the details regarding the system implementation, such as the protocol used, private. Because the access to the blockchain network is controlled, the nodes of a private blockchain network can be trusted to a higher degree than in a public blockchain network. This has important implications on the design of blockchain systems relying on a private blockchain network, which are discussed in depth in Part 2 of this book.

3.3 Data management in a blockchain node: transactions and immutable databases

The nodes of a blockchain system interact by exchanging digital messages. These messages are normally called *transactions*. A transaction is issued by one node, which we call the *originator* of the transaction. Depending on the application scenario, a transaction may contain different types of data and it may be addressed to one or more other nodes of a blockchain system. For instance, a Bitcoin transaction specifies a transfer of cryptocurrency tokens (bitcoins). This can be between two accounts (one sender and one recipient) or among multiple accounts (multiple senders and/or multiple recipients). In a blockchain system to monitor a supply chain, transactions may contain more complex data about the routing of shipping containers. These transactions may not be addressed by one user to one or more other specific users (as in the Bitcoin example), but simply issued by one user, such as a port authority, to be consulted by any other user of the system, e.g., shipping companies and custom offices.

Even if they signify a message intended to specific user(s), transactions in a blockchain system are usually broadcast to all the nodes of a blockchain. Technically, this broadcast is achieved using a so-called 'gossip protocol'. The originator node sends a transaction that it wants to issue to its peers. These, in turn, broadcast the transaction to their peers and so on until a transaction reaches all the nodes of a blockchain network. Here we see the connectivity property in blockchain network at work: a transaction can reach all nodes only if there is at least one path in the blockchain network to reach them. During the gossiping, transactions are also usually validated by each node that receives them. For instance, nodes check that transactions contain all the information required by the blockchain protocol. Transactions that fail this validation step are usually not forwarded by the nodes to other nodes. Figure 3.3 shows an example of the gossiping protocol in action. The transaction T1 transfers 10 tokens from Alice to Luna. It has originated from Alice and it has reached Alice's peers (Bob, Carol, and Dave). Each node of the network maintains a 'distributed immutable ledger' (we will explain this in detail later) with the balance of every node of the network. The transaction T1 has not reached Eva, yet. This is why, for Eva, the balance of Alice and Luna is still 35 and 2, respectively, while for all the other nodes that have received T1 the balance of Alice is 25 and Luna's is 12.

Because nodes may be offline and/or may not implement all the functionality in a blockchain protocol, the gossiping of transactions can be unpredictable. This is normal not only in blockchain networks but also in large-scale P2P networks. If one node issues a transaction A now and another node (or even the same node) issues a transaction B very close in time after A,[1] we cannot assume that all the nodes in a blockchain network receive the transaction A before the transaction B. The order in which the transactions

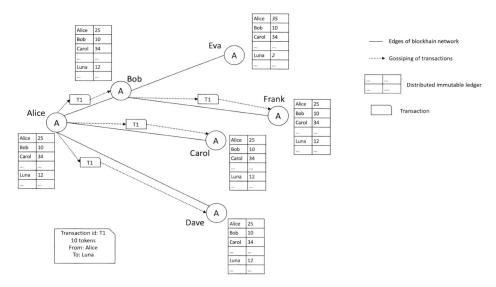

Figure 3.3 Gossiping of transactions and ledger update.

are received by a node depends on an extremely large number of variables, such as the paths of a blockchain network, the rules of the blockchain protocol, the availability of nodes, or the speed at which nodes validate transactions and forward them to their peers. This is an issue that we will revisit later in Section 3.4, where we discuss the need to introduce a consensus protocol to establish a proper order of the transactions agreed upon by all the nodes.

Based on what we have discussed thus far, it should be clear that a transaction in a blockchain system is not a direct private message issued by one node and addressed to one or more other nodes. We should instead view a transaction as a proposal to update the 'state' of a blockchain system. If such a proposal is valid, then all the nodes in the blockchain network store it in their database to be able to reproduce the change of state entailed by it. For instance, the 'state' of a cryptocurrency system is captured by the balance of tokens of every node. Then, a cryptocurrency transaction in which node A transfers 1 bitcoin to node B can be seen as an update of the system state. Every node of the network should know eventually that the balance of node A must decrease by 1 token, whereas the balance of the node B must increase by 1 token. Hence, we can now see clearly that the ledger of the nodes in Figure 3.3 shows the values of the variables describing the state of the system, i.e., the balance of every user. These variables are technically not immutable, since they are updated by every transaction. What is immutable is the sequence of the transactions that determines the value of the state variables (or, equivalently, the history of the values of the state variables).

As far as authentication is concerned, usually (ref. Chapter 2), a public key encryption mechanism is in place to guarantee the authentication of the transaction originator. Originators sign the transactions that they issue to a blockchain system using their private key. Any other node receiving a transaction verifies the identity of an originator using the originator's public key. This verification step is also part of the transaction validation. If the verification of the originator's identity fails, a node does not gossip a transaction to its peers.

Each node in a blockchain system stores the valid transactions that it receives in a database. As we discussed in Chapter 1, this database is immutable by design. This means that it is only possible to append new transactions to it, but it is not possible to modify, let alone delete, the transactions that are already stored in it. Because the first applications of blockchain technology that arose to the public attention were in finance, this database is often called a (transaction) ledger. Moreover, it is often referred to as a distributed ledger, because it is distributed among the nodes of a blockchain network. Mind, however, that being distributed in this case does not mean that every node stores only a subset of the transactions issued to a blockchain system. Every node in the network stores a complete copy of all the transactions that are issued to a blockchain system. At this stage, it should not surprise that blockchain technology, especially when relying on a private blockchain network, is often referred to as DLT (Distributed Ledger Technology). For a computer scientist, the difference between blockchain and DLT is finer-grained. It depends also on the way in which the transactions are physically stored in the database (see more details about this in the computer science focus box).

Computer Science focus: blockchain vs. DLT

Although they are often used as synonyms, blockchain and DLT are two different concepts. In particular, a blockchain – as the name suggests – requires transactions to be stored in blocks linked together in a chain-like structure.

Conversely, a DLT does not demand transactions to follow a chain-like structure. Instead, other data structures, e.g., a directed acyclic graph, can be used.

Therefore, it is correct to say that all Blockchains are DLTs, but not all DLTs are blockchains.

3.3.1 Implementing data immutability by design

An issue that has remained open until now in this book is understanding how it is possible to design a database that is immutable or, using the terminology introduced in the previous section, how to implement an immutable distributed ledger of transactions. This section solves this issue.

The fundamental technology behind the immutability of the ledger in a blockchain system is cryptographic hashing, which we introduced in Chapter 2. In a nutshell, given a digital message (like a transaction in a blockchain system), cryptographic hashing allows to create a digest of it in a fixed length that is practically unique.

Before looking at how cryptographic hashing can be exploited for building an immutable ledger, let us define the concept of block in a ledger simply as the smallest amount of data that can be appended to it. A block normally contains (see Figure 3.4) a header and a list of transactions:

- The header of a block contains metadata that describes it, such as a unique identifier, a timestamp capturing the time instant at which it was created, or the number

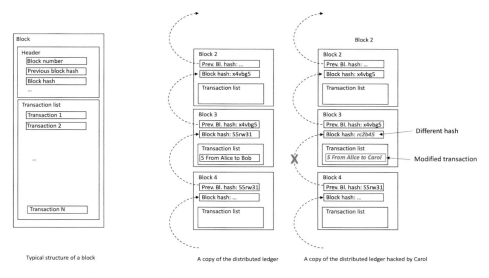

Figure 3.4 Block structure and block chaining to achieve immutability of the ledger.

of transactions that it contains. Because blocks normally can be ordered in time using the timestamp, the unique identifier of a block is often a progressive number: block 1 precedes block 2, which precedes block 3, and so forth.

- The transaction list normally contains a list of valid transactions that have been issued (recently) by nodes of the blockchain systems. The number of transactions included in a block depends on the implementation. Normally, transactions are grouped into blocks for efficiency reasons. However, there are even blockchain systems where each block contains only a single transaction.

Immutability in a ledger is created by enforcing that a block contains, normally in its header, two additional fields:

- The hash of the block, i.e., a cryptographic hash of the content of the block (header and transaction list).
- The hash of the previous block. For instance, block 3 contains the hash of block 2 in its header, block 4 contains the hash of block 3 in its header, and so forth.

As shown in Figure 3.4, the fact that a block contains the hash of its predecessor helps creating a 'chain of blocks' (sounds familiar?), in which consecutive blocks are linked by their matching hashes.

We are now ready to understand why creating a chain of blocks using the block hashes implicitly yields the immutability of the ledger storing the blocks. To do so, we should imagine what a malicious hacker (Carol in the example of Figure 3.4) should do in order to modify the content of the ledger:

- First, the hacker should modify the content of a block. Specifically, the hacker would aim at modifying the content of the transactions in a block. Figure 3.4

considers as an example a cryptocurrency system, where Carol wants to modify one transaction contained in block 3.

- Modifying the content of one block, however, changes the hash of that block. Based on what is discussed in Chapter 2, modifying even one single bit in a block changes its hash completely.
- Let us assume that the hacker succeeded somehow in modifying the content of one transaction in block 3. Now, the previous hash field in the header of block 4 no longer matches the hash of block 3. The hacker then must try to update the content of block 4, modifying the hash of the previous block to match the one of block 3, but ensuring that the hash of block 4 does not change. We know, however, that because of the property 1 of cryptographic hashing, this is (practically) impossible: if the content of block 4 changes, then its hash will also change.
- Alternatively, the hacker may try to modify the content of block 4 (for instance its header, which does not contain transactions) in the hope of making it such that the hash of block 4 stays the same. Because of property 2 of cryptographic hashing, however, we know that this is (practically) impossible, as well: it is impossible, in fact, that two 'versions' of the same block 4 map to the same hash value.
- Note that what we discussed so far applies when the hacker wants to modify the content of one specific copy of the distributed ledger. The same hacking process should also be applied to all the copies of the ledger, i.e., the copies held by every node participating in a blockchain system.

To summarize, the chain of blocks created by the chain of hashes in the header of the blocks ensures that a blockchain ledger cannot be modified. More precisely, it ensures that it is very easy for any node to quickly verify that its copy of the ledger has been modified and where (which block). This can be done simply by checking the chain of block hashes.

To conclude, there is one last (easy) problem that we need to solve when creating the chain of blocks, which concerns the start of such a chain. In other words, what is the previous block of the first block of an immutable ledger? This problem is simply solved by assuming that every ledger in a blockchain system begins with a conventional 'genesis block', for which the previous hash block is set to 0. Depending on the specific protocol implemented by a blockchain system, the genesis block may be very minimal, e.g., containing only a header, or may already contain a list of transactions.

3.4 Consensus mechanism

The last technology contributing to the functioning of blockchain systems is the consensus mechanism. The consensus mechanism ensures that all the nodes in a blockchain system maintain consistently the same copy of the ledger. In other words, the consensus mechanism ensures that all the nodes agree on the content of the ledger, i.e., which blocks and which transactions in them are included and in which order, at any point in time. This guarantees that, by replaying the transactions stored in the blocks of the ledger, every node can reconstruct the same current state of the blockchain system (or, at least, can verify that the current state that they are using is the correct one). For instance, in a cryptocurrency system, by replaying all the transactions from the creation of the system, any node can verify the correctness of the balance of every other node.

More in detail, the challenges of designing a consensus mechanism are better under-stood considering the following problem: how is it possible to establish the order of multiple transactions issued in a short time span? In the context of cryptocurrencies, this challenge goes under the label of preventing the 'double spending' of tokens.

To introduce the challenge of double spending, we consider a simple blockchain system in which every transaction records a transfer of a certain number of tokens of a cryptocurrency between two users. We call this token the CGM token (from the sur-name initials of the authors of this book). Now (see Figure 3.5), let us also assume that the user Alice has 10 CGM tokens and wants to use them to buy a mug from the user Bob for 6 CGM tokens, and a chair from the user Carol for 8 CGM tokens. Obviously, Alice does not have enough CGM tokens to pay for both items, but let us consider the following scenario:

- Alice creates one transaction (T1) transferring 6 CGM tokens to Bob and one trans-action (T2) transferring 8 CGM tokens to Carol. Alice issues both transactions to the blockchain network in a short time span. Based on what was discussed earlier in this chapter, we cannot guarantee that all other nodes receive these transactions (issued close in time) in the same order. Let us assume then that Bob receives T1 before T2, whereas Carol receives T2 before T1.
- Based on Alice's balance (10 tokens), any node considers the first transaction received between T1 and T2 valid, and rejects the second one as invalid (if T1 is processed first by a node, then for that node Alice has only 4 tokens left on her balance, which is also not enough to process T2; similarly for a node that processes T2 first).

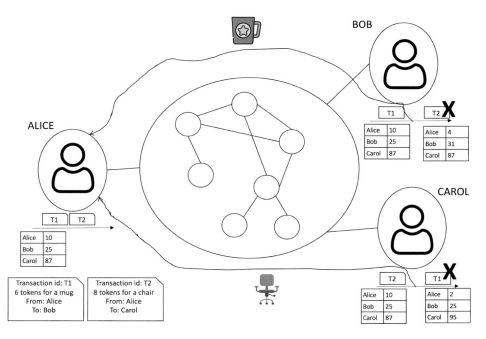

Figure 3.5 Double spending in blockchain exemplified.

- Now, if Bob receives T1 before T2, he thinks he has received the payment that he requested for the mug. Therefore, he sends the mug to Alice. Then, Bob rejects the transaction T2 because it is inconsistent with the current state of the blockchain system (i.e., Alice has only 4 tokens left). Similarly, if Carol receives T2 before T1, she thinks she has received the payment for the chair and sends it to Alice, rejecting the transaction T1.
- In the end, Alice may receive both the mug and the chair, somehow having managed to spend some of her CGM tokens 'twice' (i.e., double spending).

This simple example is archetypical of more complex issues that can arise in a blockchain system because of the ordering of transactions. We investigate more in depth this type of problems in Part 2 of the book. For now, it is important to realize that establishing an order of transactions agreed upon by all the nodes in a blockchain system is fundamental. In a blockchain system, we cannot rely on a central authority to fix this problem. If the exchange of CGM tokens among Alice, Bob, and Carol, for instance, is mediated by a bank, the problem of double spending as shown in Figure 3.5 would not exist: the bank would clear only the first transaction that either Bob or Carol originated, rejecting the second one because of insufficient funds in Alice's account. In a blockchain system, where only users exist and no central authority with 'special powers' is allowed, the users are left alone to solve this problem. In practice, the double spending problem is solved by devising rules to establish a consensus on which transactions are valid and in which order the transactions should be considered by nodes in the ledger.

The consensus mechanism is implementation-specific and more details about the consensus mechanisms used for instance by Bitcoin or Ethereum are presented in Part 2. In this chapter, our aim is not to describe specific consensus mechanisms. Instead, we only want to briefly discuss the difference between two classes of consensus mechanisms for blockchain systems: absolute and emergent consensus mechanisms.

An 'absolute' consensus mechanism is one in which the order of the transactions is determined through an explicit protocol of message exchange among the nodes of a blockchain system. This type of consensus mechanisms usually require a large number of messages exchanged among all the nodes of a blockchain system. Therefore, absolute consensus protocols are typical of private blockchain systems, where the number of nodes is usually limited and the identity of every node is known.

An 'emergent' consensus mechanism is one in which the order of the transactions 'emerges' statistically from the combination of the behavior of the nodes in a blockchain network. On the one hand, usually an emergent consensus does not involve extensive message exchange among the blockchain nodes. On the other hand, it also does not guarantee that all the nodes reach an agreement at a precise point in time. Instead, the agreement reached by the nodes has more of a probabilistic nature. Even though some uncertainty regarding the status of a transaction issued to a network may be present initially, in time all the nodes agree on the validity and the exact position of all transactions in the ledger. The consensus mechanism adopted by most cryptocurrency systems is of this kind.

3.5 A more precise specification of BC4C

To conclude this chapter, in this section we revisit the example of BC4C introduced in Chapter 1. Specifically, we discuss in depth how the elements of a blockchain system that we introduced in this chapter can be concretely defined in BC4C.

BC4C Network: BC4C relies on a public blockchain network. We assume, in fact, that anybody who is interested in playing a game of chess online and who has a computer connected to the Internet could download the software program implementing the rules of the BC4C protocol and run a BC4C node.

BC4C protocol: The most important aspect to define in BC4C is the protocol. Based on what was already discussed in Chapter 1, we can devise the following rules controlling the functioning of BC4C:

- A game in BC4C involves two nodes (i.e., the players). A new game is proposed by a player and must be accepted by the opposition player before it can start. A simple unique game id can be generated when a game is proposed by attaching a progressive number to the concatenation of the two players' names. For instance, the third game played between Alice and Bob has the id 'AliceBob3'.
- A game starts with the standard configuration of a chess board, in terms of number and type of pieces and their position on the board. We assume these are known to the readers and, therefore, we do not repeat them here.
- The players of a game take turns in making moves. We assume that the player who proposed a game moves first. A move is proposed by one player and must be accepted by the other player. We assume that the valid moves of the different pieces on a chessboard are known to the readers and we do not repeat them here. A unique id for each move can be generated following simple rules (see later for examples).
- A game terminates when a checkmate move is proposed by one player and this is approved by the counterpart.

BC4C transactions: Based on the rules of the BC4C protocol, a node of BC4C can issue different types of transactions. These are listed next (the data included in each type of transaction are listed in squared brackets):

- `CreateNewGame [gameId, counterPlayer]`: This type of transaction creates a new game between the originator of the transaction and another player, identified by the parameter `counterPlayer`.
- `ConfirmGameCreation [gameId]`: This type of transaction confirms the creation of a game. It is issued by the counter player.
- `Move[gameId, moveId, piece, new position, isCheckMate]`: This type of transaction specifies a move in a game. A move involves moving a piece to a new position on the board. A Boolean flag `isCheckMate` identifies whether the move leads to checkmate.
- `ConfirmMove [gameId, moveId]`: This type of transaction is issued by a player to confirm the validity of a move issued by a counter player.

BC4C ledger: After having specified the rules of the BC4C protocol and listed the type of transactions that can be issued by players, we can now give an example of the content of the ledger of the BC4C system (see Figure 3.6). For simplicity, we assume that each block contains only one transaction, so the content of the ledger can be simply shown as a list of transactions. The hashes of the transactions are not relevant for this example and therefore are not shown. The following should be noted regarding the state of this system:

- A total of nine transactions have been issued from the inception of the system.
- There are currently two games being played: `AliceCaroll` and `BobCaroll`. The game `DaveAlice1` has been proposed by Dave, but not confirmed by Alice, yet.

Transaction id	Transaction	Originator	Timestamp
0	Genesis of BC4C	BC4C	22-04-19 12:00:17
1	CreateNewGame[AliceCarol1, Carol]	Alice	22-04-20 09:00:03
2	CreateNewGame[BobCarol1, Carol]	Bob	22-04-20 09:00:45
3	ConfirmGameCreation[BobCarol1]	Carol	22-04-20 09:01:23
4	ConfirmGameCreation[AliceCarol1]	Carol	22-04-20 09:01:28
5	Move[BobCarol1, 1, pawn_h2, h3, false]	Bob	22-04-20 09:02:34
6	CreateNewGame[DaveAlice1, Alice]	Dave	22-04-20 09:02:48
7	Move[AliceCarol1, 1, pawn_d2, d4, false]	Alice	22-04-20 09:03:01
8	ConfirmMove[AliceCarol1, 1]	Carol	22-04-20 09:03:55
9	Move[AliceCarol, 2, pawn_a2, a3, false]	Carol	22-04-20 09:04:26

Content of the ledger (transactions)

State of the system (games currently playing)

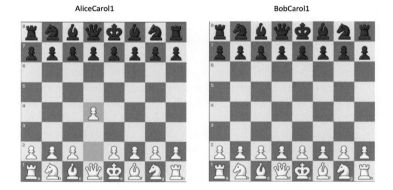

Figure 3.6 Ledger and state of the system example in BC4C.

- There are no confirmed moves played in the game BobCarol1, whereas one move has been confirmed in the game AliceCarol1 (see transactions 4 and 8). In the same game, Carol has proposed her own first move (transaction 9), but this has not yet been confirmed by Alice.

Based on the examples introduced in this chapter, it should be clear by now that, while the objective of the distributed immutable ledger in a blockchain system is always to store information regarding the state of the system, there are two possible ways in which this can be done:

1 *Storing a list of transactions*: Typically, the ledger in a blockchain system contains a list of transactions. Figure 3.4 has showed the typical structure of a block in the ledger containing a list of transactions. When the ledger contains a list of transactions, the state of the blockchain system can be reconstructed at any time by nodes by replaying all the transactions contained in the ledger from the genesis block onwards. This is the strategy that we have adopted in the design of BC4C (see Figure 3.6). Because all the transactions must be replayed any time a value of a state variable is required by a node, this strategy may be very ineffective and resource-consuming in real-world settings. In practice, blockchain systems are often designed to limit the number of transactions that must be replayed by a node to reconstruct the state

of a system. At least, given the value of a certain variable defining the state, such as the balance of a user in a cryptocurrency system, only a limited number of transactions must be checked to verify that the value of a state variable is correct.

2   *Storing the values of state variables*: Instead of a list of transactions, the ledger may store directly the values of a set of variables describing the state of the system. In this chapter, we have made this assumption when we considered cryptocurrency systems, such as in the examples of Figures 3.3 and 3.5. In this strategy, the transactions become simply instructions for the nodes to update the values of the variables describing the state of a blockchain system. Once the update entailed by it has been executed in the ledger, a transaction can be in principle discarded. When this strategy is adopted, nodes can easily and quickly consult the state of the blockchain system at any time. However, by recording only the value of the state variables, this strategy prevents nodes to reconstruct the history of individual proposed state changes, i.e., the transaction history. Some systems, such as Ethereum (see Chapter 6), use a mixed strategy, in which both the list of transactions and the values of state variables are recorded.

3.6 Case study: the predecessors of bitcoin

In this chapter, we have understood that Bitcoin is a cryptocurrency system. A cryptocurrency system is a blockchain system that keeps track of exchanges of tokens of a digital currency among nodes. The state of the blockchain system is determined by the balance of each node of the network. The transactions represent the exchange of tokens among the nodes of the network. There are no intermediaries in Bitcoin (or any cryptocurrency system). All the nodes of the blockchain network are equal and they can agree on the state of the system through a carefully designed consensus mechanism. Moreover, a fundamental feature of Bitcoin, and cryptocurrencies in general, is that they are designed to prevent the so-called 'double spending'of tokens. Double spending occurs when a poorly designed protocol allows the nodes to use their tokens more than once in the real world, e.g., transferring a token to a friend to repay a debt and, at the same time, sending the same token to another node in exchange for some physical goods.

Even though we know only relatively little about Bitcoin, and in particular we know barely anything about the more technical aspects related with its protocol, we know enough to compare, at least at a high level, a modern cryptocurrency system with the efforts made in the past to create different forms of 'digital money'. More in detail, we divide these efforts into two categories:

- 'digital cash' solutions, which still rely on a central authority to guarantee the consistency of the system state, i.e., the balance of all the users, and
- 'completely decentralized' systems, which, similarly to Bitcoin, propose to implement digital cash without assuming the existence of a central intermediary.

3.6.1 Digital (non-decentralized) cash systems

In the late 1980s, petrol stations in the Netherlands floated for the first time the idea of putting money onto smart cards that drivers could use to pay for re-fueling instead of cash. The push for such a system came from petrol station operators. Night raids of petrol stations for cash were on the rise. Operators had to find a way to keep operations safe while staying open at night for allowing the re-fueling of trucks (a particularly lucrative part of their business). Since then, the Point-of-Sale (PoS) technology, allowing payments to be taken by merchants directly from a customer's bank account, has become mainstream, both for brick-and-mortar and Internet-based merchants. Nowadays, digital money can also be stored in 'digital purses', i.e., smart cards not tied to a particular bank account or user, in which money can be loaded using cash, a debit/credit card, or a bank account transfer.

The idea of a digital form of money in which cryptographic tools enable the 'blind exchange' appeared first in DigiCash, also in the late 1980s. In DigiCash, cryptography is used to secure the anonymity of users and to equip any transfer of tokens with a digitally verifiable signature of the sender. DigiCash as a business venture ran out of money in 1998. One of the main reasons why this idea did not gather substantial mainstream interest probably lies in its focus on business customers, such as merchants and other private companies, rather than retail users. DigiCash still relied on the usual banking systems for the clearing of financial transactions.

PayPal is probably the most used form of digital money nowadays, allowing direct money transfers between (private and commercial) users. These are identified simply by an email address. Even though it can be classified as a form of digital money, from the perspective of blockchain technology, PayPal is clearly a central intermediary handling the interaction with the traditional banking system on behalf of its users.

3.6.2 *Completely decentralized digital cash systems*

In 1998, the developer Wei Dai published a white paper [Dai98] proposing the idea of B-Money, an anonymous and distributed digital cash system. B-Money relied on digital pseudonyms to identify its anonymous users. It also defined a mechanism for decentralized enforcement of money transfers among its users, i.e., a primitive form of consensus mechanism. Even though it never obtained commercial traction, some of the design features of B-Money are mentioned as a reference in Bitcoin's white paper.

Bit Gold [Sza05], proposed by cryptographer Nick Szabo, was the first decentralized form of digital money involving a consensus mechanism based on the same principles of Bitcoin's consensus protocol (the proof-of-work, see Chapter 5 for more details). Like B-Money, Bit Gold never got any substantial commercial traction.

The most successful pre-Bitcoin form of digital money completely decentralized was HashCash [Bac02]. Developed in the mid-1990s, the design of HashCash included many of the design features of modern cryptocurrencies, such as digitally signed transactions and a proof-of-work consensus protocol. Struggling to cope with a growing number of users and increased computational power to maintain the execution of the consensus protocol, HashCash become largely ineffective toward the end of the 1990s. It was then slowly abandoned by its users. The design of modern cryptocurrencies, such as Bitcoin, is clearly infused with many of the principles firstly implemented by HashCash.

3.7 Conclusions

This chapter has proposed an implementation-agnostic definition of blockchain systems. We first introduced the basic terminology that is used throughout this book when discussing concrete blockchain system implementations. This basic glossary defines terms like blockchain protocol, user, client, account, and node of a blockchain system, wallet, public and private blockchain network, and consensus mechanism. Using these definitions, we have also specified more precisely the BC4C blockchain system.

Note that concrete blockchain system implementations can be characterized by design choices that may not fit entirely with the model presented in this chapter. For instance, in this chapter we assumed that the distributed ledger of a blockchain system stores the transactions issued by the nodes. However, there are blockchain systems in which the ledger stores the variables describing the state of a blockchain system. We also discussed that the immutability of the ledger is guaranteed by a chain of blocks of transactions. There are however blockchain systems that use different 'chained' data structures to ensure immutability.

Nevertheless, we believe that the definitions introduced in this chapter are general enough to characterize blockchain technology in a broad sense and to be applied to different concrete implementations of blockchain systems. In the next chapters, we discuss in detail special cases in which specific design choices in the implementation of a blockchain system may seem to deviate from what is presented in this chapter.

The next chapter extends the implementation-agnostic definition of blockchain systems to include the concept of smart contracts. Smart contracts represent the missing feature to turn blockchain systems into full-fledged distributed information systems that can support arbitrary computations over the data stored in a distributed ledger.

3.8 Questions and exercises

1   Consider the following business scenarios: (a) the supply chain of Dutch flowers in Europe (e.g., how tulips grown and harvested in the Netherlands reach a flower market in Italy or Denmark) and (b) managing student information, like grades and degrees, in a national university system. For each scenario, discuss how blockchain can be used to support the information exchange among the stakeholders and what benefits the use of blockchain could bring. Focus specifically on: the blockchain network (Public or private? Who are the nodes?), the data exchanged (What type of transactions are exchanged? How would the ledger look like?), and the consensus protocol (What rules would you put in place to make the nodes agree?).

2   Bank cheques used to be a widespread form of payment until the early 2000s. Like cryptocurrency systems, they were also characterized by the issue of double spending. Describe the issue of double spending with bank cheques (you may need to do some research if you are too young to know what a bank cheque is), the solutions to it, and compare it with the issue of double spending in cryptocurrency blockchain systems that we discussed in this chapter.

3   Consider an instance of the BC4C system. Table 3.1 shows the ledger containing the list of transactions issued in this blockchain:

  1   Can you find errors in the ledger of Table 3.1? In which transaction(s)?
      Now consider two cases:
    1   The ledger obtained by fixing (in the most reasonable way) the errors identified at (1).
    2   The ledger obtained by deleting the transactions in which you have identified an error.
      Answer the following questions in the two cases (1) and (2):
  2   Is a game between Steph and Luka currently being played?

Table 3.1 Example transaction list in BC4C

Transaction id	Transaction	Originator
0	Genesis of BC4C	BC4C
1	CreateNewGame[LukaTrae1, Trae]	Luka
2	CreateNewGame[LukaRuss1, Russ]	Luka
3	CreateNewGame[StephLuka1, Luka]	Steph
4	ConfirmGameCreation[LukaRuss1]	Russ
5	ConfirmGameCreation[LukaTrae2]	Trae
6	CreateNewGame[StephKlay1, Klay]	Steph
7	Move[LukaTrae1, 1, …, …, false]	Luka
8	ConfirmGameCreation[StephKlay1]	Klay
9	Move[StephKlay1, 1, …, …, false]	Steph
10	ConfirmMove[LukaTrae1,1]	Trae
11	ConfirmMove[StephKlay1,1]	Klay
12	Move[StephKlay1, 2, …, …, false]	Steph
13	CreateNewGame[LukaRuss2, Russ]	Luka

   3   How many moves have been played and confirmed in game 'StephKlay1'?

   4   How many games are currently confirmed?

  4 Consider a modified version of the BC4C blockchain where:

    a Moves do not have to be confirmed by the counterpart, i.e., the correctness of moves according to the rules of chess is checked when a transaction is validated by a node.

    b Because of (a), checkmate moves do not have to be confirmed as well.

    c The players can pause and resume a game at any time. Pausing/resuming is done by a node issuing a transaction and can be done only by a node only when it is their turn to move.

     Provide a specification of this system, i.e., type of transactions and blockchain protocol rules.

  5 Using the content of Section 3.5 as a reference, imagine and describe a new block-chain system (hint: you can think of a system supporting a different type of online game, or a completely different application scenario – like the ones mentioned in this chapter). After having described the objective of the system, list the rules of the blockchain protocol, the type of transactions that can be issued by its users and give an example of the content of the distributed ledger.

Note

  1 What constitutes 'close in time' in this example depends on the specific blockchain system under consideration. Transactions spaced even minutes in time may still be considered 'close' in Bitcoin, whereas in other systems, such as Ethereum, transactions may be processed more quickly. More details are discussed for specific blockchain systems in Part 2.

4 Extending blockchain with smart contracts

Learning goals

4.A The reader can discuss the need to extend blockchain with smart contracts.

4.B The reader can explain how smart contracts extend the model of blockchain presented in Chapter 4.

4.C The reader can explain what kind of data can be handled by a smart contract and the limitations of the computation that a smart contract can carry out.

4.D The reader can explain the behavior of the example systems BC4C-CGM and BC4C-CGM+.

4.1 The case for extending blockchain with business logic

As we learnt in Chapter 3, a blockchain system can be abstracted as what could be called by a computer scientist a 'distributed state machine'. This is a combination of technological features and protocols enabling a set of computational nodes to agree on the state of a system without requiring a central intermediary. The transactions submitted by the nodes of a blockchain modify the value of the variables that capture the state of the system. Since these transactions are stored by every node locally in an immutable database, every node is always able to reconstruct the current state of a blockchain system. This can be done by replaying the transactions stored in the ledger. Thanks to the consensus protocol, all the nodes store the same transactions in the same order. This ensures that nodes reconstruct exactly the same state of the system when replaying the history of transactions.

In a cryptocurrency system, for instance, the state is captured by the value of the balance of every user. A transaction between a sender and a recipient node modifies the state of the system by increasing the balance of the recipient and decreasing the balance of the sender. In a blockchain system to monitor a supply chain, the variables describing the state of the system can be the location of a container, its content, and the shipping company in charge of delivering it. When a vessel enters a port, the location of all the containers carried by it can be updated by a transaction issued by the port authority.

Now, an interesting question that became prominent in the early 2010s is the following: would it be possible to extend a blockchain system with business logic that updates autonomously the state using the variables stored in the ledger, based on the input

DOI: 10.4324/9781003321187-5

provided by the transactions? To explain this question more in detail, next we extend the BC4C system.

Let us consider an extended version of the BC4C system that includes the CGM token as a cryptocurrency (we call this system BC4C–CGM). Besides being able to play games of chess, every node now also owns a certain number of CGM tokens. At this stage, it is not important to know how nodes obtained the tokens, let alone what is their price in US dollars or any other fiat currency. The tokens may be bought by users using fiat money, or they may have value only within the BC4C system, for instance to buy badges and other 'virtual' achievement evidence, while being worthless in the real world.

In BC4C–CGM, to make the games more competitive and exciting, both players engaged in a game are required to deposit a certain number of CGM tokens before a game starts. At the end of a game, the winner will collect all the tokens deposited by both players. This is a simple way to include, in our example system, a more general feature of e-sports, i.e., the gambling ecosystem that they enable. Simply, instead of assuming that bets on games can be placed by anybody, we restrict this capability only to the players of a game. In other words, the deposits can be seen as a way for players to bet on their ability to win a game. Moreover, this scenario looks like one that is more increasingly supported by e-sports in the real world: instead of using fiat money, bets can be placed using cryptocurrency tokens.

The first way to implement the BC4C–CGM blockchain (see Figure 4.1), is to rely on the off-chain world, i.e., involving entities outside the blockchain network. Any two

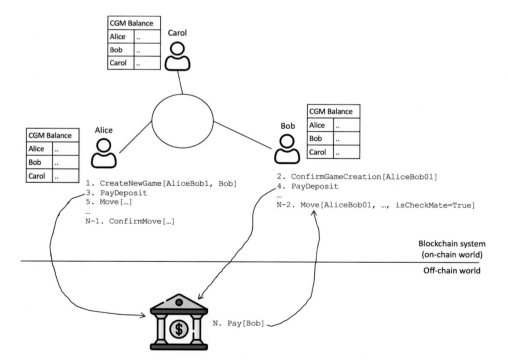

Figure 4.1 An off-chain implementation of the BC4C–CGM blockchain.

players of a game, in this off-chain implementation, must agree to pay the deposits to a trusted intermediary in the off-chain world, such as a bank, a notary, or a very good common friend. This intermediary (or central authority) keeps the deposits safe during the game and agrees to send them to the winner of a game once it is determined. We have learnt, however, that in the blockchain world central authorities are not allowed, basically because they cannot be trusted. Therefore, how can we implement BC4C-CGM fully 'on-chain', i.e., without relying on an off-chain trusted intermediary?

Before answering this question, we need to clarify that we cannot implement BC4C-CGM using only what we discussed in Chapter 3. The problem that we would face is that, without an intermediary, who or what will 'keep the deposits safe' while a game is played? And, how could the deposits be paid back to the winner? In BC4C, in fact, the state of the blockchain can be modified only by the transactions issued by the users. Moreover, the state changes entailed by a transaction are executed as soon as a transaction is processed. There is no way to (i) 'delay' the effect of a transaction (e.g., a deposit will not be available to a player to be spent as long as a game is still being played) and (ii) make the effects of a transaction 'conditional' (e.g., if a node loses a game, the node will not get back its deposit back).

The answer to the question made above lies in creating the 'business logic' required to implement the BC4C-CGM system and embedding it directly into the blockchain. Conceptually, in fact, the business logic that implements this feature requires manipulating the variables defining the state of the blockchain. The two variables to be manipulated are the balances of any two players that start a game: when a deposit is paid, the business logic should record that this has happened and decrease accordingly the balance of the players who paid the deposit; once both deposits are paid, the business logic should notify the two players that the game can start; finally, once it receives the notification of the end of a game (including the identity of the winner), the business logic should update the balance of the winner only.

Practically (see Figure 4.2), we can write a (simple) computer program that the players of a game can call only once to deposit the correct number of CGM tokens. This program keeps the deposits safe (i.e., no user is allowed to modify the deposits after they have been paid). Then, once the outcome of the game is determined, the program pays automatically the deposits to the winning player. Note that the ownership of CGM tokens is simply determined by the values of the state variables of the blockchain system. Therefore, implementing this feature means defining additional state variables for the BC4C system, such as the values of the deposits associated with each game. These can be updated by the computer program that we have described above. The computer program implementing this feature must be installed locally by every node of the system, so that every node has access to it and can call it when necessary.

In a nutshell, this computer program plays by itself the role of the intermediary. However, since it is a software program and not a human being or an organization in the off-chain world, it can be distributed to all the nodes and trusted by all nodes to always behave faithfully according to its specification. Computer programs, in fact, simply do what they are programmed to do, they cannot willfully cheat!

What we just described is technically a 'smart contract'. We could broadly define a smart contract as a software program that is deployed by all the nodes of a blockchain system and that can manipulate, autonomously or based on input from the transactions issued by the nodes, the variables defining the state of a blockchain. Being deployed

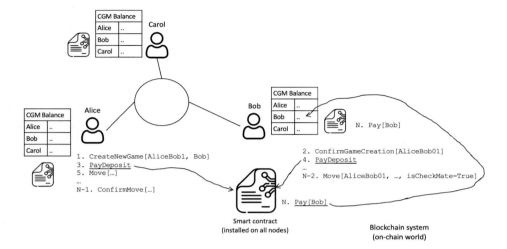

Figure 4.2 Implementing the BC4C–CGM system using a smart contract.

in every node, the nodes of a system can now issue a new type of transaction, i.e., transactions that invoke a smart contract.

The main features of smart contracts and the challenges associated with deploying them in a blockchain system are discussed more in depth in the next section. In this section, as a final note, we would like to discuss more about the meaning of the label 'smart contract'. While it is universally accepted (see the case study later in this chapter about its origin) and therefore used in this book, the label 'smart contract' may convey a misleading impression to readers not familiar with the blockchain domain. The smart contracts of blockchain systems, in fact, are not particularly 'smart'. They are not 'smarter' than any other business logic that can be coded into a traditional information system. Actually, as discussed in detail later in this chapter, the fact that smart contracts are embedded within a blockchain system poses strict limitations on the logic that can be implemented into them. Moreover, smart contracts are not necessarily common legally binding 'contracts'. In particular, they are not always contracts involving financial clauses among two or more principals. Smart contracts may be used to implement the legally binding business logic of business contracts in the real world. However, smart contracts are generally less ambitious. They simply aim at capturing the standard business logic of information processing systems that goes beyond the mere assignment of new values to state variables.

4.2 Properties of smart contracts

In this section, we present a more detailed analysis of the properties of smart contracts in blockchain systems. We divide these into three classes of properties:

1 The type of business logic that can be implemented in a smart contract
2 The data that can be manipulated by smart contracts
3 The specific properties of smart contracts entailed by their deployment into blockchain systems

4.2.1 *What kind of business logic can be implemented by a smart contract?*

The easiest way to think of a smart contract is to think of a computer program written using a procedural programming language. Such a program may receive some parameters in input and produces an output. To understand the type of output produced by a smart contract, it is important to distinguish between 'stateless' and 'stateful' smart contracts.

A stateless smart contract is one that, given an input, always returns the same output. In other words, the behavior of such smart contracts is determined only by the input that is provided. Therefore, this type of smart contracts do not maintain an internal state, which could possibly influence the behavior of the contract. As a concrete reference for a stateless smart contract, readers can think of a simple python script. A python script may be called giving some data in input. The script then may perform some calculations on the data or some modifications of the data, returning as output the results of the calculation or a modified version of the input data. No matter who invokes it, when, and under which circumstances, the output of the script depends only on the data that are provided as input.

A more interesting type of smart contracts is the 'stateful' one. Stateful smart contracts maintain an internal state. Therefore, their output depends on both the input received and their internal state when they are invoked. Figure 4.3 shows a simple example of a smart contract that, given the price of an item, returns the discount applied to it. The smart contract exposes one operation to be invoked (`calcDiscount`). This operation receives a price as an input parameter. The stateless version simply calculates a 20% discount: no matter when or by whom it is invoked, the discount returned is always 20% of the price received in input. The stateful version applies the 20% discount only to the first ten invocations. From the 11th customer onwards, the discount is not applied. This stateful version must maintain an internal state. In this case, the state is constituted by the number of invocations (or calls) received. The smart contract state is updated with every invocation, by increasing the value of the state variable `call` of one unit. Note that the state of a smart contract is different from the state of a blockchain system. The former, is local to the implementation of a smart contract, whereas the

STATELESS   STATEFUL

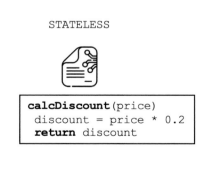

```
calcDiscount(price)
  discount = price * 0.2
  return discount
```

```
Initial state:
calls = 0
```

```
calcDiscount(price)
  if calls < 10
    discount = price * 0.2
  else
    discount 0
  calls = calls + 1
  return discount
```

Figure 4.3 Stateless and stateful smart contracts.

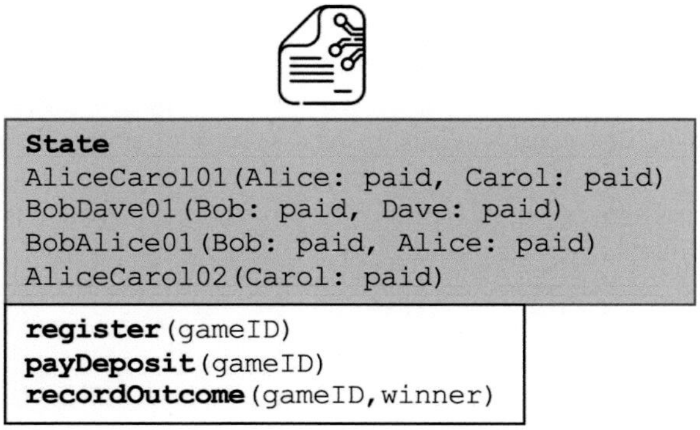

State
AliceCarol01(Alice: paid, Carol: paid)
BobDave01(Bob: paid, Dave: paid)
BobAlice01(Bob: paid, Alice: paid)
AliceCarol02(Carol: paid)

register(gameID)
payDeposit(gameID)
recordOutcome(gameID,winner)

Figure 4.4 The smart contract in the BC4C-CGM system.

latter is shared by all the nodes of a blockchain network (and possibly updated by the execution of smart contracts). This difference will become clearer as we discuss more examples of smart contracts in the remainder of the chapter.

The smart contract for the BC4C-CGM system that we introduced in the previous section is an example of a stateful smart contract (see Figure 4.4). The internal state of the smart contract is represented by the list of games for which a deposit has been paid. For instance, in Figure 4.4 there are four games registered. For one of these (AliceCarol02) only one player has paid the deposit (Carol). The smart contract can be invoked for (i) registering a new game, (ii) paying the deposit of a registered game, and (iii) recording the outcome of a registered game. For example, if a player tries to invoke the smart contract to pay a deposit for a game, then the smart contract behaves differently depending on its internal state:

- If the game has not yet been registered, then the smart contract returns an error (i.e., 'the game does not exist!'). For instance, the call payDeposit(BobAlice01) made either by Bob or Alice would return such an error.
- If the game is already registered, then the smart contract accepts the deposit and updates its own state (recording the fact that a player has paid the deposit). For instance, Alice can pay the deposit of the game AliceCarol02 by calling payDeposit(AliceCarol02).

After both players of a registered game for which the deposits have been paid have recorded the outcome of a game (and the outcome declared by both players is the same), the smart contract triggers the payment of the deposits to the winner. Note that any transfer of CGM tokens by the smart contract is implemented simply as an update of the blockchain state (which for simplicity is not represented in Figure 4.4):

- When a deposit is paid, the CGM balance of the player paying the deposit is simply decreased.
- When the outcome of a game is determined, the CGM balance of the winner of the game is increased by a quantity equal to the sum of the deposits paid by both players.

To summarize, from the point of view of the business logic that they can implement:

- Smart contracts are computer programs written in some computer language understood by all the nodes of a blockchain system.
- Smart contracts expose different functions, which may be invoked (called) by the nodes of a blockchain system.
- Smart contracts may maintain an internal state, which can be modified by the node invocations.
- The execution of a smart contract does at least one of the following:
  - Modifies the internal state of the smart contract
  - Returns a value as the result of an internal computation of the smart contract
  - Modifies the state of the blockchain system

4.2.2 Which data can be handled by a smart contract?

To some extent, the answer to this question is already included in the answer to the previous one. Smart contracts handle three different types of data:

- *Input parameters*: As we discussed in the previous section, smart contracts are invoked by the nodes of a blockchain system. The invocation of a smart contract can be seen as a function call of a procedural programming language. This can involve one or more input parameters. For instance, in our example, a smart contract invocation to pay the deposit for a registered game should include an id of the game for which the deposit is paid. If we assume that the deposit is fixed for all games, then no other parameter is required. Otherwise, another parameter to specify the amount deposited must be provided. Practically, these input parameters are provided as part of a transaction. Indeed, since transactions are the only messages that users can issue in a blockchain system, we must use transactions even to invoke smart contracts. Therefore, the nodes issue (digitally signed) transactions to invoke the smart contracts. If necessary, these transactions include also input parameters for the invocation.
- *Internal state variables*: A smart contract may define and maintain a set of variables describing its internal state. In our example, the variables describing the internal state of the smart contract are the list of registered games, the addresses of the players, and Boolean variables for each of them recording whether the deposits have been paid by the players. Note that, even though internally a smart contract may define many variables necessary for the computation, the ones that describe the internal state are only the ones that can influence the computation carried out by the smart contract across different invocations. For instance, a temporary variable necessary to check whether the deposit paid by a player is correct does not live beyond the scope of a single invocation of a smart contract. Therefore, it is not relevant to define the internal state of the smart contract. In a procedural programming language, internal state variables are the global ones, whereas variables local to individual functions would not be considered as defining the state of a program.
- *Blockchain state variables*: A smart contract should have access to and should be able to modify the variables describing the state of a blockchain system. In our example, smart contracts should be able to access and modify the balance of every user in the system.

An additional type of data that can be handled by smart contracts and that makes their design more challenging are the so-called 'off-chain' data. The three types of smart contract data listed above are in fact 'on-chain' data. On-chain data are intrinsic to the blockchain system. They are either fed by its users or are instrumental in describing its state. Off-chain data are the ones that are available outside the blockchain system (or outside the 'blockchain world' of Figure 4.1) and that are relevant for the computation that a smart contract must perform. The challenges of handling off-chain data in blockchain systems are discussed more in detail in the next section.

4.2.3 What specific requirements are introduced by smart contracts by their need to be deployed in a blockchain system?

If you think carefully, the features of smart contracts that we have discussed until now do not differentiate a smart contract from any other computer program. In other words, any of you who have taken a basic computer programming course would be thinking by now that smart contracts bear no difference whatsoever with traditional computer programs.

There are, however, specific features of smart contracts distinguishing them from traditional computer programs. These features derive directly from the fact that smart contracts must be deployed within a blockchain system. In fact, a fundamental characteristic of blockchain systems is that the nodes in them must agree on the system state without the need for any intermediary or central authority. In practice, in a blockchain system without smart contracts, this is achieved through the immutability of the distributed ledger and the consensus protocol: the nodes maintain a consistent local copy of an immutable ledger in which every transaction submitted to the system is appended and can never ever be modified. This ensures that any node can always reconstruct the current state of the blockchain systems by replaying the transactions stored in the ledger.

From the discussion made thus far in this chapter, it follows that, since they can modify the state of the blockchain system, smart contracts should also be 'immutable'. Somehow, smart contracts should therefore obey the rules of the consensus protocol. Nodes should be able to invoke them whenever they need to reconstruct the correct state of a blockchain. Moreover, the invocations should lead the nodes to update their copies of the ledger in a consistent way.

However, what does it mean for a smart contract to be 'immutable'? The immutability of smart contracts is more complex than the immutability of the data (transactions) stored in the distributed ledger. Practically, it is defined by the following properties:

1 The code of a smart contract should be available to all the nodes of a blockchain. In this way, every node can invoke a smart contract whenever needed.
2 The nodes must not be able to modify the code of a smart contract. Once it is deployed in a blockchain system, for instance by one of its users, nobody should be able to modify the code of a smart contract, let alone delete it.
3 Smart contracts must enable consistent state updates by all the nodes in a blockchain network.

How can the three properties listed above be implemented in a blockchain? Regarding the first property, the immutability of the code of a smart contract is achieved by making the code of a smart contract available as part of a transaction. As we discussed in the previous chapters, any transaction of a blockchain system is usually broadcast to all the nodes of a blockchain system. Hence, if the code of a smart contract is part of a transaction, it will reach all the nodes of a blockchain system. Once the transaction is received, every node has access to the code of the smart contract. There are also blockchain implementations in which the smart contract code is not delivered as part of transactions. For instance, in a private blockchain system, it may be installed by the consortium of organizations running the system. However, even in these cases, the code of the smart contract is stored by the nodes in the immutable database. Therefore, it could not be modified.

The implementation of the second property follows from the first one. In fact, all the transactions in a blockchain system are digitally signed by an originator and then stored by each node in a local copy of the immutable ledger. Now, a transaction containing the code of a smart contract follows the same path: it is stored by every node in their immutable copy of the distributed ledger, so that every node can access it. Most importantly, nodes can neither modify it nor delete it.

Finally, regarding the third property, once every node has received the transaction containing the code of a smart contract, they are able to replay every transaction containing invocations to it. The consensus mechanism ensures the correct ordering in the ledger even of transactions invoking smart contracts. Hence, the nodes do not have to modify their behavior to consistently update the state of their local copy of the ledger: they simply can keep replaying the transactions in the order determined by the consensus mechanism.

The implications of the last property, however, are more complex than we think. In order to be able to replicate the state changes entailed by the execution of smart contracts, every node executing a smart contract should get exactly the same output when invoking a smart contract using the same input (no matter whether the smart contract invoked is stateless or stateful). While this may seem like a straightforward property to enforce, there are two situations in which guaranteeing this property is challenging:

* When off-chain data are needed by the smart contract.
* When the computation involves random numbers.

As mentioned above, handling off-chain data is discussed more in depth in the next section. In this section, we concentrate on understanding the relation between smart contracts and random numbers (see Figure 4.5).

The issue introduced by using random numbers in smart contracts is a direct consequence of the role that smart contracts play in updating the state of a blockchain system when executed. By executing a smart contract, every node of a blockchain system must be able to obtain the same state change. Then, the computation executed by a smart contract simply cannot rely on random number generators. By definition, in fact, random number generators return a different number randomly chosen every time that they are invoked.

To better understand the impossibility of using random number generators in a smart contract, let us consider the following additional feature of the BC4C-CGM system (see Figure 4.5). To keep things simple, the smart contract of BC4C-CGM in this example is extended with an operation `returnDeposit()` that can be invoked only by the winner of a game to get the deposits back. The `returnDeposit()` function is now implemented as follows: the smart contract generates a random number between

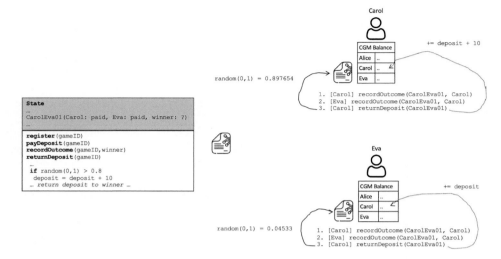

Figure 4.5 Smart contracts and random numbers.

0 and 1; if the number generated is greater than 0.8, then the winner is paid, besides the deposits, additional 10 CGM tokens. In other words, if we assume that the random number is extracted from a uniform distribution, this gives the winner a 20% chance of earning 10 CGM tokens extra when winning a game.[1] Let us now consider two nodes (Carol and Eva), who have just finished playing a game (CarolEva01), won by Carol. Figure 4.5 shows the list of transactions received by the nodes of the system. Each transaction includes information about the originator (in square brackets) and the smart contract operation that is invoked. First, both players confirm the outcome of the game that they have played (transactions 1 and 2), then Carol invokes the smart contract to obtain the deposit. To update the state of the blockchain, each node executes the operations that are invoked on their local copy of the smart contract. Now, the execution of the transactions 1 and 2 result in the same output for both Carol and Eva. They both update the state of the smart contract, recording (and confirming) the winner of the game. Transaction 3 is the critical one. Its execution in fact may result in an inconsistent update of the blockchain state by the two nodes. If, for instance, Carol's and Eva's invocations generate random numbers greater and lower than 0.8, respectively, then in Carol's ledger the CGM balance of Carol is increased of the deposits plus 10 additional tokens, whereas Eva's ledger update does not include the 10 additional tokens. Clearly, the execution of the smart contract has led the two nodes to update the state of the blockchain system inconsistently.

This simple example should be sufficient to demonstrate that random number generators cannot be used in smart contracts. This has obviously important implications for the type of business logic that can be implemented by a smart contract.

4.3 On-chain, off-chain data, and smart contract oracles

While discussing the type of data handled by a blockchain system in the previous section, we briefly mentioned the need to handle 'off-chain' data. Off-chain data are data generated outside a blockchain network that are required by a smart contract to execute its business logic. In this section, we discuss this issue more deeply.

To provide an example of off-chain data, we extend again the BC4C-CGM blockchain. In this extended blockchain (which we call BC4C-CGM+), we assume that CGM tokens have become immensely popular. Therefore, a market for them has emerged. In practice, this means that CGM tokens could be bought and sold (in a so-called 'crypto-exchange', i.e., a marketplace for cryptocurrency tokens) using fiat money, such as US dollars or Euros. This in turn entails that the price of CGM tokens, expressed in US dollars or Euros, fluctuates continuously depending on the supply and the demand of these tokens. Given this premise, we now want to design the BC4C-CGM+ smart contract in a different way. Specifically, we would like to guarantee that a player is never rewarded more than the equivalent of 100 US dollars from playing a game: if the value in US dollars of the deposit paid by the players when a game terminates is less than 100 US, then the deposit is paid in full to the winner of the game; otherwise, an equivalent of 100 US dollars in CGM tokens is paid to the winner. The remainder deposit returned is equally split between the two players.

For its implementation, this smart contract requires access to the price in US dollars of the CGM tokens. This price keeps fluctuating, and it is clearly available only in the 'off-chain' world. Hence, we must devise a way to make it available to the smart contract.

Unfortunately, there are not many solutions to this problem. The price in US dollars of CGM tokens can be provided only by an external actor, like a crypto-exchange that handles CGM tokens (see Figure 4.6). While technically feasible, this solution can be accepted only if the following two conditions hold:

1 All the players, i.e., the nodes of the blockchain system, trust that the crypto-exchange behaves faithfully, reporting to the smart contract a correct CGM token price whenever required. In practice, this cannot be enforced through the design of the technology. The best we can do is to choose a popular crypto-exchange that all the nodes can trust.
2 We create a mechanism to inject this information into the smart contract whenever necessary. Most importantly, this mechanism must ensure that every smart contract invocation to determine the amount of deposit paid back for a given terminated game receives the same CGM price from the crypto-exchange. Only in this way, in fact, it is possible to guarantee that all the nodes will update consistently the state of the BC4C-CGM+ blockchain system.

While the implementation of the second property listed above is addressed differently by different blockchain systems,[2] the first property can be satisfied in an implementation-agnostic way. It requires, in fact, that the nodes identify an external actor (like the 'Old crypto-exchange' in Figure 4.6) who is entrusted with the task of providing correct values of the off-chain data needed by a smart contract. This external actor is usually called an oracle. In ancient Greece and Rome, oracles were priests and priestesses considered to always provide insightful counsel and prophetic predictions. Oracles for blockchain smart contracts are not really prophetic. Rather than providing actual predictions, they always provide truthful values of off-chain data in a consistent way to a blockchain system (or, more specifically, to smart contracts deployed within it).

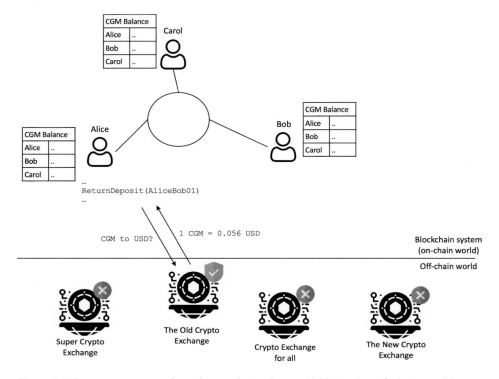

Figure 4.6 Smart contracts and oracles to obtain data available in the off–chain world.

Note that the use of oracles seemingly contradicts a basic principle of blockchain technology that we have held dear until now, i.e., avoiding intermediaries and central authorities. The trusted crypto-exchange is obviously such an intermediary. However, there is not much more that we can do solve this issue without relying on oracles. Because of the nature of oracles, there is also an ongoing debate on whether a blockchain system using oracles can actually be called a blockchain system.

Leaving the philosophical debate about the nature of blockchain systems aside, oracles highlight how challenging it is to manage off-chain data in a blockchain system. Note that, in many business scenarios, off-chain data play a fundamental role in the exchange of information and value among business actors. As an example, let us consider the case of an insurance company. Many claims can be lodged by customers at a given time because a tornado (or any catastrophic weather event) occurred in a certain geographical area. Traditionally, an insurance company must trust a weather forecast service and/or its own weather experts to provide important information regarding the tornado, such as the exact time of occurrence and its path on the ground. This allows the insurance company to assess the faithfulness of the claims. If a blockchain system is adopted in this scenario, then the nodes (like customers, the insurance company itself, independent experts, etc.) must elect a trusted oracle to provide this weather information to the smart contracts implementing the application logic of the claim management.

4.4 An architecture for blockchain systems

To give structure to the implementation–agnostic model of blockchain presented in the first part of the book, we propose here a conceptual architecture of blockchain systems. Generally, the architecture of a software system defines that system in terms of computational components and interactions between those components [SG96]. The objective of the architecture proposed here is to establish a common ground for the concrete blockchain systems and applications that are discussed later in this book. Whenever needed, in fact, we will extend and customize the architecture to fit specific blockchain system implementations considered in this book.

The conceptual architecture of blockchain systems is shown in Figure 4.7. To structure the architecture, we have made use of architectural styles, which are high-level structuring approaches. Our blockchain system architecture combines two styles: the layered style and the component-oriented architectural style [Gref16a]. Layering defines structure in an information system by organizing the functionality into several layers of functional abstraction. The component-oriented style gives structure by combining the grouping of coherent functionality into components with explicit interfaces.

The architecture defines the business, blockchain, and data layers:

- The blockchain layer, in the middle, contains the blockchain functionality that we described in the first part of this book.

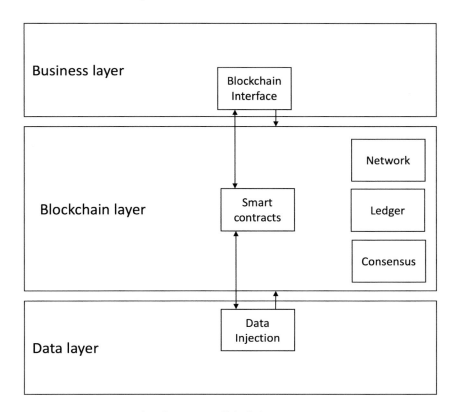

Figure 4.7 A conceptual architecture of blockchain systems.

- The business layer sits on top of the blockchain layer. It uses the functionality of the blockchain layer to realize the functionality required by business users to achieve specific business objectives.
- The data layer sits below the blockchain layer. It contains functionality to feed the blockchain layer with the data required for the realization of the business layer functionality.

While conceptually separated in Figure 4.7, the business and data layers may often refer to the same users or client applications of a blockchain system. A user at the business layer, in fact, may also provide the data required for the realization of the business layer functionality.

Regarding the components of the architecture, the blockchain layer comprises three internal components that implement the functionality described in this chapter and in Chapter 3. These are the functionalities to manage the blockchain network (e.g., gossiping and validation of the transactions), to manage the distributed ledger (e.g., storing transactions and blocks), and to execute the consensus mechanism. Smart contracts are the only 'active' component of the blockchain layer. They can in fact be invoked directly by the other layers, to execute specific business logic or simply to store data required for their execution. The functionality of the business and data layers are aggregated

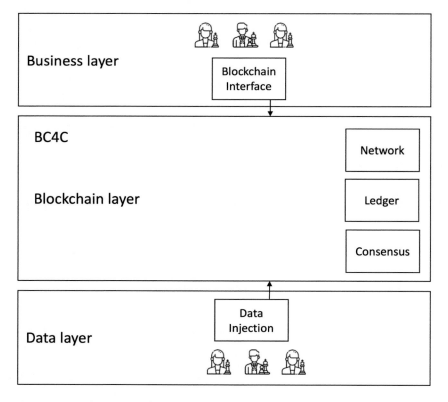

Figure 4.8 Architecture of BC4C.

into one component, i.e., the blockchain interface and the data injection component, respectively. These components can interact with the blockchain layer in two ways:

- They can issue transactions to the blockchain layer. Technically, this is done by creating a transaction and forwarding it to the peers of a blockchain node.
- They can directly invoke the smart contracts of the blockchain. Note that the interaction with smart contracts is bi-directional: the smart contracts may in fact be able to notify proactively the other layers, usually by emitting events. For instance, a smart contract can emit an event to signal the termination of its execution.

To show the value-in-use of this architecture, we conclude this chapter by considering the concretization of the architecture into the three blockchains that we considered in this chapter: BC4C, BC4C-CGM, and BC4C-CGM+.

Figure 4.8 shows the concretization for the BC4C system. Simply put, the only users of this system are the chess players. They use both the business and the data layer. On the one hand, the system allows the players to complete business-meaningful operations, like starting new games and recording the termination of games. On the other hand, the system collects from the users the data required to complete the business operations, i.e., the moves played in each game. There are no smart contracts in this system.

Figure 4.9 shows the concretization of the architecture for the BC4C-CGM blockchain. Compared to BC4C, the difference is the smart contract in the blockchain layer.

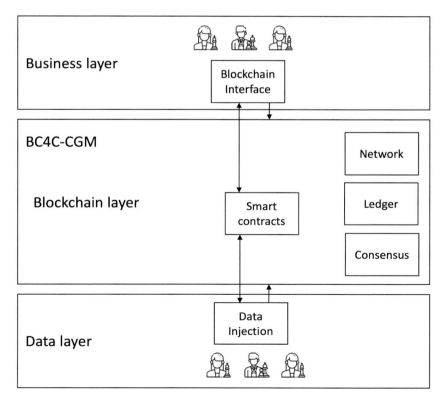

Figure 4.9 Architecture of BC4C-CGM.

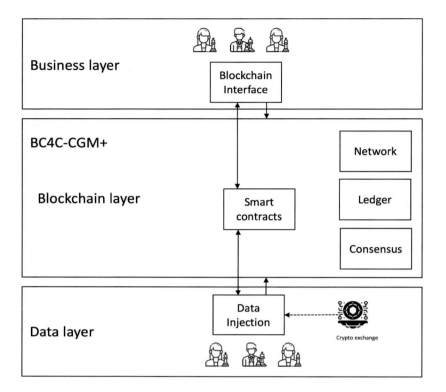

Figure 4.10 Architecture of BC4C–CGM+.

The smart contract implements the additional business logic required to handle the deposits from the players.

Finally, Figure 4.10 shows the concretization of the architecture for the BC4C–CGM+ blockchain. Compared to the BC4C–CGM system, the difference is in the data layer. In the data layer, the crypto-exchange is a new client application. It uses the data injection function to inject the CGM token exchange rate in the blockchain layer. This is required by the smart contract to implement correctly the functionality provided to the business layer (i.e., calculating the deposit payback correctly to the winner of a game).

4.5 Case study: the original definition of smart contract

The term 'smart contract' was introduced for the first time by cryptographer and legal scholar Nick Szabo in an article originally written in 1994 and edited in 1996 [Sza94]. First, the article praises the robustness of the common law of contracts that had been regulating business and other types of agreements (e.g., marriages) for centuries. Then, Szabo introduces the concept of contract 'smartness' as the idea of embedding contractual clauses 'in the hardware and software that we deal with'.

As the simplest example of a smart contract, the article mentions the vending machine. As soon as enough money is introduced by the customer into a vending machine, the contract between the vendor and the customer (i.e., the principals of the contract) is executed: the vending machine delivers the product, returning also the change if needed. The vending machine is programmed to execute precisely the terms of the contract. The contract execution cannot be physically stopped by the customer. In other words, the contract between the vendor and the customer is embedded 'by design' into the hardware of the vending machine.

Szabo then discusses what technology can be used to implement 'smartness' into contracts. Interestingly, Szabo's smart contracts build on 'cryptographic building blocks', such as keys to sign and verify digital messages related to the contract execution. The spectrum of tools discussed in the article includes also more centralized solutions, such as public digital notaries. These could certify the performance of the principals in the contract (based on evidence provided by digitally signed messages related with the contract execution).

As far as contract design is concerned, the article lists four principles that normally define 'well-designed' contracts in the real world:

- *Observability*: the principals should be able to observe each other's performance relevant to a contract.
- *Verifiability*: the principals should have the ability to prove contract violations when they occur.
- *Privity*: information regarding the content of a contract and performance of the principals should be distributed to the principals and other parties only as much as necessary.
- *Enforceability*: there should be a way to enforce the principals to fulfill the terms of a contract.

The common law of contracts often requires third parties and central authorities to realize the principles listed above. For instance, arbitrators are introduced to settle disputes when a principal claims that the other one has not performed according to the terms of the contract (an issue of 'verifiability'). However, in order to perform their role, arbitrators may require access to private information about the principals ('privity'). They may also rely on a police authority to enforce the principals to perform ('enforceability').

In this context, it is interesting to notice that the blockchain smart contracts that we discussed in this chapter implement by design three of the four principles listed above:

- *Observability*: all the interactions between the principals (i.e., the blockchain nodes using a smart contract) and a smart contract are completely transparent and observable in the transactions recorded on the immutable ledger. Since every transaction is digitally signed by its originator, it is also impossible for a node to repudiate its interactions with a smart contract. For instance, in the BC4C-CGM blockchain, every node can verify whether the players of a game have paid the required deposit before starting a game.
- *Verifiability*: since all the interactions between the principals and a smart contract are observable, any attempt to breach the contract is also observable. Note, however, that blockchain smart contracts will reject any interaction not conforming with their implementation. For instance, in BC4C-CGM the smart contract automatically returns an error message if a player tries to pay a lower deposit than what is due.

- *Enforceability*: a smart contract in a blockchain system is by design enforceable. As we have seen in this chapter, any time it is invoked, a smart contract executes its business logic. Nobody can stop the execution of a smart contract once it is invoked. Moreover, because the code of a smart contract is delivered in a transaction stored on the immutable ledger, none of the nodes of the system can modify the code of a smart contract (i.e., trying to enforce a different business logic than what intended).

A principle where the blockchain smart contracts presented appear to fail is the one of 'privity'. Every interaction with a smart contract by any node in a blockchain system is known to every other node, since it is recorded in the immutable ledger. Therefore, it is virtually impossible for a node (or a set of nodes) in a blockchain system to hide their interaction with a smart contract. In the BC4C-CGM system, for instance, all nodes know exactly which player has won every game and when the deposits were paid back to the winner.

Implementing privity in smart contracts is challenging when these are deployed in a public blockchain system. In fact, if anybody can join a public blockchain, anybody who joined must be able to know the current state of the system. This is achieved by giving full access to the smart contract(s) deployed in the system and the history of their invocations. More can be done to achieve smart contracts privity in private blockchain systems (see Chapter 7). For instance, private blockchain systems may allow the creation of different 'sub-channels' to which only a selected set of nodes can subscribe. Smart contracts can be deployed only into specific sub-channel, thus limiting their visibility.

Finally, a fundamental limitation of common law contracts mentioned by Szabo is the one of the observability of hidden actions during the contract execution. Basically, the execution of a contract can trigger or enable other actions that may remain neither observable nor verifiable by the principals. As an example, Szabo considers the case of Point-of-Sales (PoS) systems in shops and supermarkets. By allowing the customer to pay, these systems have access to sensitive client information, such as credit card numbers and purchase expenses. The issue of observability of private actions is one of assessing to what extent a common contract between a merchant and a vendor using a PoS terminal should concern also the actions that may be triggered by/on this sensitive information: Can they be recorded? Can they be sold by the merchant to advertisers and other agencies? Can they be linked to other data from the same client recorded by other PoS terminals at different merchants?

Normally, in common law contracts it is practically impossible to anticipate all the hidden actions that can originate from a contract. Therefore, the best way to address this issue is to devise regulations that guide or enforce the principals to include specific clauses in the contracts and/or to follow specific execution mechanisms. Regarding the example of the PoS system and, more generally, the issue of managing the data provided by the customers of a service, the General Data Protection Regulation (GDPR, https://gdpr.eu) in the EU and similar efforts in other parts of the world, can be seen as a regulation of this type. The GDPR forces the principals of a contract to worry, for instance, about the right of the customer to ask the service provider to delete the data that they have provided.

With blockchain smart contracts, the hidden actions may become in practice observable. Since the code of every smart contract in a blockchain system is available to all the nodes, every action taken by a smart contract is fully observable and predictable simply by analyzing the code of the smart contract. It is therefore impossible for a smart contract to take actions that remain hidden to the nodes of a blockchain system. In the BC4C-CGM system, for instance, inspecting the smart contract code can reveal whether the smart contract may secretly behave maliciously, such as paying hidden rewards to colluding nodes, or whether the smart contract is collecting and selling the data regarding the games played to advertisers.

To conclude, the blockchain smart contracts discussed in this chapter represent an implementation of the smart contracts envisioned almost 30 years ago by Nick Szabo in his seminal article. While Szabo also envisioned centralized mechanisms for smart contract implementation, blockchain smart contracts focus on the completely decentralized implementation of smart contracts.

4.6 Conclusions

This chapter has presented the concept of smart contracts in blockchain. Smart contracts are computer programs that can manipulate the state of the blockchain based on the input provided by the transactions. They can execute arbitrary business logic, except logic involving random numbers. Randomness in smart contracts would prevent the nodes to achieve consistent state updates when executing them. We also discussed how off-chain data can be included into smart contracts. The concept has been exemplified using evolutions of the BC4C blockchain: BC4C-CGM, including a smart contract to handle the deposits paid by the players to start a game, and BC4C-CGM+, an evolution in which the values of the deposits are linked to the exchange rate between CGM tokens and fiat currencies.

This chapter concludes the first part of the book. Besides providing the required background on cryptography, in this chapter we have explained the concept of blockchain and smart contracts using a model that is independent of any specific implementation. We concluded this first part by introducing, at the end of this chapter, a general architecture of blockchain systems. This architecture combines the elements of blockchain introduced in the first four chapters in a single conceptual framework. It is used throughout the book to give structure to concrete applications of blockchain that we will discuss. The second part of the book focuses on these concrete applications. We present Bitcoin, a cryptocurrency, Ethereum, a cryptocurrency that also provides smart contracts, and other frameworks to develop private blockchains and, finally, we focus specifically on the applications of blockchain in the IoT.

4.7 Questions and exercises

1 Consider the scenarios in which blockchain can be applied that you have identified to answer question 1 of Chapter 3. Discuss how smart contracts can be used to improve or extend the application of blockchain in each of the scenarios that you have identified.

2 Consider the definition of smart contracts provided by Nick Szabo in [Sza94]. Provide two different lists of quotes from the paper: (i) quotes that support the definition of smart contracts that we presented in this chapter and (ii) quotes that support an implementation of smart contracts based on centralized authorities or intermediaries.

Table 4.1 Example of ledger for the BC4C-CGM system

Transaction id	Transaction	Originator
…	…	…
T789	Move[CrisLeo21, 56, …, …., false]	Cris
T790	CreateNewGame[SungLeo92, Leo]	Sung
T791	ConfirmGameCreation[SungLeo92]	Leo
T792	PayDeposit[LeoSung7] (SC call)	Leo
T793	PayDeposit[LeoMin5] (SC call)	Min
T794	ConfirmMove[CrisLeo21, 56]	Leo
T795	Move[DiegoMin4, 45, …, …, true]	Min
T796	PayDeposit[SungLeo92] (SC call)	Sung
T797	Move[SungCris23, 78, …, …, true]	Sung
T798	ConfirmMove[DiegoMin4,45]	Diego
T799	ConfirmMove[SungCris23, 78]	Cris
T800	CreateNewGame[MinCris4, Cris]	Min
…	…	…

3 Even though smart contracts cannot handle random numbers, blockchain and smart contracts can still be adopted to address specific issues in the gambling industry. Discuss one application of blockchain and smart contracts that could improve the gambling industry.

4 Show how the reference architecture of Chapter 4 can be customized to the application of blockchain that you have considered to answer question 5 in Chapter 3.

5 Consider an instance of the BC4C-CGM system for which a list of consecutive transactions recorded in the ledger is shown in Table 4.1:

Consider the following assumptions:

a Deposits are fixed to 5 CGM tokens for all games.

b The smart contract SC handling the deposits is a bit 'smarter' than the one introduced in this chapter. It has only one function 'payDeposit[gameID]'. The originator of the transaction calling this function uses this call to pay the deposit for the game 'gameID'.

c The SC monitors the state of the blockchain and automatically knows when a new game is confirmed and, most importantly, it knows when a new game terminates, i.e., after a checkmate move is confirmed by the counterpart. When a game terminates, the SC immediately pays back the deposits to the winner. In other words, assume that the SC does not have the functions register() and recordOutcome()].

Consider the following state of the system before T789 is issued:

CGM balance of users:

• Cris: 78
• Leo: 45
• Diego: 90
• Min: 45
• Sung: 89

ID of games currently played (i.e., confirmed and deposits paid):

- CrisLeo21
- DiegoMin4
- SungCris23

ID of games confirmed, but waiting for the deposit to be paid:

- CrisLeo22 (no deposit paid)
- LeoSung7 (only Leo paid the deposit)
- LeoMin5 (only Leo paid the deposit)

ID of games proposed, but not confirmed by counterpart:

- SungCris87

Answer the following questions:

1 One transaction has one error, i.e., it registers something that has already happened, which one?
2 Ignoring the transaction with an error that you have identified at Q1, what is the new state of this blockchain after transaction T800?

Notes

1 Note that there is no 'law of conservation' of the tokens, unless we define it explicitly. Ten CGM tokens (or any arbitrary number of CGM tokens) can be created at any time in the BC4C-CGM system simply by updating the balance of the nodes. The supply of CGM tokens is in principle infinite and only subject to the rules of the blockchain protocol and the smart contracts embedded in the system.
2 More details regarding the challenges of handling off-chain data using oracles are discussed in Chapter 6, which introduces the issue of smart contract implementation in Ethereum.

Part II

Blockchain platforms – the systems that provide blockchain functionality

In Part 1 of this book, we have presented blockchain as a mechanism. Specifically, blockchain is a mechanism that creates trust among a set of business partners who face the need to exchange valuable assets and information, while not necessarily trusting each other. We have showed that this mechanism is enabled by a set of cryptographic tools, which we have presented avoiding as much as possible the more technical details. In all the discussions of Part 1, we have been careful in maintaining an implementation-agnostic standpoint.

In Part 2, we look at how the blockchain mechanism is implemented into real-world blockchain systems. To this aim, we must abandon the implementation-agnostic standpoint and we must look at the implementation details of different blockchain technologies. We begin by discussing the most famous examples of (public) blockchain systems, of which most of you probably have heard already in the news: Bitcoin and Ethereum, presented in Chapters 5 and 6, respectively. Then, in Chapter 7, we discuss the peculiarities of private blockchain and how we can build private blockchain systems. Specifically, we discuss how Ethereum can also be used for private blockchain, and we additionally present two frameworks for building private blockchains: Corda and Hyperledger Fabric. Finally, in Chapter 8, we look in detail at the relationship between blockchain and IoT technology. In this context, we introduce another blockchain framework, IOTA, which has been created specifically to implement blockchain systems handling IoT data.

DOI: 10.4324/9781003321187-6

5 Bitcoin and public blockchain

Learning goals

5.A The reader can define the characteristics of the Bitcoin network and its user nodes.

5.B The reader can describe the content of the Bitcoin transactions and the Bitcoin ledger.

5.C The reader can explain the mechanism of unspent transaction outputs to determine the state of the Bitcoin blockchain.

5.D The reader can explain how transactions are digitally signed in Bitcoin.

5.E The reader can describe the proof-of-work consensus mechanism of Bitcoin and discuss its implications on the Bitcoin blockchain.

5.F The reader can discuss the positive and negative characteristics of Bitcoin as an enabler of business applications.

5.1 The Bitcoin network

Bitcoin is surely the most famous of cryptocurrencies. It was created in late 2008 by an unknown author (or group thereof) who published a white paper under the pseudonym of Satoshi Nakamoto [Nak08]. Since then, what was born as a pioneering computing project has become a worldwide phenomenon that affects the global economy.

Bitcoin is a public blockchain. It is also a cryptocurrency system. That is, the Bitcoin blockchain records the exchange of a digital token among its users. The state of the Bitcoin blockchain is therefore represented by the balance of this digital token held by all users, i.e., the amount of tokens owned by them. In global markets, e.g., crypto-exchanges and other investment platforms, Bitcoins are denominated as 'BTC'. Hence, in the remainder of this chapter, we refer to the digital tokens of the Bitcoin blockchain simply as 'BTC' or 'Bitcoins'. As we mentioned briefly in Chapter 3, Bitcoin is a public blockchain. Anybody can download the software required to run a Bitcoin node from https://bitcoin.org, install it on a computer connected to the Internet, and run a node of the Bitcoin network.

Besides the main Bitcoin network, there is also a Bitcoin test network. The test network allows interacting with a blockchain similar to the Bitcoin blockchain, without the need to use 'real' Bitcoins. It is deployed for curious users, but most importantly for developers who need to test their applications that use the Bitcoin blockchain, like digital wallets. The nodes of the test network run exactly the same protocol as the main network. The test network is smaller than the main one, i.e., it has a lower number of

DOI: 10.4324/9781003321187-7

nodes. The other main difference concerns the nature of the Bitcoin tokens: the ones used in the test network are fake. They have no value in the real world. They can even be requested at will by nodes to special accounts. Running a node of the test network can be a good experience to get a concrete experience of using the Bitcoin blockchain.

A node of the Bitcoin network is associated with a unique private key, public key, and address (see Figure 5.1).

The private key k is created when a new node is initiated. It is used by a node to sign the transactions that it issues on the Bitcoin blockchain. A Bitcoin private key is 256-bit long. Hence, creating a Bitcoin private key means to pick randomly a number between 1 and 2^{256}. The way in which this number is picked does not matter, as long as it is not predictable, nor repeatable. Nodes must not reveal their private key to anybody at any time. Hence, it would be very unsafe to generate private keys using an algorithm that is easily repeatable or predictable. A hacker could in fact use the same algorithm to easily generate 'valid' private keys of existing nodes. The software that we install to run a node can generate a private key for our node securely. The private key must be always kept secret by the owner of an account. Knowing a private key of an account means to control the Bitcoins on it. A hacker who has obtained our private key can in fact sign transactions transferring our Bitcoins on our behalf. Private keys must also be stored carefully. If we lose or forget our private key, we can no longer use our Bitcoins. There is no 'forgot your password?' button in Bitcoin!

The public key K of a node is generated from its private key using Elliptic Curve multiplication. The digital signature mechanism adopted by the Bitcoin blockchain is in fact the Elliptic Curve Cryptography (see Chapter 2). The public key is used by other nodes to validate the transactions originated by a node. To enable this, the public key of the originator is normally included in every transaction originated by a node. Note that public keys are made to be distributed by the owners to enable the digital signature

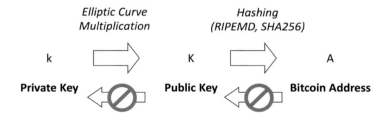

Figure 5.1 Private and public key, and addresses in the Bitcoin network.

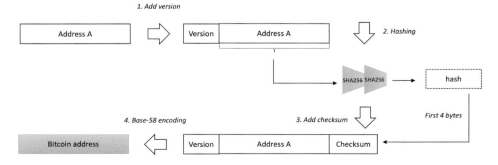

Figure 5.2 Encoding of Bitcoin address to improve readability by humans (Base-58-check).

mechanism. As shown in Figure 5.1, in any cryptography system it is practically impossible to infer the private key *k* from the corresponding public one *K*.

Finally, a Bitcoin address is derived from the public key using a cryptographic hashing function. The Bitcoin address is in practice equivalent to the details of a bank account, like an IBAN code in the European SEPA system or the combination of account number and sort code in the United Kingdom. Users distribute their Bitcoin addresses to other users who need to send them Bitcoins. More in detail (see Figure 5.1), a Bitcoin address A is derived from a public key K using a double cryptographic hashing function:

$$A = \text{RIPEMD160}(\text{SHA256}(K))$$

That is, the address A is obtained by applying first the SHA256 hashing function on the public key, and then applying the RIPEMD160 hashing function to the output of the latter. As we know from Chapter 2, this operation returns a 160-bit number.

To facilitate the understanding by human users, Bitcoin addresses are usually encoded using the so-called 'Base-58-check' encoding (see Figure 5.2). Before encoding A using the Bitcoin's Base-58 encoding, a version number is added in the first position of A, identifying the type of account associated with the address. For instance, the version value '1' identifies the normal Bitcoin accounts that we mostly consider in this chapter. The version values 'm' or 'n' identify normal accounts of the Bitcoin test network. The version value '3' identifies 'pay-to-script' accounts. These are automated accounts not controlled by human users, which we do not discuss in this book (if you are interested, more technical details regarding the Bitcoin protocol are presented extensively in [Ant17]). Then, address A, preceded by the version number, goes through a double hashing (SHA256) operation. The first 4 bytes (32 bits) of the result of this hashing are attached to the address A as a checksum. Finally, the sequence of version number, address A, and checksum is encoded using the Bitcoin's Base-58 encoding discussed in Chapter 2. The result of this encoding is the Bitcoin address of a node commonly handled by wallets and other applications.

The Base-58-check encoding of Bitcoin addresses achieves two objectives:

- First, it produces compact addresses that are human-readable (thanks to the Base-58 encoding, which yields short and better readable numbers than, for instance, Base-16 and Base-64).
- Second, it embeds a safety mechanism to verify the correctness of an address. A Bitcoin address includes the first 16 bits of its hash. Therefore, these can be used to establish whether an address is correct or not. In this way, every software application handling Bitcoin transactions can quickly verify the correctness of a Bitcoin address simply by verifying the correctness of the checksum.

5.2 Bitcoin transactions

Bitcoin is a cryptocurrency. As discussed in Chapter 3, the state of a cryptocurrency system is captured by the balance of all the nodes in the system. This state is modified by the transactions issued by the nodes. This section discusses in detail the structure of the Bitcoin transactions. Implicitly, the structure of the Bitcoin transactions also defines how the Bitcoin network can keep track of the system state. More in detail, the discussion is split into two sections. First, we discuss the main content of the Bitcoin transactions, with the aim of understanding how the Bitcoin blockchain manages the balances of the nodes (Section 5.2.1). Then, we discuss how the Bitcoin transactions can be digitally signed by their originator nodes (Section 5.2.2).

5.2.1 *Transactions and node balances in Bitcoin*

The nodes of the Bitcoin network interact by issuing transactions. Transactions signify exchanges of Bitcoins among the nodes of the Bitcoin blockchain. Figure 5.3 shows the contents of a real Bitcoin transaction, obtained from a Bitcoin 'explorer'. An explorer of a public blockchain is a public Web site publishing the information regarding transactions and blocks issued in the blockchain. It is usually run by a node or a set of nodes with high availability, i.e., which normally never disconnect from the blockchain network. For each public blockchain, there are usually several explorers available online. In this book, we focus on the main information contained in a transaction. The understanding of other very specific fields of a transaction requires technical knowledge of the Bitcoin protocol that goes beyond the scope of this book.

In this transaction, one sender (identified by the address '15TUAsp...') has sent some Bitcoins (0.1184 BTC, to be precise) to a recipient (identified by the address '1CTtPA5...'). Note that both addresses start with '1'. This tells us that the sender and the receiver are normal users (and not, for instance, users of the Bitcoin test network). The transaction has a unique identifier (its hash 'e27824...') and it is included in the block n. 543028. The transaction includes a 'fee', which is calculated as the difference between the input (0.11847874 BTC) paid by the sender and the output of the transaction (0.1184 BTC received by the recipient). In practice, this fee is paid by the originator of the transaction and it is collected by the node that 'mined' the block in which this transaction is included. The mining mechanism, which underpins the execution of Bitcoin's consensus mechanism, is discussed in detail in Section 5.4. For now, it is enough to understand that using the Bitcoin network is not free of charge for its nodes. Nodes must pay a fee to issue a transaction. Note that usually, this fee is small. In the transaction of Figure 5.3, the fee (0.00007874 BTC) is several orders of magnitude lower than the actual amount of Bitcoins transferred. To sum up, the total output of a transaction is equal to the amount of Bitcoins actually received by the recipient. The total input is the amount of Bitcoins taken from the originator's account (which includes the fee).

Figure 5.4 shows the content of another real Bitcoin transaction. This transaction looks more complex than the previous one. It involves two inputs, for a total of 11.23500889 BTC, owned by the user 'bc1q7cyr...'. Note that the prefix 'bc1' identifies a new type of 'normal' Bitcoin address recently introduced that allows segregated witnesses for the transaction validation (do not worry if you do not understand this, it is outside the

Figure 5.3 Content of a real Bitcoin transaction elaborated by blockchain.com/explorer (one sender, one receiver). Available at: https://www.blockchain.com/btc/tx/e27824e8c9a8f2fdd4c731c13ea6a057b21d5940a4d0b85473431d10ce6aea9e.

Figure 5.4 Content of a real Bitcoin transaction (one sender – many inputs, multiple receivers). Available at: https://www.blockchain.com/btc/tx/578fa2731059 bde959e2418903e2c717f81bc9bf883b10560fff9a66c3f20428.

scope of this book!). The transaction transfers Bitcoins from the user 'bc1q7cyr…' to many users, like 'bc1qtj2n…' or '15yQZN…'. The highest amount (6.54324413 BTC) is transferred to the same node that provided the input. This looks odd, but do not worry, by the end of this section you will understand what this means. Some of the outputs are associated by to a green 'globe' icon, others to a red one. The red icon means that an output has been spent. The green one means that it has not been spent yet. The concepts of spent and unspent outputs are also clarified later in this section. Note that the status of the outputs depicted in Figure 5.4 is the one captured at the time this chapter was written (late Spring 2022). We cannot predict the future, but it is likely that the unspent outputs may be spent (and their icon turned red) by the time this book goes to the press.

To understand how the balance of the nodes is managed in Bitcoin, we need to look at the actual data contained in a Bitcoin transaction. In reality, Figures 5.3 and 5.4 do not show the actual content of Bitcoin transactions. They show instead a human-reada-ble elaboration of the content of transactions made by a Bitcoin explorer.

Figure 5.5 shows the content of the transaction of Figure 5.3 in a machine-readable format, i.e., the actual transaction data exchanged by the nodes of the Bitcoin network. For the computer scientists, Figure 5.5 shows the JSON format of this transaction. In Figure 5.5, there is no trace of a lot of the information shown in Figure 5.3. For instance, where is the total input? Where is the total output? Where is the transaction fee?

Some of the information available in the elaboration of Figure 5.3 is also readily available in the machine-readable format of Figure 5.5, like the transaction id ('txid') or the size in bytes ('size') of the transaction. This information basically concerns the so-called metadata of a transaction. It is not the information regarding the actual amount of Bitcoins that changed ownership through this transaction. To understand the latter, we need to look at the elements '*vin*' and '*vout*' of the machine-readable format of Figure 5.5. The element '*value*' nested within '*vout*' appears to match the value of the total output of the transaction (0.1184 Bitcoins) in Figure 5.3. Moreover, the '*address*' element of '*vout*' matches the recipient of this transaction in the human-readable format.

```
{
    "txid": "e27824e8c9a8f2fdd4c731c13ea6a057b21d5940a4d0b85473431d10ce6aea9e",
    "hash": "e27824e8c9a8f2fdd4c731c13ea6a057b21d5940a4d0b85473431d10ce6aea9e",
    "version": 1,
    "size": 192,
    "vsize": 192,
    "weight": 768,
    "locktime": 0,
    "vin": [
        {
            "txid": "1d09a97d881c0ae4f6a7095686a0d759564b312014a7ea9ace92b1005c95f455",
            "vout": 1,
            "scriptSig": {
                "asm": "3045022100ea ...",
                "hex": "483045022100ea..."
            },
            "sequence": 4294967295
        }
    ],
    "vout": [
        {
            "value": 0.1184,
            "n": 0,
            "scriptPubKey": {
                "asm": "OP_DUP OP_HASH160 ...",
                "hex": "76a9147dbf17155ee3019b0ca180ec0e8f9bdff43d5e4e88ac",
                "address": "1CTtPA5hCgtydSCMbcWWnNTfdTRLBm1rVG",
                "type": "pubkeyhash",
                "addresses": [
                    "1CTtPA5hCgtydSCMbcWWnNTfdTRLBm1rVG"
                ],
                "reqSigs": 1
            }
        }
    ]
}
```

Figure 5.5 Machine-readable content of the transaction of Figure 5.3.

The '*vin*' element appears to describe the input of this transaction. However, it does not contain any actual values. It only points to another transaction (identified by the transaction id '1d09a9…') and to a '*vout*' element of it (i.e., the one with id equal to 1). Figure 5.6 shows the content of the transaction referenced by this '*vin*' element (see the matching transaction id '1d09a0…' at the beginning). We can see that this transaction has two '*vout*' elements (with id '*n*' equal 0 and 1). The '*vout*' element with n = 1 has a value of 0.11847874 (i.e., the total input of the transaction of Figure 5.5) associated with the address '15TUAsp…' (i.e., the sender of the Bitcoins in the transaction of Figure 5.5).

After this brief trip into the world of machine-readable Bitcoin transactions, we are now ready to understand how the state of the Bitcoin blockchain is defined and managed. The Bitcoin transactions create and consume the so-called transaction out-puts. Specifically, a transaction produces (as output) one or more transaction outputs and consumes (as input) one or more transaction outputs produced by other transactions issued in the past. Each transaction output produced by a transaction is associated with a node of the Bitcoin network (i.e., a Bitcoin address). We say that this node controls the transaction output. There is one basic rule to respect when creating a transaction: the sum of all the outputs produced by it must be lower than the sum of all the inputs used by it. There is no specific rule regarding, for instance, the number of inputs that can be consumed, the number of outputs that can be produced, or the value of the outputs produced. Finally, the difference between the sum of the values of the inputs used by a transaction and the sum of the outputs produced by it is the fee paid by the transaction originator to issue the transaction.

A transaction output produced by a transaction and not yet used by any other transaction as input is called a UTXO (Unspent Transaction Output). The balance of a node of the Bitcoin network is given by the sum of all the UTXOs that the

```
{
  "txid": "1d09a97d881c0ae4f6a7095686a0d759564b312014a7ea9ace92b1005c95f455",
  "hash": "1d09a97d881c0ae4f6a7095686a0d759564b312014a7ea9ace92b1005c95f455",
  "version": 1,
  "...
  "vin": [
    {
      "txid": "785397b83f201e50db8154e93e5996bb698cfef20c10fb6ff1a63f46d3e51b31",
      "vout": 0,
      "scriptSig": {
        "asm": "...",
        "hex": "..." },
      "sequence": 4294967295
    }
  ],
  "vout": [
    {
      "value": 0.01986368,
      "n": 0,
      "scriptPubKey": {
        ...
        "address": "3FdkDy6xaKvaugDtCaEiXqXW6oDt5hw9NC",
        "type": "scripthash",
        ....
      }
    },
    {
      "value": 0.11847874,
      "n": 1,
      "scriptPubKey": {
        "asm": "OP_DUP OP_HASH160 30e1ffaddbf133ead74cb356b77c7698412e3817 OP_EQUALVERIFY OP_CHECKSIG",
        "hex": "76a91430e1ffaddbf133ead74cb356b77c7698412e381788ac",
        "address": "15TUAsp5G8k18gXBdJA7jdMvPEaPr2KxLx",
        "type": "pubkeyhash",
        "addresses": [
          "15TUAsp5G8k18gXBdJA7jdMvPEaPr2KxLx"
        ],
        "reqSigs": 1
      }
    }
  ]
}
```

Figure 5.6 Another Bitcoin transaction in machine-readable format.

node controls. Consequently, the state of the Bitcoin blockchain is defined collectively by all the UTXOs. These in fact can be used to determine the balance of every node.

In practice, the mechanism determined by transaction inputs and outputs in Bitcoin can be understood by drawing an analogy with traditional banknotes. At the end of the day, in fact, the Bitcoin blockchain was invented as a new form of electronic cash:

- A UTXO controlled by a user (say Alice) can be seen as a banknote owned by that user. For example, if Alice controls a UTXO valued 20 Bitcoins, it is like she has a banknote worth 20 Bitcoins in her wallet.
- Let us assume that Alice now wants to transfer 6 Bitcoins to Bob. To do so, Alice issues a new transaction that uses as input the 20 Bitcoins UTXO that she controls and produces two UTXOs as output: one controlled by Bob, valued 6 Bitcoins and one controlled again by Alice, valued 14 Bitcoins (actually a little less, because Alice also needs to pay a small fee!).
- So, somehow, UTXOs are like magic banknotes that can be split by the owner into as many other banknotes as necessary.

A more elaborated example of the UTXO mechanism is shown in Figure 5.7. In the example, we start from a situation in which only the transactions T1 and T2 include UTXOs. Therefore, they are the only two transactions required to define the state of the system (33 tokens controlled by Alice, 4 by Bob and 0 by Emma). The transaction T3 consumes two of the three UTXOs included in T1 and T2 (the output n. 0 of T1 and the output n. 0 of T2) and produces two new UTXOs as output. Based on the values of the new UTXOs included in T3 and considering the UTXO that have been consumed by T3, the net effect is that Alice has transferred 27 tokens to Emma using T3. Finally, T4 is used to transfer 2 more tokens from Bob to Emma.

5.2.2 Digital signature of Bitcoin transactions

After having understood how Bitcoin transactions define the state of the Bitcoin blockchain, i.e., the balance of the nodes, we can now focus on how the Bitcoin transactions are digitally signed. In Chapter 3, when discussing cryptocurrency systems (e.g., the CGM token), we said that every transaction in such a system is digitally signed by its originator. However, the transactions that we considered in Chapter 3 were somehow simpler that the Bitcoin transactions that we have described in this chapter. In Chapter 3, in fact, we assumed that one transaction transferred some cryptocurrency from one sender node to one recipient node. However, in the Bitcoin blockchain: (i) transactions do not specify simply a transferred amount between two users, but they combine transaction inputs from other transactions and (ii) they can even transfer Bitcoins between many nodes (see Figure 5.4).

Then, how are Bitcoin transactions digitally signed in practice?

In Bitcoin, the UTXOs, rather than the transactions as a whole, are the 'basic unit' that are digitally signed. When used in a transaction, a UTXO must be digitally signed. The signer in this case is the node that controls a UTXO, rather than the originator of a transaction. More in detail, the following happens:

- Each UTXO produced by a transaction is controlled by one node (identified by the '*address*' element of the corresponding '*vout*' element in the transaction that generated a UTXO).

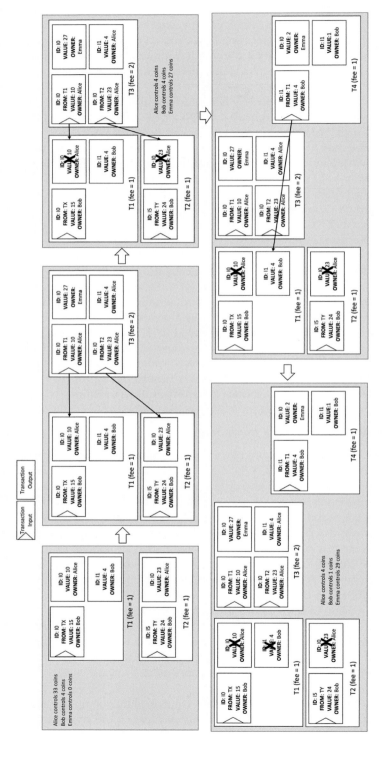

Figure 5.7 Transaction inputs and outputs in Bitcoin: a simplified example.

- Each UTXO is also associated with a so-called 'cryptographic puzzle' (identified by the '*scriptPubKey*' element of the UTXO).
- Understanding the nature of the cryptographic puzzle and how it can be 'solved' requires knowledge of cryptographic tools that go beyond the scope of this book. For us, it is enough to know that:
    - A cryptographic puzzle can only be solved by the node controlling a UTXO using their private key. We say that a UTXO is 'locked' by the cryptographic puzzle and can be 'unlocked' only by the node controlling it using its private key.
    - Every other node can verify the correctness of the solution provided by a node to unlock a UTXO, using the node's public key.
- When a node controlling a UTXO wants to use that UTXO as input of a transaction, the node unlocks it by providing in the input the solution of the cryptographic puzzle (see Figure 5.5, where the '*scriptSig*' element contains the solution of the cryptographic puzzle that only the node controlling that UTXO can calculate using their private key). However, thanks to the power of asymmetric encryption, every other node can verify the correctness of the solution to the puzzle provided. This is done using the node's public key (which is also normally included in a transaction, even though it is not shown for brevity in Figure 5.5). Note that this verification is done by every node of the Bitcoin network when validating a transaction. The same mechanism applies also to transactions including inputs from multiple nodes: to use an output in another transaction, a node must unlock it using their private signature; every other node then verifies the solution provided using the node's public key.

To sum up, in Bitcoin the transactions are not digitally signed as a whole by their originator. Instead, each UTXO must be digitally signed by its owner when used as input for another transaction. Practically, this happens by providing a solution to a cryptographic puzzle. This solution can only be calculated by the owner of the UTXO using its private key and it can be verified by any other node using the owner's public key. Based on what was discussed in Chapter 2, this mechanism is clearly a digital signature mechanism: the solution of the cryptographic puzzle represents the 'digital signature' of a transaction input, which can be verified by every other node.

5.3 Bitcoin blockchain as a data structure: the Bitcoin ledger

In the previous section, we have discussed the structure of Bitcoin transactions. We have understood that, particularly regarding the way in which they are digitally signed, transactions in Bitcoin are fairly different from the ones that we introduced in the implementation-agnostic discussion of Chapter 3. Nevertheless, the principles that characterize the transactions in a blockchain system still hold: the transactions in Bitcoin specify the transfer of cryptocurrency tokens; every transfer is digitally signed by the owner of the transferred funds.

In this section, we focus on Bitcoin as a data structure. That is, we discuss the structure of the Bitcoin ledger. As we learnt in Chapter 3, this is the data structure that is replicated by every node of the Bitcoin network. The rules of the consensus protocol (presented in the next section) allow the nodes to agree on the content of this data structure at any point in time. Luckily, unlike transactions, the Bitcoin ledger is pretty much similar to the implementation-agnostic blockchain data structure that we introduced in Chapter 3.

Figure 5.8 shows the high-level structure of the Bitcoin ledger. It is a chain of blocks. Unsurprisingly, each block contains a header and a list of transactions. The header contains, among others, the following important fields:

- The *hash of the block*: this is the SHA256 hash of the content of the block. Since, as we know from Chapter 2, a hash is practically unique for the data from which it is generated, the block hash is also used as a unique id of the block.
- The *block height*: this is a progressive number identifying the block. The genesis block has a height equal to 0.
- The *hash of the previous block*: as we discussed in Chapter 3, including the hash of the previous block in a block guarantees the immutability of the blockchain data structure.
- The *Merkle root*: this value is calculated based on the data structure in which the transactions belonging to this block are stored. We do not discuss this aspect of the Bitcoin blockchain in detail in this book. It is enough to know that this is an important piece of information used by the nodes to quickly verify whether a given transaction (identified by its unique id) belongs or not to a block.
- The *nonce*: this is an integer number. The value of this integer number is set by the 'block mining' process underpinning the execution of the consensus mechanism. From the point of view of the functioning of the Bitcoin blockchain (i.e., transfers of tokens and state updates), it has no particular meaning. More details about how the value of the nonce is calculated are discussed in the next section.

Figure 5.9 shows the information in the header of a real block of the Bitcoin blockchain elaborated by a Bitcoin explorer. This particular block is at height 738656, it was created (mined) on May 31st, 2022 at 11.30. The block contains 1,758 transactions.

A block contains many transactions, usually around a few thousands. The first transaction of each block is a special one. It is called 'coinbase' transaction and it deserves to be discussed more in detail.

A coinbase transaction does not use any UTXO as input. It produces in output one UTXO valued to the sum of the fees paid by all the transactions included in the block,

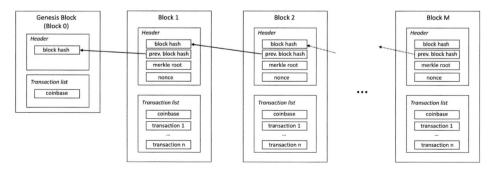

Figure 5.8 The structure of the Bitcoin ledger.

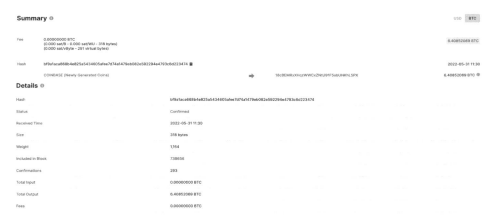

Figure 5.9 The header of a real Bitcoin block. Available at: https://www.blockchain.com/btc/block/00000000000000000000073ef06543252dce1cc24c9e31a6d6848d892ffc824f71.

Figure 5.10 Details of the coinbase transaction of block 738656. Available at: https://www.blockchain.com/btc/tx/bf9a1aca668b4e825a5434605afee7d74a1479eb082e592294e4793c6d223474.

plus an additional fixed number of Bitcoins (i.e., the 'fixed reward'). The value of the fixed reward is established by the Bitcoin protocol. Currently, it stands at 6.25 BTC. The motivation behind including a fixed reward in the coinbase transaction, as well as the way in which this fixed reward is updated over time by the Bitcoin protocol are beyond the scope of this book. In a nutshell, it has to do with the vision of designing a currency with a fixed supply, which should prevent the inflation of prices.

The node controlling the UTXO created by a coinbase transaction is the node that has mined the block to which the coinbase belongs. Figure 5.10 shows the coinbase transaction of the block shown in Figure 5.9. It can be seen that it creates a transaction output of about 6.4 BTC controlled by the node '18cBE…' (that is, the miner of this block).

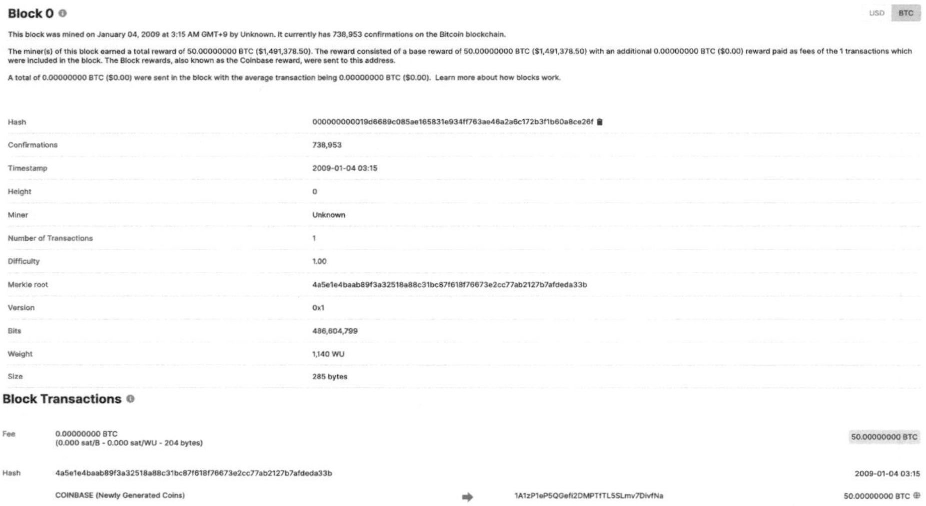

Figure 5.11 The genesis block of the Bitcoin blockchain. Available at: https://www.block chain.com/btc/block/0.

Now, what is the point of adding the coinbase transaction to a block? Based on what we discussed above, the role of the coinbase transaction is twofold:

1 It allows the node that mined the block to collect the fees of the transactions included in it.
2 It rewards the node that mined the block with an additional fixed amount of Bitcoins. Note that the reward is pretty high (currently 6.25 BTC).

To conclude, the coinbase transaction provides a monetary incentive to a node for having mined a block. More about the incentives for nodes to mine new blocks are discussed in the next section when introducing the Bitcoin consensus mechanism.

Before discussing the Bitcoin consensus mechanism, let us conclude this section by presenting the genesis block of the Bitcoin blockchain (see Figure 5.11). This block was created on January 3rd, 2009. It contains only one coinbase transaction (at that time, in fact, there were no other transactions with UTXOs that could be spent!). This transaction assigns 50 newly created Bitcoins to the node '1A1zP...'. These 50 Bitcoins are the first ever created. Since January 3rd 2009, the Bitcoin blockchain has been running smoothly with a new block created on average every ten minutes. The entire history of every block created in the Bitcoin network is stored by every Bitcoin node in their immutable ledger. It can also be consulted at any time by anybody through any of the online Bitcoin explorers. More about the history of Bitcoin is discussed in the final section of this chapter.

5.4 Bitcoin consensus mechanism

The nodes of the Bitcoin blockchain need a consensus mechanism to agree on the content of the Bitcoin ledger. Agreeing on the state of the Bitcoin ledger means to agree on which blocks are added to it and in which order. Since blocks contain transactions ordered in time, agreeing on the order of the blocks means to agree on the order of the transactions issued on the Bitcoin network. Through the UTXO mechanism described in the previous section, knowing the order of the transactions allows to establish the balance of every node. The balance of a node is in fact the sum of the value of the UTXOs that a node controls.

At the core of the Bitcoin consensus lies the Proof-of-Work (PoW) mechanism. The PoW is one of the defining aspects of the Bitcoin blockchain. It is practically implemented through the mechanism of mining new blocks (we use in fact 'PoW' and 'block mining' interchangeably in the remainder of this section and this book).

We divide the discussion of the Bitcoin's consensus mechanism into three parts. First, we discuss the life cycle of Bitcoin transactions. This captures at a high level what happens to a transaction from the moment it is issued by a node of the Bitcoin network until it ends up in a block that is stored by every node in their local copy of the ledger. Then, we zoom into the mechanism that nodes use to assemble new blocks and to broadcast them to the other nodes of the network. Finally, we zoom even further into the so-called 'mining' of new blocks. Specifically, we discuss how nodes are created by calculating a correct value of a block's nonce.

5.4.1 The life cycle of Bitcoin transactions

We split the life cycle of Bitcoin transactions into two phases. The first phase (see Figure 5.12a) concerns the creation and gossiping of a transaction across the nodes of the Bitcoin network. The second phase (see Figure 5.12b) concerns including a transaction in a new block and the gossiping of this block:

* A transaction T is first created by a node and sent to its peers. Figure 5.12a shows two transactions issued by a node, one valid and one invalid. In the remainder we focus on the valid one.
* Every peer validates the transaction T and, if it passed the validation: (i) forwards T to its peers and (ii) stores the validated transaction T in a local transaction repository, named the 'memory pool'. This mechanism is recursive across the nodes and defines the gossiping protocol in Bitcoin. Through this mechanism, a valid transaction T reaches all the nodes in the Bitcoin network.
* A node that runs the 'mining' functionality of the Bitcoin protocol removes T from its memory pool and includes it in a 'candidate' block. The mining node runs the PoW mechanism on the candidate block. If this is successful, then the node has succeeded in creating and new block. The node can now forward the newly mined block to its peers (see step 4 in Figure 5.12b).
* Every peer validates the new block (the details of this validation are discussed later in this chapter). If the new block is valid, then a node: (i) removes all the transactions in it (including T) from the memory pool and (ii) forwards the valid new block to its peers. In this way, the validated transaction T, included in a valid new block, reaches all the nodes of the Bitcoin network. Every node is now able to calculate the balance of all the nodes in the network by considering also the transfer of Bitcoins specified by the transaction T.

When validating a transaction T, a node verifies the following:

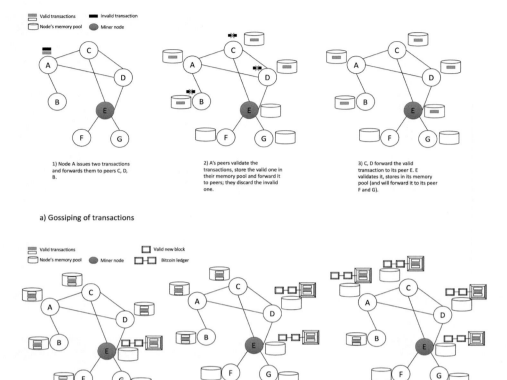

Figure 5.12 The life cycle of Bitcoin transactions. (a) Gossiping of new transactions. (b) Gossiping of new blocks.

- That T is well-formed according to the rules of the Bitcoin protocol. For instance, this includes verifying that the list of transaction inputs is not empty or that every output is associated with an existing node of the Bitcoin network. A node also verifies that every input used by T is digitally signed.
- That the sum of the transaction inputs in T is greater than the sum of the transaction outputs. If that is not the case, in fact, then T is trying to force the creation of Bitcoins that do not exist. This can be done only by coinbase transactions, which can be created only when assembling a new block.
- That every transaction input in T matches a UTXO of a transaction issued in the past. That is, a transaction T can use as input only transaction outputs generated by preceding transactions that have not yet been spent.

An invalid transaction normally never makes it beyond the peers of the issuing node. Therefore, the transaction validation mechanism guarantees that all the transactions that are gossiped across the nodes of the Bitcoin network are valid. Valid transactions are stored by a node in the so-called 'memory pool'. This is simply a local repository, i.e., a database. The transactions stored in the memory pool are 'unconfirmed'. This basically means that they have never been included in a valid block. Therefore, they do not contribute to defining the balances of the nodes of the Bitcoin network. The validation and gossiping of the blocks are similar to the ones of transactions. However, to understand them in detail, we first need to discuss in depth how new blocks can be created by miner nodes.

5.4.2 Creating a new block

When creating a new block, a node must solve the following three problems:

1 Which transactions should be included in the block?
2 Which should be the 'nonce' of the block?
3 Where should the block be included in the ledger, i.e., which should be its previous block?

In fact, a block first and foremost contains a list of transactions (Problem 1). To complete the header of a block, however, we also need to know the value of the nonce (Problem 2) and the hash of the previous block (Problem 3).

Regarding the first problem, a new block can only include valid transactions that are stored by a node in its memory pool. Since, at any time, the number of transactions in the memory pool may be higher than the number of transactions that could be included in a block, a node must choose which transactions to include in a new block. In principle, nodes do not have any particular constraint when selecting which transactions to include in a block. In practice, the nodes usually choose transactions considering both the fee that they pay and the time at which they were created:

• Nodes tend to prefer transactions with earlier timestamps, i.e., which have been issued earlier. These, in fact, are the older transactions in the memory pool. They may be necessary to validate new transactions and, therefore, they should be included in a block as soon as possible. Somehow, including the older transactions in a candidate block fulfills a social welfare objective of the Bitcoin network. It increases the chance, in fact, that the new transactions can be validated.
• Nodes also prefer transactions that pay a higher fee. This is because nodes also have an incentive to be selfish. The fees paid by the transactions in a block (plus the fixed reward) are in fact collected by the node that mines a new block through the coinbase transaction. Hence, the higher the fees of the transactions included in a block, the more Bitcoins a node makes from mining this block. Note that the mining of a new block, i.e., finding its correct nonce, is not an easy task. As we will see, it takes time and, most importantly, a lot of energy (electricity). Hence, the selfishness of nodes mining new blocks is also driven by the need to cover the expenses that they must sustain to do that.

Once the list of transactions to be included in a block is determined, a miner node must decide which is the previous block of the new block and then calculate a correct nonce. To calculate the nonce (Problem 2), a node must solve a computational problem. This problem is determined by the information contained in the block. Most importantly, calculating the solution of this problem requires a high amount of computational work. More specifically, this computational problem has a given level of 'difficulty', which is set by the Bitcoin protocol. The level of difficulty determines the amount of computational work required on average to solve the problem. From this, it is also possible to determine the expected time required by an 'average' Bitcoin node to solve the problem.

The details about this problem, its difficulty, and how it can be solved, are discussed in the next section. For now, it is important to understand the main characteristic of the calculation of the nonce of a new block: it is 'computationally expensive'. This means that a node consumes (a lot of) computational resources, and therefore electricity, to create a new block. Note that ultimately the resources used by a node become monetary ones, i.e., the money needed to pay for the electricity required to run the computational work. Because nodes, like any other rational agent, do not want to waste resources, this mechanism creates an incentive for nodes to assemble only valid new blocks. Nodes in fact have no incentive in wasting computational resources (and therefore money) to create blocks that are not valid (and that, therefore, will never be validated and broadcasted by the peer nodes). This obviously makes the Bitcoin blockchain more robust against malicious attacker nodes.

The computational work required to create the nonce is the first element of the PoW mechanism. The word 'work' in PoW, in fact, refers to computational 'work'. In other words, a correct nonce proves that a miner node ran a certain (high) amount of computational work to create a new block. The second element of the PoW mechanism concerns selecting the previous node of a new block. This solves the last problem (Problem 3) enumerated above.

The rule of the Bitcoin protocol in this case is simple: a node must always mine a new candidate block at the top of the chain in its local copy of the ledger. More in detail, the previous block of a new block must always be the one characterized by the highest height in the local copy of the ledger of a miner node. Why choosing the node with the highest height? The reason for this is to extend the chain characterized by the highest amount of computational work performed to create it. If a new block extends the local ledger from the highest point, then it extends the longest chain of blocks in the local ledger. The longest chain of the blocks is, by definition, the one that required the most computational power by the nodes of the Bitcoin network to be created.

At this point, we understand that you may be confused. You may be asking yourself, among many others, a fundamental question: why should a local copy of the ledger have multiple chains that can be extended? Based on what is discussed in Chapter 3, shouldn't a ledger contain only one chain of blocks, the order of which is agreed upon by all the nodes of a blockchain network?

This question is obviously legitimate. The answers to it unveils (i) the concept of 'forks' of the chain of blocks in the Bitcoin ledger and, consequently, (ii) the probabilistic nature of the Bitcoin consensus mechanism.

To answer this question, let us consider the gossiping of new blocks. The Bitcoin network is constituted by millions of nodes and, at any time, many of them (at least hundreds) are continuously running the mining functionality, trying to create new blocks. When a miner node succeeds in finding a new block (i.e., it solves the computational problem of finding a correct nonce for it), it broadcasts this node to its peers. As mentioned above, the gossiping of new blocks is similar to the one of transactions: a node receiving a new block validates it and, if the validation succeeds, it forwards it to its peers. In this way, a valid new block can reach all the nodes of the Bitcoin network. To validate a new block, a node verifies the following:

- That the block is well-formed. For instance, it verifies that the list of transactions is not empty and that it includes a coinbase transaction.
- That the information in the block header is correct: For instance, the hashes (of the block and of the previous block) must be correct and, most importantly, the nonce of the block must be correct. Verifying the correctness of the nonce is very easy and it is discussed in detail in the next section.
- That the content of the coinbase transaction is valid, i.e., the output generated by it matches the sum of the fixed block reward and the fees paid by all the transactions in the block.

Now, a node must store the valid new block into the ledger. This implies to extend the current chain of blocks with the new block. Intuitively, most of you are probably thinking that this is trivial. If the chain of blocks looks like a linear data structure, a new block simply extends the existing chain in the only possible way: adding one block on top of the highest block. This, however, is only one of the possible scenarios at this stage. You should in fact consider that, at any point in time, multiple miner nodes may succeed in finding a new block and, consequently, gossiping this across the Bitcoin network. Like for transactions, even for new blocks we cannot guarantee (i) that, at a particular point in time, every node has received all the successfully mined new blocks until that time, and (ii) that the new blocks are received in the same order by all the nodes.

Depending on the value of the hash of the previous block, a new block may extend the current chain locally stored in the ledger by a node in one of the four possible cases depicted in Figure 5.13:

- *Case 1*: this is the case already discussed. The previous block of the new one is the highest in the local ledger. Hence, the new block extends the longest chain in the local ledger.
- *Case 2*: the previous block of the new one is not the highest one. This means that the new block does not extend the local chain of blocks from the top, but it creates a sideway 'fork', which may or may not be extended by other blocks in the future.
- *Case 3*: the previous block of the new one does not exist yet in the local ledger (probably, it has not yet been received by the node). In this case, the new block does not extend any chain in the local ledger immediately (but it might in the future, should the missing block be received by this node).
- *Case 4*: the previous block of the new one extends the local chain at some height and it is also the one missing by one or more blocks already received. This is an extension of Case 3. In this case, a node extends the chain using the new block and also the other blocks that have been received before.

Note that the forks (created in Figure 5.13 by Case 2 and Case 4) normally concern only the last few blocks in the local ledger. That is because miner nodes always create a new candidate block extending the longest chain in their ledger. Thus, it is extremely unlikely (and impossible in practice) that a new block has a very old block (deep into the chain of blocks) as the previous one.

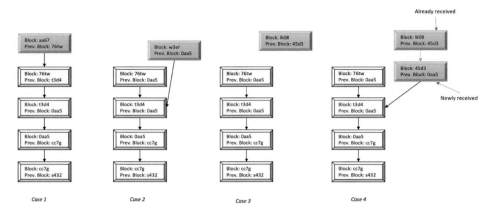

Figure 5.13 Extending the local ledger with a new valid block. For simplicity, blocks are identified by a four-character hash.

The four cases discussed above shed some light on a number of aspects of the Bitcoin consensus mechanism that perhaps have remained unclear to many of you until now. More in detail:

- It should now be clear what we meant earlier that a miner node must create a new block extending the longest chain. In practice, among the many chains determined by the (possible) forks in the local ledger, a miner node must always use the last block of the longest chain as the previous block of a new block.
- Because forks may occur in the ledger, nodes should not trust the transactions belonging to the most recent blocks. These blocks, in fact, may belong to forks that will not be extended in the future and that, therefore, will not be part of the longest chain of blocks in the ledger.

As a rule of thumb, nodes should trust only blocks that are at least 6-block deep into the main chain in the ledger. Based on the rules of the Bitcoin protocol, a 6-block or deeper block belonging to the main chain is not likely to ever be forked by a new block. Since in the Bitcoin network a new block is mined every ten minutes on average, a transaction issued on the Bitcoin network should be fully trusted only after one hour (i.e., 60 minutes) it has been issued. After one hour has elapsed, in fact, a transaction is certainly likely to have been included into a block that is 6-block deep into the main chain and that, therefore, can be trusted to remain on the longest chain forever.

Finally, we can now clarify why the PoW is usually referred to as an 'emergent' consensus mechanism. In the Bitcoin consensus mechanism, it is impossible to define a precise time instant in which all the nodes agree on accepting a new block in the ledger. In practice, the process of creating and gossiping new blocks is continuous. The nodes continuously receive new blocks. A new block may fork the current longest chain in their local copy of the ledger, may fork another chain, or may even not find its previous block in the local ledger. Therefore, the nodes cannot trust that any of the most recent blocks received will remain on the longest chain. However, they can trust blocks once they are deep enough in the current longest chain (6-block deep).

5.4.3 Calculating a correct nonce for a candidate new block

After having discussed the general functioning of the PoW, we can finally focus on how the nonce is calculated. That is, we now discuss the computational problem that miner nodes must solve to calculate a correct value of the nonce for a new block. Then, we also discuss the implications that this has on the nature of the nodes and, more in general, on the Bitcoin network as a whole.

To understand the computational work involved in calculating nonces, we begin with an example that, at a first glance, has not much to do with Bitcoin or blockchain in general. Let us consider a game of dice. We play with two traditional cube six-sided dice. A player throws the two dice simultaneously. The players 'win' if the sum of the dice is below a certain target score S. Now, if S = 13 or higher, players have a 100% of winning every time they throw. The maximum score that can be achieved with one throw of two dice is in fact 12 (six on both dice). The winning chances become less than 100% if S is equal to 12 or less. For instance, if S = 12, then the only non-winning combination (out of 36 possible combinations that can be thrown) is to get two times 6. Hence, the chances of winning with one throw are 35/36 = 97.22%. If S = 3, then the wining chances are 1/36 = 2.78%. There is in fact only one possible winning combination in this case (throwing two times 1). We can slightly modify the game, allowing the players to cast the dice multiple times until they get a winning throw. Then, if S = 12, players can have a fair certainty of throwing a winning combination casting the dices only a few times. The chances of getting a non-winning throw are in fact very low. If S = 3, then players should cast the dices many more times to have a comparable chance of getting a winning throw.

What is the lesson to be learnt from designing this simple game? We created a game in which a target value S determines the 'amount of work' (i.e., the number of times that dice should be cast) required to have a 'fairly high' chance of succeeding (i.e., throwing less than the target S). Also, we should note that, while it takes some effort to play the game, i.e., throwing the dice multiple times, it takes very little effort to verify whether a player has cast a winning combination. Anybody can quickly verify this simply by adding up the value obtained on each dice and verifying whether this sum is less than S. For now, let these considerations sink in the back of our memory. They will be needed later. First, let us present the 'game' or, better, the computational problem, that miner nodes must solve to find a correct nonce for a candidate block.

Let us consider a miner node that has selected the transactions to include in a new block and determined the previous block on which the local ledger should be extended. The only missing information in this new block is now the nonce (and the hash of the block, but this is also set by the process that we are about to discuss). To determine the value of the nonce, a miner node must solve the following computational problem:

> Find a value of a nonce such that the value of the SHA256 of the hash of the new block is less than a given target S.

The problem formulation is rather simple. However, the devil often hides in the details. First, we need to understand that the output of the SHA256 hashing function is a sequence of 256 bits. Recalling what we discussed in Chapter 2, this sequence of bit can always be interpreted as a number expressed in Base-2. Hence, the problem of assessing whether a SHA256 hash is less than a target number S is well-defined (i.e., it is solved by comparing two numbers: the hash obtained and the target S). Then, how can this problem be solved? Is there a 'smart' algorithm that we could use to solve this problem efficiently? Unfortunately, the answer is no, and in this impossibility lies the essence of the PoW.

As we discussed in Chapter 2, a cryptographic hash function must not be invertible. That is, given a hash value h, it must be impossible to find the message M that generates it. Now, what happens if, instead of a single hash value h, we consider a range of values or, more specifically, the range $[0,h]$, that is, all the possible hash values lower than h? In other words, is it possible to find a message M whose hash value is lower than a given target $S = h$? First, we should realize that it is impossible to devise a smart algorithm that finds a solution to this problem efficiently (for instance, for the computer scientists, in 'polynomial time'). We do not go in depth in this matter, but we can try at least to sketch an explanation. Any efficient algorithm to solve this problem would require the ability to 'predict' somehow the value of a hash based on the content of an input message (the block in this case). This would in fact allow to explore the space of possible messages values efficiently. By definition of cryptographic hash function, however, this is practically impossible. A well-designed hashing function is such that it is impossible to predict the value of a hash (or its range) based on the content of the input. The only way to solve this problem is to try all the possible messages, i.e., a 'brute force' approach, hoping to find sooner or later the message that we are looking for.

The range of the allowed hashes, i.e., the target S on the value of the hash, can be used to control how difficult it is to find an allowed hash. The larger the target S, the easier to find an allowed nonce. Then, the difficulty of solving this problem can be evaluated considering the number of hashing operations that, on average, a node should perform to be fairly confident to find a successful hash.

Can you see now the analogy with the game of dice discussed earlier? The work required by players to play the game (throwing the dice) is equivalent to the hashing operations required to calculate a nonce; the target S on the value obtained by throwing the dice is equivalent to the target S on the value of the hash; the target S can be manipulated (increased or decreased) to control the average amount of 'work' required to solve the problem (or to win the game).

Now, there are only a few pieces missing to fully understand the PoW mechanism. The role of the nonce should now be clear. The nonce is an integer number that allows to enumerate the number of hashing operations that a node has performed to find an allowed hash. There is no smarter way for a node to find an allowed nonce than a 'brute force' approach. Hence, when mining the nonce of a new block, a node simply starts from the value 0 of the nonce, hashes the block obtained by considering that nonce value, and verifies whether the hash is lower than the target S. If that is not the case, the node increases the value of the nonce of one unit and keeps trying. This process continues until a value of the hash lower than S (and therefore a correct nonce) is found.

Then, while finding a correct value of the nonce may take a significant amount of hashing operations (and computational power), validating the value of a nonce takes only one single hash operation. Upon receiving a new block, in fact, any node can verify if its nonce is correct simply by recalculating the SHA256 hash of the block and verifying that it matches the block hash (and therefore it is indeed below the target S).

The difficulty of the problem of finding a correct nonce can be adjusted by increasing or decreasing the value of the target S. Given the average computing power of the nodes of the Bitcoin network, the average number of hashing operations to succeed in finding an allowed hash can be translated into an average amount of time that it may take to an 'average' node of the Bitcoin network to find a value of a correct nonce. As mentioned before, the Bitcoin protocol dynamically adjusts the difficulty of the PoW to guarantee that, on average, a new block is mined successfully every ten minutes. The algorithm that dynamically sets this difficulty uses as the main input the average computational power of the nodes of the Bitcoin network that implement the mining functionality.

Figure 5.14 shows the hashes of different blocks in the main Bitcoin blockchain mined at different times since 2009. At first glance, it can be noticed that the hashes differ for the number of initial 0s. Specifically, the number of initial 0s in the hash tends to increase over time. This is a direct consequence of the design of the PoW mechanism. For instance, the target S = 5,000,000 in Base-10 is represented in Base-16 by the characters '4c4b40'. In the PoW mechanism, this level of difficulty means that a miner must find a nonce such that the SHA256 hash of a candidate block is less than:

00000000000000000000000000000000000000000000000000000004c4b40.

This means that, in order to be lower than S, the hash of a block should start with at least 56 zeros. The more the 0s at the start of a hash of a block, the lower the range of allowed hash values, i.e., the higher the difficulty that has characterized the mining of that block.

Finally, let us briefly discuss what are the implications of the PoW mechanism for the nodes of the Bitcoin network.

- First, individual miner nodes have an incentive to use more and more computational power in order to be able to find a correct nonce, on average, quicker than other miner nodes. When receiving a new block, in fact, a miner node discards the mining of its current new block, assembles a new one, and then starts assembling and mining a new block. All the time spent mining a new block that is then discarded is time completely wasted by a miner node. To minimize the occurrence of such an event, the best that a miner can do is to increase its computational power.
- The collective push to build miner nodes with increased computational power obviously increases the average computing power of mining nodes of the Bitcoin network. This, in turn, tends to increase over time the difficulty of the PoW set by the Bitcoin protocol. Hence, the intrinsic design of the PoW mechanism creates a positive feedback loop that requires miner nodes to implement more and more computational power.

```
0000000000000000000d36a105e1f07e697fdabf36bde99b275f2e0427d26d6e
```
(mined on 2019-03-14 06:05:08, height = 566,975)

```
00000000000011906b491883ab0f16f0e690b133ca860b199b775c3cf6581c21
```
(mined on 2011-06-11 09:11:11, height = 130,000)

```
00000000f093cf2c5865f2bb851d5fa65ff1794b02fea4b0d90ff451e6e5d1c0
```
(mined on 2009-01-10 20:20:48, height=56)

Figure 5.14 Hash of Bitcoin nodes mined at different times.

These considerations are reflected in the history of the Bitcoin mining. Mining of Bitcoin blocks started as a hobby activity for computer science enthusiasts in 2009: the Bitcoin network was known to very few, the difficulty of PoW was very low, and mining was feasible using any high-spec desktop computer, e.g., a well-performing gaming desktop computer. In 2010, the first implementation of the mining mechanism on GPUs was proposed. This began a first race in the Bitcoin mining: miner nodes became increasing complex, with architectures involving several GPUs working in parallel; stand-alone desktop computers were cut off from the mining competition. Starting from 2011, the first implementations of the mining algorithm on hardware bundles (ASIC – Application Specific Integrated Circuits) were proposed. These implement the hashing operation logic required to calculate nonces on pure hardware. Any application running only on hardware is orders of magnitude faster than any software implementation of it. Since then, Bitcoin mining has become an extremely specialized computing task that can be successful only by an ASIC-based miner and, more recently, by the so-called mining consortia.

A mining consortium is a set of computing nodes that apply a 'divide & conquer' strategy to find the correct nonces: the range of possible nonces is split across different computing nodes and each node tries to find a correct nonce only in the range assigned to them. In this way, the consortium can explore the range of possible nonces in a parallel way. The eventual rewards of the successful mining (i.e., the fixed rewards and fees in the coinbase transaction of a successfully mined node) are then split among the nodes of the consortium according to the range of nonces that each explored.

It should now be clear that Bitcoin mining is not particularly sustainable from an energetic standpoint. The hardware circuits that a miner keep running consume a very large amount of energy. It is estimated that the industry of Bitcoin mining as a whole consumes as much energy as a medium-sized developed country [SBF+20][Tru18]. It is a staggering amount of energy, which, in practice, is used simply by mega computers that do only one simple thing: running SHA256 hashing operations increasingly faster. Moreover, the energy consumption of Bitcoin mining, for the reasons discussed above, is only likely to grow forever.

5.5 Case study: Bitcoin in the real world

While, in this chapter, we have approached the Bitcoin blockchain mainly from a mechanism design standpoint, in this case study we want to look at the adoption of Bitcoin in the real world. To this aim, we focus on the usage and acceptance of Bitcoin and on the implications that the design features that we have discussed in this chapter have on real-world applications of Bitcoin.

Bitcoin is used in the real world as a payment means and as an investment asset. The latter is the use of Bitcoin that is most popular and discussed mostly in the news. In the last five years, Bitcoin has become an investment asset globally. It is now part of the portfolio diversification strategies of even major investment banks. The price of Bitcoin in fiat currencies, like US dollars or Euros, has seen a substantial increase, albeit extremely fluctuating and unpredictable, since the mining of the Bitcoin's genesis block in 2009. The first noticeable race of the Bitcoin price happened in late 2013: BTC traded at 123 USD in October, then raced to 1,237 USD in December, but fell again below 700 USD in the same month. More recent races (see Figure 5.15) occurred in 2017, where BTC price raced from about 200 USD in May to almost 20,000 USD in December, and

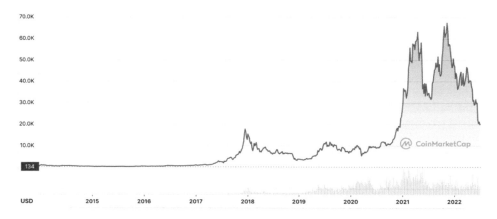

Figure 5.15 Price of BTC in US dollars from 2015 until late October 2022.
Source: coinmarketcap.com.

more recently in 2021, when the price climbed above 60,000 USD in April. Since then, however, the price of BTC has more than halved again during the so-called 'crypto winter' of 2022. Like any other financial asset, the price of BTC in US dollars is primarily determined by the levels of supply and demand. At the same time, however, important factors such as the cryptocurrency regulations passed by different countries or the hype given in the news to new cryptocurrency developments (like the bankruptcy of major crypto-exchanges), are also important factors inflating and deflating the price of Bitcoin in unpredictable ways. As an investment asset, BTC has been extremely lucrative during the last few years, but also extremely risky. Many young investors have seen their investments in BTC almost completely wiped out by the wild price fluctuations that we see in Figure 5.15. Investors tend to agree that Bitcoins, and cryptocurrencies in general, should be considered only as the very risky (and probably small) component of a balanced investment portfolio.

Bitcoin is not regulated, or only very mildly regulated, in most countries and financial markets. The United States and most European countries, for instance, have yet to develop clear regulatory frameworks for the use of Bitcoin and other cryptocurrencies. Other countries, like Ecuador, Qatar, and, most prominently, China, have completely banned cryptocurrency transactions, preventing even financial institutions to invest in BTCs. Such strict regulations however may be bypassed easily, thanks to the regulations of other countries that do not enforce restrictions on foreign investors in Bitcoin and other cryptocurrencies.

The general lack of clear regulations regarding Bitcoin is a major issue affecting the adoption of Bitcoin in the real world. On the one hand, such a lack of regulation is intrinsic to the inner design of Bitcoin. Regulations, in fact, must be imposed by a central authority. Bitcoin, however, was created as a form of digital cash that does not involve central authorities. So, any form of regulation could be seen as violating the inner spirit of the Bitcoin system. On the other hand, the lack of regulation has pushed Bitcoin to become a major payment means for illegal activities (e.g., weaponry, narcotics) on the so-called 'Dark Web' [KR19], that is, the part of the Internet not indexed by the search engines that we commonly use.

As a means of payment, currently Bitcoin is 'legal tender', i.e., recognized by a state as a viable form of payments on its national territory, only in El Salvador and the Central African Republic [Her21]. In these countries, any merchant is legally allowed to receive payments from customers in BTC. Both countries cited a need to increase the reach of digital payments and to decrease digital financial exclusion as major reasons to pass regulations making Bitcoin legal tender. Both countries have struggled mightily from a technical standpoint to implement BTC payment systems [Haw22]. For instance, there is no standard for a Bitcoin wallet, which in turn prevents the development of standard digital payment devices to handle Bitcoin payments. As a consequence, customers often are prevented to use their BTC simply because they are using a wallet not supported by the payment device used by the merchant. The fluctuations of the BTC price in fiat currency also have been a major impediment for Bitcoin adoption. For instance, merchants struggle with pricing correctly their good or services in BTC. Moreover, they tend to accept BTC payments only when the price of BTC is high.

The evidence discussed thus far seems to point to a future in which it may not be impossible to see Bitcoin used more often as a means of payment in everyday life. However, such a diffusion can only occur with appropriate regulations of Bitcoin in the national and global financial markets. Stabilizing the price of BTC in fiat currency also seems like a major concern for the adoption of Bitcoin in everyday life.

Finally, a major issue with Bitcoin is its sustainability. As we discussed in this chapter, the Bitcoin's PoW consensus mechanism enforces miners to constantly improve their computational capabilities. Practically, this means that miners tend to consume more energy over time on average to mine new blocks. In 2021, it was estimated that Bitcoin miners consumed the 0.55% of the electricity globally produced [KV22]. This does not seem to be sustainable in a world where resources are limited and where there is a growing concern over the role that high energy consumption has, for instance, on the changes in weather patterns. Luckily, such a concern can be addressed by acting on the design of a blockchain. Specifically, sustainability concerns could be addressed by a different consensus mechanism. Bitcoin does not have any plan to change its consensus mechanism in the near future. However, Ethereum, which we discuss in the next chapter, has managed to switch in September 2022 from a PoW-based consensus to a much more sustainable consensus based on the principle of the Proof-of-Stake (PoS, also presented in the next chapter).

5.6 Conclusions

In this chapter, we have presented the Bitcoin blockchain. We first presented it as a public network of computational nodes. Then, most part of the chapter was spent in discussing the Bitcoin transactions and the mechanisms through which Bitcoin manages the state, i.e., the BTC balance of all the nodes, the Bitcoin ledger, and the Bitcoin consensus mechanism. Regarding the latter, we discussed how the consensus in Bitcoin 'emerges' from the interaction of the nodes and how nobody should trust Bitcoin transactions that are included in blocks that are not 6-block deep in the ledger. Finally, we also understood why the Bitcoin blockchain is characterized intrinsically by a race among the miner nodes to improve their computational power.

To conclude this chapter, we briefly summarize what are the 'good' and the 'bad' aspects of the Bitcoin blockchain. Regarding the 'good' aspects, we first should mention that Bitcoin has been a surprisingly stable system thus far. It has been in use since 2009, becoming the premium alternative for a digital cash system completely decoupled from national central banks. In this regard, you might have read of the Bitcoin blockchain being 'hacked'. However, these news items refer to cases in which the private keys of (careless) Bitcoin users have been stolen. They never refer to the actual hacking (i.e., modification to achieve a private benefit) of the data stored by the nodes in the Bitcoin ledger. Because of this overall stability and its nature decoupled from individual governments, Bitcoin is valued today by many corporate and private investors as one of the alternatives for financial portfolio diversification.

There are obviously several 'bad' aspects of Bitcoin. However, only a few of them relate specifically to the design of the Bitcoin blockchain that we discussed in this chapter. From a design standpoint, Bitcoin consumes an enormous amount of energy. This is obviously a detrimental factor on a planet where resources are limited. Moreover, it is operationally slow, which may be a problem for everyday small-scale monetary transactions. Most importantly, the two main problems of the Bitcoin blockchain concern its lack of regulations within the financial markets. Being completely unregulated in most countries, BTCs are often used as the means of payment in the 'Dark Web' [KR19], to regulate, for instance, drug of weaponry dealings. Moreover, the exchange rate between BTC and fiat currency varies wildly. This can be very lucrative for speculative short-term investments. However, it can be a problem for investments that require more stability. One of the main reasons for the failure of the El Salvador initiative, in fact, was that the state spent at least 100 million USD to buy Bitcoins in September 2021, which in early 2022 became worth around 50 million USD because of the massive drop of the exchange rate. Wise regulation, rather than improved design and technology, is perhaps the silver bullet for seeing Bitcoin, and cryptocurrencies in general, more widely adopted.

5.7 Questions and exercises

1   Use a Bitcoin explorer (e.g., https://www.blockchain.com/explorer) to find:
    a   A transaction in which at least one of the outputs has not yet been spent
    b   A coinbase transaction
    c   A transaction consuming two or more inputs
    d   A transaction producing two or more outputs
2   Consider the transactions in a blockchain that, like Bitcoin, uses the mechanism of UTXOs to manage its state shown in Figure 5.16. Assume that T1 is processed before T2, T2 before T3 etc. and that TX and TY are processed before T1.

    Complete the transactions with the missing information (i.e., '??') and, assuming there are no other transactions except the ones shown above, calculate the blockchain state (i.e., the balance of all the nodes) after T5 is processed.
3   Consider the fragment of a real Bitcoin transaction in Figure 5.17.
    Answer the following questions:
    a   What is the id of this transaction?
    b   How many UTXOs does this transaction consume? From which previous transaction(s)?
    c   Which address controls the output n.1 of this transaction?
        Use a Bitcoin blockhain explorer (e.g., https://www.blockchain.com/explorer) to answer the following questions:
    d   Have the outputs of this transactions been spent?

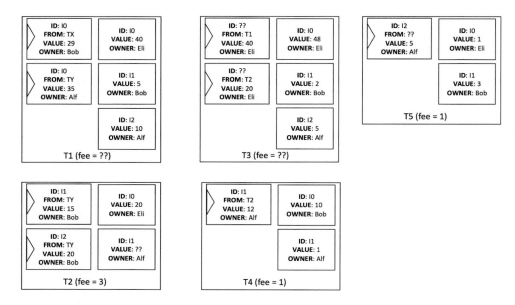

Figure 5.16 Transactions in a blockchain system using the UTXO mechanism.

    e   List the address(es) of the account(s) controlling the input(s) of this transaction

    f   What is the fee paid by this transaction?

    g   In which block was this transaction included on the main Bitcoin blockchain? (Indicate block number/height)

    h   How much fees have been paid to the miner by the block in which this transaction was included?

4 Consider a hashing algorithm that returns hashes of 40 bits, e.g., 0x78ab6f6712. Consider then a blockchain system adopting PoW in which the mining 'difficulty' D is the inverse of the probability of finding an hash for a given block satisfying a given target with only one hashing operation. For instance, difficulty D = 60 means that there is a 1/60 probablity to find, given a block, a hash that satisfies a given target.

    Design a target for this blockchain system for D = 16, D = 256, D = 65,536

    Is it possible to design a target for D = 64?

5 Consider the information about blocks mined received by node X in a blockchain adopting the same consensus mechanism of Bitcoin shown in Table 5.1.

    Considering that the memory pool of node X contains the following transactions at t = 1: {T1, T2, T3, T4, T5, T6, T7, T8, T9}, answer the following questions:

    a   Which blocks are in the main blockchain (and in which order) of node X at time t = 22?

    b   Which transactions are in node X's memory pool at time t = 15?

    c   Which transactions are in node X's memory pool at time t = 22?

```
{
        "txid": "3c7aba2b158db5c0344f041b4cecb7ad493d8820da7b4cee064046968b5c5b60",
        "hash": "80178bebe9c2c52e7b1e9116df807c78352161e2fe9f6fc29b11ea738ea4e4a5",
        "version": 2,
        "size": 284,
        "vsize": 202,
        "locktime": 565138,
        "vin": [
            {
                "txid": "9558cbb413c83cf7069e4895c3a943d5f683977328513b9d072ff550914babf0",
                "vout": 1,
                "scriptSig": {
                    "asm": "00143ce91c9867cc3fe5c0e4a315c24b883ada38d551",
                    "hex": "1600143ce91c9867cc3fe5c0e4a315c24b883ada38d551"
                },
                .....
            }
        ],
        "vout": [
            {
                "value": 0.00080000,
                "n": 0,
                "scriptPubKey": {
                    ...
                    "addresses": [
                        "1Ma2DrB78K7jmAwaomqZNRMCvgQrNjE2QC"
                    ]
                }
            },
            {
                "value": 0.00996313,
                "n": 1,
                "scriptPubKey": {
                    ...,
                    "addresses": [
                        "3GpDFSM5vWqVUPQHTctME8NgpNTJsFVzgF"
                    ]
                }
            },
            {
                "value": 0.00293842,
                "n": 2,
                "scriptPubKey": {
                    ...,
                    "addresses": [
                        "1Q532MYAXwRbcvEAsYxD4bELinnwdX2QDk"
                    ]
                }
            }
        ],
        "hex": "....",
        "blockhash": "00000000000000000000262846807fcfe0f6db136d33f32711f6414fe5f92d72a6",
        "confirmations": 1534,
        "time": 1551413037,
        "blocktime": 1551413037
```

Figure 5.17 Machine-readable version of a real Bitcoin transaction.

Table 5.1 Blocks received by node X

Time	BlockId	Previous block Id	Transactions included
t1 = 2	A	…	T1, T2, T4
t2 = 5	B	A	T2, T6
t3 = 10	C	A	T2, T5
t4 = 14	D	B	T5, T7
t5 = 18	E	C	T7, T8
t6 = 21	F	E	T9,T6

6 Ethereum and smart contract-enabled blockchain

Learning goals

6.A The reader can describe the Ethereum network and the mechanisms characterizing the Ethereum transactions, such as transaction nonce and gas.

6.B The reader can define the Ethereum consensus mechanism and compare the proof-of-work and proof-of-stake consensus mechanisms.

6.C The reader can define the concept of the Ethereum Virtual Machine and explain the life cycle of transactions and blocks in Ethereum.

6.D The reader can understand simple Ethereum smart contracts written in Solidity.

6.E The reader can explain the concept of Ethereum token and compare the characteristics of fungible and non-fungible tokens.

6.F The reader understands the concept of Ethereum DApp and can discuss their benefits and drawbacks.

6.1 Ethereum network

In the first part of this book (Chapter 4), we introduced the concept of smart contracts. Smart contracts equip a blockchain with the ability of executing arbitrary business logic. As such, they allow a blockchain to transition from a system to implement cryptocurrencies to a system supporting more general asset exchange scenarios. Ethereum is the first and most prominent example of public, smart contract-enabled blockchain. It was conceived in 2013 by Canadian programmer Vitalik Buterin and it went live in 2015. Like Bitcoin, Ethereum has its own cryptocurrency. Unlike Bitcoin, it allows its users to define and utilize smart contracts. Thanks to smart contracts, the Ethereum blockchain is currently used by several real-world applications, ranging from IoT applications to decentralized finance and digital art exchange applications.

Ethereum is a public blockchain. Like Bitcoin, it has a cryptocurrency. The Ethereum cryptocurrency is called 'Ether'. It is denominated ETH in the international asset markets. Unlike Bitcoin, the information that can be recorded in the Ethereum ledger is more than cryptocurrency exchanges among the nodes. Unlike Bitcoin, Ethereum also has smart contracts. As discussed in Chapter 4, with smart contracts the state of a blockchain is captured by the value assigned to all the variables used by the smart contracts deployed in the system. The ETH balance of a node (see Figure 6.1), i.e., the amount

DOI: 10.4324/9781003321187-8

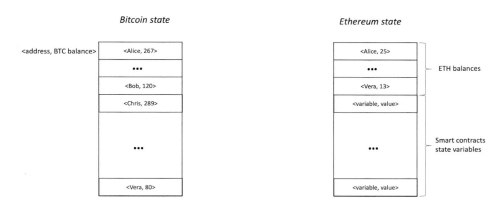

Figure 6.1 Comparing the state of Bitcoin and Ethereum.

of Ether owned by it, is simply one of the variables, among many others, defining the state of the Ethereum blockchain. The Ethereum state and the content of the Ethereum ledger is analyzed more elaborately later in the chapter.

Like Bitcoin, the Ethereum network is a connected network of computational nodes with Internet access. Standard implementations of the Ethereum clients for different devices and operating systems are available at https://ethereum.org. Like Bitcoin, the Ethereum nodes have a private key, a public key, and an address. The private key is used by the nodes to digitally sign the transactions that they issue on the Ethereum network. The public key is used by other nodes to verify such signatures. The address is a unique identifier of a node. It is used, for instance, when transferring ETH to a node, or to uniquely identify a node in the code of a smart contract.

The 'normal' nodes of the Ethereum network discussed above are called EOA (Externally Owned Accounts). They are very much similar to the nodes of the Bitcoin network: they have an address, they own ETH, and they can exchange it using transactions.

EOAs are not the only entity in Ethereum associated with an address. Smart contracts in Ethereum also have an address. This has the same format as an EOA address. To distinguish smart contract accounts from EOAs, in this book we call the former SCA (Smart Contract Accounts[1]). An SCA cannot issue transactions. Hence, it is not associated with public/private keys. An SCA is simply a means to uniquely identify a specific smart contract in the Ethereum network. As discussed later, a smart contract can be invoked by a node by addressing a transaction to it. That is, the address of a SCA is the recipient in this type of transactions. This type of transactions must contain the details of the invocation, such as the name of the function to be invoked and, if needed, the value of the input parameters.

From a technical standpoint, the format of the keys and addresses in Ethereum, and the technology used to generate them are not the same used by Bitcoin. For instance, Ethereum also uses Elliptic Curve Cryptography to implement digital signatures. However, the format and size of the keys are not the same as discussed in the previous chapter for Bitcoin. Knowing these technical details is not necessary to understand the functioning of Ethereum as discussed in this chapter. Hence, we do not discuss further these aspects here. Readers who want to know more about these technical aspects are referred to technical publications about Ethereum, like [AW18].

6.2 Ethereum transactions

Like Bitcoin, Ethereum EOAs can issue transactions to modify the state of the Ethereum blockchain. Because Ethereum includes smart contracts, an Ethereum transaction can do either of the following three actions:

1   Transfer ETH from one EOA (the sender) to another EOA (the recipient), in a manner similar to a Bitcoin transaction
2   Create a new smart contract (that any EOA can invoke in the future)
3   Invoke an existing smart contract, specifying the function to be invoked and, if needed, the input parameters

These three types of transactions are discussed more in detail next.

6.2.1 Transactions transferring Ethereum tokens between EOAs

First, we discuss Ethereum transactions transferring ETH between nodes. Unlike Bitcoin, where one transaction can transfer BTC to/from multiple nodes, in Ethereum a transaction can transfer ETH only between two EOAs: the sender and the recipient. The sender issuing a transaction must own an amount of ETH greater than the amount transferred. The recipient receives the ETH transferred by the sender.

In Ethereum, the balance of a node is simply one of the many variables describing the taste of the blockchain. Unlike Bitcoin, there is nothing equivalent to the UTXOs in Ethereum. When executing a transaction, a node of the Ethereum network updates the value of the two variables capturing the ETH balance of the sender and the recipient. The ETH amount that is transferred (plus the fee, which we discuss later) is deducted from balance of the sender. The balance of the recipient is increased by a corresponding amount.

Figure 6.2 shows the content of a transaction elaborated by one of the online 'explorers' of the Ethereum blockchain. At a first glance, this transaction is very similar to a Bitcoin transaction. It has its hash as a unique id (the hash '4957...'[2]), belongs to a block (number '15038026'), and it transfers approximately 1.92 ETH from the EOA '3cd7...' to the EOA 'dd6e...'. The fee paid by the sender is approximately 0.00045 ETH. A closer inspection, however, clearly reveals information fields in Figure 6.2 that we do not know how to interpret. For instance, what is the gas (price, limit, usage)? What is the nonce? What are the input data? We explain the meaning of these fields next.

6.2.1.1 Transaction nonce

The nonce of an Ethereum transaction is a progressive number that counts the number of transactions originated by the EOA that issued this transaction. In Figure 6.2, the nonce is equal to 8194637. This means that this transaction is the 8194637th issued by the originator EOA '3cd07...'. Obviously, it is not to be confused with the nonce of blocks in Bitcoin (we will see soon that a similar nonce for blocks exists also in

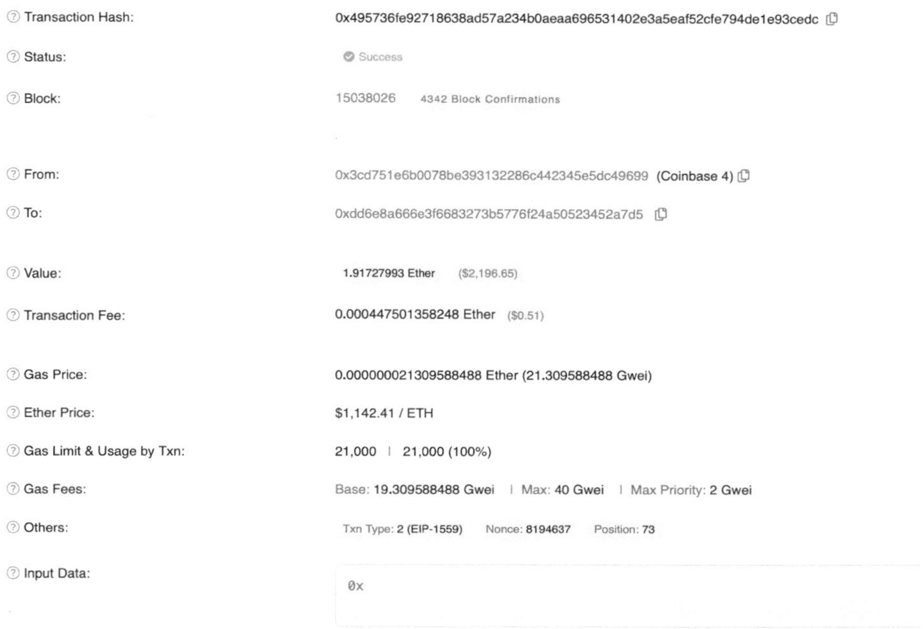

⑦ Transaction Hash:	0x495736fe92718638ad57a234b0aeaa696531402e3a5eaf52cfe794de1e93cedc ⃞
⑦ Status:	⊘ Success
⑦ Block:	15038026 4342 Block Confirmations
⑦ From:	0x3cd751e6b0078be393132286c442345e5dc49699 (Coinbase 4) ⃞
⑦ To:	0xdd6e8a666e3f6683273b5776f24a50523452a7d5 ⃞
⑦ Value:	1.91727993 Ether ($2,196.65)
⑦ Transaction Fee:	0.000447501358248 Ether ($0.51)
⑦ Gas Price:	0.000000021309588488 Ether (21.309588488 Gwei)
⑦ Ether Price:	$1,142.41 / ETH
⑦ Gas Limit & Usage by Txn:	21,000	21,000 (100%)
⑦ Gas Fees:	Base: 19.309588488 Gwei	Max: 40 Gwei	Max Priority: 2 Gwei
⑦ Others:	Txn Type: 2 (EIP-1559) Nonce: 8194637 Position: 73
⑦ Input Data:	0x

Figure 6.2 A real Ethereum transaction transferring ETH between two EOAs, obtained at:
https://etherscan.io/tx/0x495736fe92718638ad57a234b0aeaa696531402e3a5eaf
52cfe794de1e93cedc.

Ethereum). The real question, though, is, why is such a nonce needed, that is, why is it necessary to count the transactions issued by an EOA?

The nonce contributes to solving the issue of double spending or, more precisely, it allows to order the transaction issued by an EOA. In Bitcoin, we have seen that the UTXO mechanism prevents a node to double spend the BTC that they own. A UTXO used by a node as input of one transaction cannot be used also as input of a different transaction. In Ethereum, however, UTXOs do not exist. The balance of a node is simply determined by the value of one of the many variables that determine the Ethereum state. In such a situation, ordering the transactions issued by an EOA node and making such an order explicit in every transaction is the only way to prevent double spending. The transaction nonce has precisely this role: to order the transactions issued by an EOA.

To better understand the role of the transaction nonce, let us consider a typical double spending scenario (see Figure 6.3, expanded from Figure 3.5 in Chapter 3). Here Alice is trying to double spend part of her ten ETH to buy both a mug and a chair from Bob and Carol. Without a transaction nonce, Alice would be able to replicate exactly the double spending mechanism described theoretically in Chapter 3: if Bob and Carol receive the transactions T1 and T2 in a different order, then Alice may succeed in double spending her Ether. The transaction nonce, however, forces Alice to make the order of her transactions explicit. This obviously prevents the double spending of her tokens.

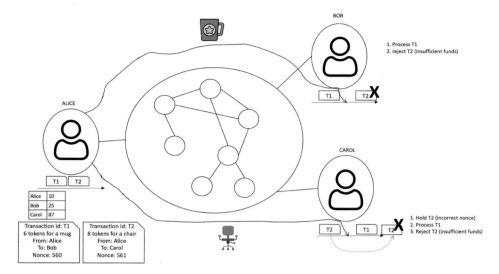

Figure 6.3 Transaction nonce and double spending in Ethereum.

In fact, it guarantees that other nodes know exactly the order in which the transactions issued by Alice must be validated and processed. So, Carol, considering the value of the transaction nonce, in this particular example holds the processing of T2 (which is eventually rejected) until T1 is received and processed.

The transaction nonce introduces other issues that did not exist in Bitcoin. Most importantly, it must always be set correctly by an EOA. If that does not happen, then the transactions issued by an EOA may never be validated and processed by the nodes. In Figure 6.3, because of the values of the transaction nonces, the transaction T2 cannot be validated by Carol until she received the transaction T1. Now, if a node is using only one client application (a single wallet) to interact with the Ethereum blockchain, then setting a correct transaction nonce is trivial. The client application can easily take care of it, counting the number of transactions issued by the EOA. The problem is technically more complex to solve when a node uses multiple client applications. The different client applications must coordinate themselves whenever issuing a new transaction to ensure a correct setting of the transaction nonce value.

6.2.1.2 Transaction input data

An Ethereum transaction also contains 'input data'. This because, unlike Bitcoin, there are different types of transactions in Ethereum. Depending on the type of transaction, the 'input data' is treated differently. Table 6.1 summarizes the role of the input data field for different types of transactions.

For transactions that transfer Ethereum tokens between two EOAs, like the one of Figure 6.2, the 'input data' field is simply ignored. This means that, when validating or executing this transaction, the nodes ignore the content of this field. In practice, for this type of transaction this field often remains empty (like in the transaction of Figure 6.2),

Table 6.1 Input data field content in Ethereum transactions

Type of Ethereum transaction	Content of input data field
Transactions transferring ETH between EOAs	Ignored
Transactions deploying a new smart contract	Byte code of the smart contract
Transactions invoking an existing smart contract	Function to invoke and (if necessary) input parameters

or it is used to specify information relevant to the sender and/or the recipient (like a 'reason for payment', or a 'payment reference').

When a transaction deploys a new smart contract into the Ethereum blockchain, the 'input data' field contains the so-called 'bytecode' of the smart contract. This is basically the executable code of the smart contract that every node can install locally to execute the smart contract in the future. When a transaction invokes a smart contract, the 'input data' specify the function of the smart contract to be invoked and, if necessary, the invocation parameters. More details about Ethereum smart contracts are discussed later when presenting the smart contract-related transactions.

6.2.1.3 *Transaction gas*

The transaction gas is the mechanism to specify the value of the transaction fee in Ethereum. In Bitcoin, the fee of a transaction is calculated by a node basically considering the size (expressed in bytes) of a transaction. The larger a transaction, the higher the amount of computational power that nodes require to validate and execute it, hence the higher the fee. The Bitcoin nodes may also increase the fee paid by a transaction to improve the chances that it would be picked up earlier by a miner node when assembling a new block.

Now, in Ethereum, the spirit of the transaction fee is the same as Bitcoin's: the more the computation required to process a transaction, the higher the fee. However, in Ethereum there are also transactions that trigger the execution of smart contracts. A smart contract invocation triggers the execution of some computational logic that processes the input and/or the variables describing the state of the Ethereum blockchain. Such logic can be more or less complex, depending on the nature of the smart contract. For instance, in the BC4C-CGM system introduced in Chapter 4, the smart contract is invoked by the players to pay a deposit. This practically means that a certain amount of cryptocurrency is transferred from a player's account to the temporary balance of the smart contract. This sounds like a fairly simple operation from a computational standpoint. However, as discussed also later in this chapter, smart contracts can execute any arbitrary computation, including for instance loops that are executed hundreds of times.

In this context, the mechanism to specify the transaction fee in Ethereum must adapt to the different types of transactions that exist in Ethereum. The gas mechanism represents exactly this adaptation. The metaphor of a fuel-propelled car comes in handy to understand the concept of gas. The gas price and limit represent the 'fuel' with which a transaction is equipped by its originator. Specifically, the gas limit represents the size of the 'tank'. When executing a transaction, a node carries on the execution as long as the gas limit is not reached, that is, as long as there is still gas in the tank. Now, this is normally not an issue for simple transactions that transfer ETH between EOAs, like the one of Figure 6.2. The computation required by this type of transaction is minimal: simply updating the value of the balance of the sender and the recipient EOAs. When a transaction invokes a smart contract, however, the gas limit becomes more important. It ensures specifically that the nodes cannot get stuck into very long (even infinite) computations during the execution of smart contracts. Note that, in normal situations, setting an appropriate value of the gas limit is trivial for a node. The Ethereum client can in fact estimate pretty reliably the amount of gas required for a transfer of ETH or a smart contract invocation based on a quick inspection of the smart contract code. Finally, we remark that a fee must be paid also by transactions deploying a new smart contract. The gas used, in this case, depends on the size (lines of code) of the contract's byte code.

The gas price is the price that the originator is willing to pay for one unit of fuel (gas) consumed during the execution of the transaction. In Figure 6.2, the sender has set a limit of 21,000 gas units to execute this transaction. The gas price per unit specified by the sender is approximately 21.3 Gwei.[3] Like in Bitcoin, nodes may decide to set higher gas prices to pay a higher fee. This, in turn, can increase the likelihood that their transactions are picked up earlier when nodes assemble new blocks. The gas used in this case is the gas actually used by nodes to execute a transaction. It could be the case that not all the gas in the tank is consumed by the execution of a transaction. In case a transaction triggers the execution of a smart contract, the amount of computation required to complete the execution may depend on the values of the input parameters contained in a transaction. In the transaction of Figure 6.2, all the gas in the tank ('100%') was used to execute this transaction.

6.2.2 Smart contract–related transactions

As mentioned earlier, there are two types of smart contract–related transactions in Ethereum: the ones that deploy new smart contracts and the ones that invoke smart contracts already deployed. These are discussed next.

6.2.2.1 Transactions deploying a new smart contract in the Ethereum network

With a transaction of this type, a node deploys a new smart contract into the Ethereum network. Deploying a smart contract means to distribute the code of the smart contract to all the nodes of the Ethereum network. Once every node of the Ethereum network has received the code of the smart contract, they can install it locally in their client. After the code of a smart contract is installed locally, a node can execute any transaction that invokes that particular smart contract.

Practically, to deploy a new smart contract, a node creates a transaction having the following characteristics:

- The recipient of the transaction is a fictitious node with address '0'.
- The input data of the transaction contains the byte code of the smart contract. As we said earlier, this is basically the executable code of the smart contract. More technical details from a computer science standpoint are available in the Computer Science Focus.
- The value of the transaction represents the initial balance (in ETH) of the smart contract.

Computer Science Focus: Ethereum smart contract languages

Several new programming languages have been invented to write Ethereum smart contracts, like Solidity, Vyper, or Yul. Like other programming languages, they differ in the syntax used and the level of abstraction provided in the definition of variables, variable types, etc. For instance, Vyper has a more Python-like syntax, whereas Solidity's syntax is more similar to Java's. Solidity is the most used Ethereum smart contract-programming language.

To be executed, programs written in all Ethereum smart contract languages are compiled into the so-called Ethereum bytecode. The bytecode is then interpreted by the Ethereum Virtual Machine (EVM) to be executed. The EVM is part of any Ethereum client and its behavior is specified by Ethereum community. While developers can write their smart contracts in any language that allows it (like Solidity, Vyper, Yul, etc.), the transactions deploying the smart contracts only distribute the bytecode. This can be executed by any Ethereum node running the EVM.

Combining compilation and interpretation for the execution of computer programs is not new in software engineering. It mainly facilitates the execution of computer programs across different platforms. The programming language Java works exactly in the same way: a Java program can be written by a developer using any platform, like Windows, Macos, or Linux. It is then compiled into the Java bytecode. The Java bytecode can be executed by any platform (even different from the one in which the program was originally written) that runs the Java Virtual Machine (JVM). This mechanism is different from the one adopted by fully compiled languages, like C or C++. For those, the executable code generated when compiling a program on a Windows platform is not likely to run on a Macos or Linux machine.

As we discuss more in detail in the next section, in fact, smart contracts can control ETH. To do so, each smart contract has an ETH balance. This balance can be initialized directly when the smart contract is deployed using the 'value' field of the transaction deploying it.

For smart contracts that do not handle ETH, the value of the ETH balance is always 0. The balance of the smart contract changes whenever ETH is paid into/from the smart contract from/to other nodes of the network. For example, in a hypothetical implementation in Ethereum of the smart contract of the BC4C-CGM system, the smart contract is created with a balance equal to 0. Then, before a new game is started, the smart contract receives the deposits from the players. At any point in time, the balance of the smart contract is equal to the deposits paid for the games that have started and have not yet terminated. At the end of a game, the smart contract pays the deposits for that game to the winner.

As a result of the deployment of a smart contract, a new Ethereum network account is created (a SCA). An SCA allows assigning a unique address to a smart contract. The transactions that invoke a smart contract are in fact addressed to an SCA as the recipient.

⑦ Transaction Hash:	0xe5af36d9162a89e2da2b99b5afb5fefe85569bc2b0945ed97a36b7333c2b4bfe 🗐
⑦ Status:	⊘ Success
⑦ Block:	11380284 3662636 Block Confirmations
⑦ Timestamp:	⊙ 572 days 12 hrs ago (Dec-03-2020 02:49:24 PM +UTC)
⑦ From:	0x4b5057b2c87ec9e7c047fb00c0e406dff2fdacad 🗐
⑦ To:	[Contract 0xfbddadd80fe7bda00b901fbaf73803f2238ae655 Created] (StrongBlock: Service) ⊘ 🗐
⑦ Value:	0 Ether ($0.00)
⑦ Transaction Fee:	0.02988225 Ether ($34.35)
⑦ Gas Price:	0.00000005 Ether (50 Gwei)
⑦ Ether Price:	$616.55 / ETH
⑦ Gas Limit & Usage by Txn:	597,645	597,645 (100%)
⑦ Others:	Nonce: 1570 Position: 24
⑦ Input Data:	0x6080604052604051610cb7380380610cb78339818101604052606081101561002657600080fd5b810190808051906020019092919080519060200190929190805160405193929190849640100000000082111561005a57600080fd5b838201915060208201858111156100705760000080fd5b8251866001820283011164010000000082111171561008d57600080fd5b8083526020830191250505090805190602001908383600005b838110156100cc157808201518184015260208101905060100a6565b5050505050905090509081019060011f1680156100ee5780820380516001830360200361010100a0319185157602801915850b5060640525050590500828160061600160405180807f6559783313036372a70726f78792696d70c656d656607a617406f56a... *View Input As*

Figure 6.4 A transaction deploying an Ethereum smart contract, available at: https://etherscan.io/tx/0xe5af36d9162a89e2da2b99b5afb5fefe85569bc2b0945ed97a36b7333c2b4bfe.

🛢 Contract 0xFbdDaDD80fe7bda00B901FbAf73803F2238Ae655				
Contract Overview		StrongBlock: Service ☑	**More Info**	❤ More ⌄
Balance:	44.515664009390368344 Ether		⑦ My Name Tag:	Not Available, login to update
Ether Value:	$51,149.39 (@ $1,149.02/ETH)		Contract Creator:	0x4b5057b2c87ec9e7c0… at txn 0xe5af36d9162a89e2da…
Token:	$18,050.40 **12**	⌄ 📇		

Figure 6.5 Details of an Ethereum SCA account, available at: https://etherscan.io/address/0xfbddadd80fe7bda00b901fbaf73803f2238ae655.

Figure 6.4 shows the information about a transaction deploying a smart contract elaborated by an Ethereum explorer. The contract was deployed by the node '4b50…' on December 3rd, 2020. Note that the 'To' field does not contain the address of the recipient of this transaction (which is simply the conventional address '0'), but only the SCA address of the smart contract created by this transaction ('FbdD…'). Since the 'value' of this transaction is 0 ETH, the smart contract was created with a balance equal to 0 ETH. The 'input data' field contains the byte code of the deployed smart contract. Figure 6.5 shows the information regarding this contract[4] elaborated by an Ethereum explorer. We can see that the smart contract has a balance of about 44.5 ETH. The contract also holds a balance of 12 Ethereum 'tokens'. We will learn more about these later in this chapter. The 'Contract creator' field references the transaction of Figure 6.4.

6.2.2.2 *Transactions invoking smart contracts*

Once a smart contract is deployed, it can be invoked by the nodes of the Ethereum network. As mentioned in the previous section, to invoke a smart contract an EOA creates

⑦ Transaction Hash: 0xc0705963ac05171b2ebbccedee9d8a98ddec8979cf9a52f3ba4408ac49d3e9ca   ⎘

⑦ Status: ⊘ Success

⑦ Block: 15042903   95 Block Confirmations

⑦ Timestamp: ⏱ 27 mins ago (Jun-29-2022 02:57:52 AM +UTC) | ⏱ Confirmed within 1 min

⑦ From: 0x3e266ed242524635192d9fbf69adbb4f5fb6fcaf ⎘

⑦ To: ⧉ Contract 0xfbddadd80fe7bda00b901fbaf73803f2238ae655 (StrongBlock: Service) ⊘ ⎘
                          ↳ TRANSFER 0.004440694748365599 Ether From StrongBlock: Ser... To ⇒ 0x4a5057b2c87ec9e7cb47fb00c...

⑦ Tokens Transferred: ‣ From StrongBlock: Ser... To 0x3e266ed242524... For 8.420685714285714285 ◐ Stronger (STRNGR)

⑦ Value: 0.0044407022820153 Ether   ($5.10)

⑦ Transaction Fee: 0.01377559349974528 Ether ($15.81)

⑦ Gas Price: 0.000000061439214592 Ether (61.439214592 Gwei)

⑦ Gas Limit & Usage by Txn: 229,411 | 224,215 (97.74%)

⑦ Others: Txn Type: 2 (EIP-1559)   Nonce: 18   Position: 270

⑦ Input Data:

```
Function: claim(uint128 nodeId, uint256 blockNumber, bool toStrongPool, uint256 claimedTotal, bytes signature)

MethodID: 0x03a9ea6d
[0]:  0000000000000000000000000000000000000000000000000000000000000003
[1]:  000000000000000000000000000000000000000000000000000000000e58954
[2]:  0000000000000000000000000000000000000000000000000000000000000000
[3]:  0000000000000000000000000000000000000000000000000000000000000000
[4]:  00000000000000000000000000000000000000000000000000000000000000a0
[5]:  0000000000000000000000000000000000000000000000000000000000000041
```

Figure 6.6 A transaction invoking the smart contract of Figure 6.5, available at: https://etherscan.io/tx/0xc0705963ac05171b2ebbccedee9d8a98ddec8979cf9a52f3ba4408ac49d3e9ca.

a transaction addressed to an SCA. The input data contain the details of the invocation, i.e., the function of the smart contract to be invoked and, if needed, the values of the input parameters. The 'value' field of this transaction contains, if needed, the amount of Ethereum tokens that are transferred to the smart contract and that will increase its balance.

Figure 6.6 shows a transaction addressed to the smart contract of Figure 6.5. The recipient address is the contract SCA address ('xfbd...'). The transactions transfer approximately 0.0045 ETH to the contract (see the field 'value'). The 'input data' field shows that this transaction is invoking the function called 'claim' of this smart contract.

One final aspect of Ethereum transactions concerns how they are digitally signed. In Bitcoin, digital signatures apply to transaction outputs and inputs. More easily, in Ethereum transactions are digitally signed as a whole. Simply, the originator EOA signs a transaction using its private key. Any other EOA (or SCA) can verify this signature using the EOA's public key.

6.3 Ethereum ledger and consensus mechanism: the Ethereum Virtual Machine

Now that we have a deeper understanding of the Ethereum transactions, we are ready to understand the life cycle of transactions in Ethereum. More in detail, this section describes, without going too much into the technical details, the functioning of the so-called EVM. The EVM is the core component of an Ethereum client. Specifically, it processes transactions and, if necessary, it executes the smart contracts invoked by them.

For a large part, the life cycle of transactions in Ethereum is similar to the one of transactions in Bitcoin:

- A transaction is created by an EOA and it is gossiped through the Ethereum network. When receiving a new transaction, each node validates it before forwarding it to its peers. Similarly to Bitcoin, the validation checks whether the transaction is well-formed and it contains all the required information. For instance, if a transaction invokes a function of a smart contract that requires input parameters, a node checks if these input parameters are present in the 'input data' field.
- A validated transaction is stored by a node in a temporary repository of the unconfirmed transaction (similar to Bitcoin's memory pool).
- The so-called 'validator' nodes continuously try to create new blocks using the transactions that they have validated and temporarily stored. Similarly to Bitcoin, a new block includes a number of unconfirmed transactions and a reward for the creator. The principles of the Ethereum's consensus mechanism and its evolution over time are discussed in detail in the next section.
- Once created, a new block is gossiped by a validator node through the Ethereum network. A node receiving a new block validates it and, upon successful validation, executes all the transactions included in it.

In the remainder of this section, we discuss in detail the last step listed above, i.e., the execution of the transactions belonging to a new valid block received by a node. This step allows us to present, at least at a high level, the functioning of the EVM.

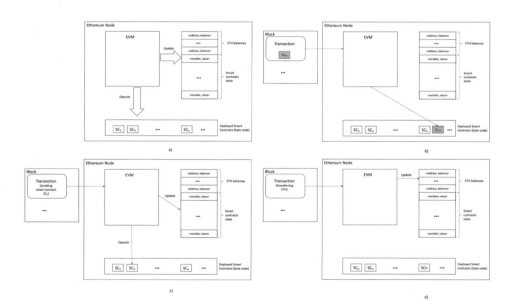

Figure 6.7 Ethereum node structure and processing of transactions in a valid block. (a) Internal architecture of an Ethereum node. (b) Processing a transaction that deploys a new smart contract. (c) Processing a transaction that invokes an existing smart contract. (d) Processing a transaction that transfers ETH.

Figure 6.7a sketches the structure of an Ethereum node. At any given time, a node contains:

- The EVM. As mentioned earlier, the EVM is a piece of software that can process the transactions and execute smart contracts. For the computer scientists, this is a 'virtual machine' that can interpret the bytecode of smart contracts.
- A set of deployed smart contracts. These are the bytecode of all the smart contracts that have been deployed in Ethereum throughout its history.
- The Ethereum ledger. This basically contains (i) the value of the variables describing the state of the Ethereum blockchain, like the ETH balance of every node and the value of the state variables of every deployed smart contracts, and (ii) the transactions, organized into blocks (i.e., the blockchain). More details regarding the way in which the data are stored in the Ethereum ledger are in the Computer Science Focus.

Computer Science Focus: the Ethereum ledger

In principle, every Ethereum node could reconstruct the state of the whole blockchain by replaying all transactions in all blocks in chronological order. However, this would require each node to store a copy of the whole blockchain, which would require several terabytes of storage available. Also, nodes joining the Ethereum blockchain would have to download the whole blockchain, with a significant bandwidth usage.

To avoid such issues, Ethereum relies on an efficient data structure, named 'trie', to keep track of the whole blockchain. Explaining the inner details of how the trie structure works goes beyond the scope of this book. However, you can understand the main advantages that this data structure brings. Firstly, the trie structure allows a node to store locally only a portion of the blockchain (e.g., only the smart contracts deployed by that node), while ensuring that this portion is consistent with the whole blockchain. Secondly, the trie structure significantly reduces the bandwidth and computation requirements for a node to synchronize with the blockchain. Finally, the trie structure is tamper-resistant, that is, nodes can detect if updates received from other nodes are not consistent with the actual state of the blockchain. To keep track of the state of the blockchain, Ethereum relies on four trie structures:

- The **Transaction Trie**, which keeps track of all the transactions submitted. For each transaction, this stores the nonce, the gas price, the gas limit, the address of the recipient, the amount of ETH transferred, the digital signature of the sender, and additional data (e.g., smart contract creation or invocation parameters). This information is never updated once the block containing the associated transactions is mined. Each block includes a hash of the Transaction Trie at the moment that it was mined.
- The **Receipt Trie**, which hosts the outcome of the transactions submitted. For each transaction, it stores its position in the blockchain (block hash, block number, transaction hash, and transaction number), the addresses of

the parties involved (sender, receiver, and contract if the transaction deployed a smart contract), the post-transaction state (e.g., succeeded, failed, out of gas, etc.) and the gas units effectively used for processing the transaction. This information is never updated once the block containing the associated transactions is mined. Each block includes a hash of the Receipt Trie at the moment that it was mined.
- The **State Trie**, which hosts all Ethereum accounts. For each account, its balance and nonce are stored, as well as a hashed reference to the Storage Trie. This information is constantly updated. Each block includes a hash of the State Trie at the moment that it was mined.
- The **Storage Trie**: which hosts the deployed smart contracts and their data. For each smart contract, its variables and their current values are stored. Each account has its own Storage Trie, which is referenced in the State Trie.

We can see that the Ethereum ledger contains both the list of transactions (in the Transaction and Receipt trie) and the state of the system (account balances in the State trie and smart contract state variables in the Storage trie).

Now, Figure 6.7 also sketches the role of the EVM in respect of the three types of transactions described in Section 6.2. The EVM recognizes that a transaction deploys a new smart contract if the recipient is the address '0' (Figure 6.7b). In this case, the EVM deploys a new smart contract in the node. This is done by copying and storing locally the bytecode contained in the 'input data' field of the transaction.

If a transaction invokes a smart contract (Figure 6.7c), then the EVM extracts the information regarding which function to invoke and, if needed, the value of the input parameters. Then, it invokes the smart contract. As a result, the smart contract invocation may modify the value of one or more state variables of the Ethereum blockchain. For instance, it may update the ETH balance of a node or update the value of one or more smart contract state variables.

The easiest case is the one in which a transaction transfers ETH between two nodes (Figure 6.7d). No smart contracts are involved in this case. The EVM simply updates the ETH balances of the nodes involved, increasing the balance of the recipient and decreasing the one of the sender.

6.4 Ethereum consensus mechanism

The Ethereum consensus mechanism is a perfect way to introduce, besides the Proof-of-Work (PoW), a new class of consensus mechanisms, that is, the Proof-Of-Stake consensus.

Until September 15th 2022, Ethereum used a PoW consensus mechanism, called Ethash. While it is similar to Bitcoin's consensus in many aspects, Ethash was based on a slightly different principle. In the last step of Ethash, the nodes still had to find the value of a nonce making the hash of a given 'blob' of binary data lower than a given target value. In Bitcoin, this blob of data is the actual new block. In Ethereum, this blob of data was a large DAG (Directed Acyclic Graph) combining some random data extracted from the new block with other historical data extracted from the Ethereum ledger. The DAG kept growing in size to control the difficulty of the PoW.

The main characteristic of Ethash was that fetching the data to assemble the DAG and load it into a node's memory was much more computationally intensive than calculating the correct value of a nonce in the last step. In other words, Ethash was 'memory hard' – it required from a node a large amount of fast memory – rather than 'computationally hard', like Bitcoin's PoW. This rather technical detail had fundamental implications for practice. Specifically, in Ethereum we did see the computational power of miners increasing over time. However, we did not see such a fierce race to build more and more energy-hungry miner nodes as we saw in Bitcoin. This is mainly because lightning-fast calculations of cryptographic hashes were not ideal for an Ethereum miner to succeed. An Ethereum miner node has to be fast at handling its memory, while a Bitcoin miner must be extremely fast at executing simple hashing operations. From this standpoint, Ethereum has always been a more sustainable blockchain than Bitcoin. Still, the amount of energy required to run Ethash was very high.

For years, the Ethereum consortium has tried to move to an even more sustainable mining algorithm, based on the Proof-of-Stake (PoS) principle. The general principle of PoS is the following: while in PoW the nodes (miners) invest a scarce off-chain resource (i.e., the electricity required to run the required computational work) in the hope of being rewarded with cryptocurrency, in PoS the nodes invest, for a similar reward, a resource that is intrinsic to the blockchain (i.e., their cryptocurrency).

In Ethereum's PoS consensus, the nodes creating and validating the new blocks are called 'validators'. To become a validator, a node must 'stake' 32 ETH. This is done by a node by sending 32 ETH to a smart contract. The smart contract locks a stake and manages it until a node decides to withdraw it. At every epoch (a period about six-minute long), a group of validators are randomly selected. Within this group, validators take turns proposing new blocks, while the other validators 'check' the correctness of the new blocks proposed. If valid, the new blocks are gossiped to the rest of the network. The nodes can increase their chance to be selected as validators during an epoch by providing multiple 'stakes' of 32 ETH.

The validators are rewarded (i) by interest rate paid on the ETH that they stake and (ii) by a reward obtained when proposing or validating new blocks. Given the value B of a 'base' reward, a validator is rewarded with $1/8$ B ETH for proposing a valid new block, while the other validators of an epoch split $7/8$ B ETH when validating the new block. The value B is adjusted dynamically by the Ethereum protocol to control the length of the validation phase. The validators may also lose their stake, though. This may happen when they submit an invalid block. In this case, the smart contract will 'burn' the stake: a validator will never see their 32 ETH again. Validators may lose part of their stake when they fail to validate within one epoch the new blocks that are proposed (for instance because they went offline) or even when they are slow at doing so.

The Ethereum's PoS consensus mechanism has cut down the Ethereum blockchain network energy consumption (to assemble new blocks) by at least 99%. This may have huge implications for seeing Ethereum rising as the most used public blockchain in the future. The PoS consensus mechanism is probably also more secure than PoW by design. In PoW, a miner could get control of the mining of new blocks by accumulating 51% of the mining power in the network. This is hard to achieve, but not impossible. Most importantly, it can be done in principle by a miner without colluding with any other. A miner would 'just' need to buy and run (a lot of) more powerful computers. In PoS, a validator may get control of the mining process by staking more Ether than all the other validators combined. This could be achieved in principle by a malicious validator. However, this can happen only if other nodes owning some of the existing ETH collude to transfer their ETH to the malicious validator to pay the stakes. Finally, Ethereum's PoS allows for much more flexibility regarding how the Ethereum ledger can be extended by new blocks. We are not going to go into details on this topic in this book. We will only mention that Ethereum's PoS enables the 'sharding' of the main chain in the Ethereum ledger, i.e., creating multiple 'legal' forks at the top of the existing chain, which are reconciled in a single chain at a later stage. The sharding of the main chain could improve the performance of the Ethereum blockchain, increasing the transaction throughput from a few transactions per second to thousands of transactions per second.

6.5 Ethereum smart contracts and tokens

In this section, we deep dive into the implementation of the Ethereum smart contracts. We do so in two steps. First, we provide and discuss examples of real smart contracts. Then, we focus on the so-called Ethereum 'tokens'. These are a special class of smart contracts capturing the behavior of digital and possibly physical assets exchangeable by the nodes. Tokens are by far the most famous class of smart contracts in Ethereum.

6.5.1 Smart contracts

A smart contract in Ethereum is a piece of software code, which executes some well-defined business logic. This logic manipulates the state of the Ethereum blockchain, possibly using also input parameters provided by the EOAs in the transactions invoking the smart contracts. There are many programming languages in which an Ethereum smart contract can be written. Among them, however, the language of Solidity has emerged as the most used one. Hence, all the examples that we provide in this section are written in Solidity. Obviously, this section is not a tutorial on Solidity. For that, interested readers are referred to [ZGH+21]. Nevertheless, we believe that examining and understanding the code of real smart contracts is important to grasp the full potential of smart contract implementations. Therefore, we provide and discuss a few examples of Solidity code. Do not worry though, the examples that we provide here are simple and understandable by anybody with only a basic computer programming background.

Like most programming languages, e.g., Java, Python, or C++, Solidity is a 'Turing complete' programming language. In a nutshell, this means that it can execute any computation that we can think of, which can be expressed using the typical statements of programming languages, like conditional statements (if-then-else) or loops (for, while, etc.). More in detail, a Turing complete language also allows to specify codes that could execute indefinitely (e.g., a while loop controlled by a condition that may never become false). As briefly discussed earlier in this chapter, Ethereum's 'gas' is a mechanism created to control the execution of transactions that trigger the execution of smart contracts. Even if, by mistake or on purpose, a transaction triggers an infinite execution of a smart contract, the nodes execute a smart contract only as long as the gas of the transaction invoking it does not run out.

A major difference between traditional programming languages and Solidity (and, more generally, Ethereum smart contracts) concerns random number generators. As we discussed in Chapter 4, because every node must be able to obtain the same output from the execution of a smart contract at any point in time, the computation specified in a smart contract cannot rely on the generation of random numbers. Hence, the Solidity language does not provide constructs to generate random numbers.

Figure 6.8 provides an example of a very simple Solidity smart contract. It is not the usual 'Hello world' example that you might be familiar with, but it gets close. The code looks like any other computer code that you might be used to, such as Python or Java. The syntax may be only a little different. For instance, in Python we do not use semicolons at the end of each instruction. In Java, we put the function qualifiers, like 'public' or 'private', before the function name, and not after it.

The Demo smart contract of Figure 6.8 allows nodes to do one simple thing: store the value of one integer number. The value to be stored can be set by invoking the `store()` function and it can be retrieved using the `retrieve()` function. The function `store()` is public, which means that it can be invoked by all the nodes of the Ethereum network. Conversely, a private function would not be visible to the nodes of the Ethereum network (it could only be called by other functions of the same smart contract). The function `retrieve()` returns, obviously, an integer value (`uint256` stands for 'unsigned integer of 256 bits', i.e., an integer lower than 2^{256}). It is also declared to be a `view` function. The keyword `view` distinguishes functions that do not modify the state of the Ethereum blockchain from the ones that do. The `store()` function, in fact, does modify the Ethereum state: the variable `number` defines the state of the smart contract and, as said earlier, all the state variables of smart contracts are part of the Ethereum state. The `retrieve()` function simply reads the value of the state variable number and returns it. Finally, the function `getBalance()` reads the value of the balance of this contract. This is available in the special variable `address(this)balance`. Note that the function `getBalance()` is also a `view` function: it reads and returns information regarding the state of the Ethereum blockchain, without modifying it.

```
contract Demo{

    uint256 number;

    function store(uint256 num) public{
        number = num;
    }

    function retrieve() public view returns (uint256){
        return number;
    }

    function getBalance() public view returns (uint256){
        return address(this).balance;
    }

}
```

Figure 6.8 A simple solidity smart contract.

```solidity
contract Purchase {

  uint public constant depositFee = 2000000000;
  uint public constant price = 50000000000;

  address public buyer;
  address public seller;
  bool public paid;
  bool public shipped;
  bool public delivered;

  event ItemBought ();
  event ItemShipped ();
  event ItemDelivered ();

  constructor() public {
     seller = msg.sender;
  }

  function buy() public payable {
     require(!paid, "The item has already been sold");
     require(msg.value == depositFee + price, "Value must be item price + the deposit fee");
     paid = true;
     buyer = msg.sender;
     emit ItemBought();
  }

  function ship() public {
     require(msg.sender == seller, "Only the seller can ship the item");
     require(paid, "The item is still for sale");
     require(!shipped, "The item has already been shipped");
     shipped = true;
     emit ItemShipped();
  }

  function confirmDelivery() public {
     require(msg.sender == buyer, "Only the buyer can confirm the delivery");
     require(shipped, "The item has not been shipped yet");
     require(!delivered, "The deposit has already been returned");
     (bool sent, bytes memory data) = payable(msg.sender).call{value: depositFee}("");
     require(sent, "Failed to return the deposit fee to the buyer");
     delivered = true;
     emit ItemDelivered();
  }

  function getPayment() public {
     require(msg.sender == seller, "Only the seller can retrieve the payment for the item");
     require(delivered, "The delivery has not been confirmed yet");
     (bool sent, bytes memory data) = payable(msg.sender).call{value: price}("");
  }
}
```

Figure 6.9 A Solidity smart contract for safely buying an item using cryptocurrency.

Another example slightly more complex is the Purchase smart contract of Figure 6.9. This smart contract regulates the sale of an item using cryptocurrency, ensuring that the buyer eventually gets the item requested, and the seller gets the payment from the buyer. The Boolean variables `paid`, `shipped`, and `delivered` track the phases of the sale. In addition, the events `ItemBought()`, `ItemShipped()`, and `ItemDelivered()` are declared. An event, as the name suggests, is a notification that the contract sends to the transaction log and it is accessible to applications outside the blockchain. Using events, the outside world can be made aware regarding when a change in the state of the smart contract occurs, without having to periodically invoke its functions. Events are particularly useful when implementing DApps, which are introduced later in this chapter.

Similarly to object-oriented programming languages, the `constructor()` function is a special function, which is automatically invoked when the smart contract is deployed. In this way, the identity of the seller is associated with the address of the account that deployed the contract, and it can no longer be changed.

To buy the item, the buyer has to invoke the `buy()` function. The `buy()` function is `payable`. Payable functions allow the account invoking them to also transfer cryptocurrency to the smart contract. The `buy()` function must ensure that the item has not already been paid, and that the amount transferred by the buyer is equal to the price of the item plus a deposit (defined by the `price` and `depositFee` constants, respectively). The `buy()` function invokes the `require(condition, message)` library function provided by Solidity, which checks the `condition` provided as the first parameter. If that condition is not met, the transaction is aborted, and the `message` provided as the second parameter is returned. Otherwise, the execution continues. If both conditions are met, the function `buy()` sets the `paid` variable to `true`, associates the identity of the buyer to the address of the account who invoked the function, and emits the `ItemBought()` event to notify the seller that the item has been bought.

Once the buyer has bought the item, the seller can invoke the `ship()` function, notifying that (s)he has shipped the item. In particular, the `ship()` function ensures that the address of the account that invokes it corresponds to the one of the sellers. Also, it ensures that the item has been paid, but it has not been shipped yet. If all conditions are met, this function sets the `shipped` variable to `true`, and emits the `ItemShipped()` event to notify the buyer that the item has been shipped.

Once the seller has shipped the item, the buyer can invoke the `confirmDelivery()` function, notifying that (s)he has received the item. This function ensures that the address of the account that invokes it corresponds to the one of the buyer. Also, it ensures that the item has been shipped, but has not been delivered yet. If all conditions are met, this function returns the deposit to the buyer. To do so, the address of the sender is firstly cast to a `payable` address, that is, an address that can receive cryptocurrency units. Then, for that address the `call{value: depositFee}("")` library function is invoked. This function enables the smart contract to increase the balance of a payable address of an amount equal to `depositFee`. This function returns also the Boolean value `sent`, indicating whether the paying transaction succeeded or not. In this way, it is possible to check the outcome of the paying transaction by using the `require(condition, message)` library function. If the payment fails, the current transaction is aborted (i.e., the one that directly invoked the `confirmDelivery()` function). If the payment was successful, the function sets the `delivered` variable to `true`, and emits the `ItemDelivered()` event to notify the seller that the item has been successfully delivered.

Finally, once the buyer has confirmed that the item was delivered, the seller can invoke the `getPayment()` function to receive an amount of cryptocurrency units equal to the price of the item sold. Firstly, this function ensures that the address of the account that invokes it corresponds to the one of the sellers. Also, it ensures that the seller has confirmed that the item was successfully delivered. Then, the address of the sender is cast to a payable address, and the `call{value: price}("")` function is invoked.

To sum up, the smart contract of Figure 6.9 can be generalized to any scenario in which an Ethereum node wants to safely buy a product or service from another node using cryptocurrency units. The item bought could be for instance real estate, a fancy car, or even a digital identifier of a piece of unique digital art. You might have heard of the latter as 'NFTs'. These are presented in the next section.

6.5.2 Ethereum tokens

Ethereum tokens are smart contracts that define the behavior of digital assets in the Ethereum blockchain. The 'behavior' of a digital asset must be intended as a combination of (i) what users are allowed to do with these assets and (ii) how the status of these assets, most importantly their ownership, is modified by the user interactions.

More technically speaking, a token smart contract defines a set of variables of the Ethereum state. Typical variables of this kind are the identifiers of the digital assets and other variables capturing the ownership of these assets by Ethereum nodes. The smart contract manipulates the value of these variables. A token can represent any digital asset. It can also represent the digital equivalent of a physical asset existing in the real world. Typical classes of resources that can be associated with Ethereum tokens are listed in Table 6.2. The same table also classifies the digital assets according to their 'fungibility', i.e., whether these digital assets are fungible or non-fungible.

Fungibility is a fundamental property of (digital) assets, which determines also the behavior of the smart contracts implementing their related token in Ethereum. An asset is 'fungible' when its individual units are essentially interchangeable, and 'non-fungible' otherwise. Currency, gold, equity in an organization, or storage capacity of a computer system are typically fungible assets. In fact, it does not matter which particular

Table 6.2 Examples of digital assets that could be 'tokenized' in Ethereum

Class	Description/examples	Type
Currency	Private cryptocurrencies, like a cryptocurrency that can be used only on a university campus, or one that users can spend only to pay for the services provided by a network of private hospitals	Fungible
Computing Resources	Storage capacity of CPU time provided by a cloud service	Fungible
Asset	Digital equivalent of physical assets, such as gold, paintings, cars, real estate, or diamonds	Depends on the physical asset (e.g., fungible for gold, non-fungible for paintings or cars)
Access	Access rights to physical property, such as a hotel room or an exclusive Web site	Non-fungible
Equity	Shareholder equity of an organization	Fungible
Voting	Right to vote in a digital or legal system	Fungible
Identity	A digital or legal identity	Non-fungible

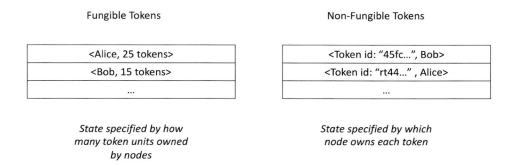

Figure 6.10 Ethereum state variables and fungibility of Ethereum tokens.

banknote, gold bar, shareholder certificate, or physical sector of a hard disk we own. The only thing that matters is 'how much' or 'how many units' of that asset we own. Conversely, with assets such as paintings, cars, or access to hotel rooms, it is fundamental to distinguish which particular unit of that asset we own. Owning an old second-hand car is much different from owning a shiny new sports car!

An Ethereum token defines what the Ethereum nodes can do with it and how the variables defining the state of the token are modified by what the nodes do. For fungible tokens (see Figure 6.10), similarly to the example of cryptocurrency that we have extensively discussed until now in this book, these variables capture the amount of assets owned by each user. For non-fungible tokens, given each specific asset available associated with a unique 'token id', a state variable captures its current owner. Private cryptocurrencies, such as tokens created and distributed by blockchain startups to raise funds, are typical examples of fungible Ethereum tokens. Digital non-fungible tokens have become particularly popular in the past few years, with the emergence of the so-called market of NFTs. From a technical standpoint, NFTs are simply Ethereum non-fungible tokens. From a business standpoint, NFTs are like unique digital trading cards, for which a marketplace may exist. For instance, recently the market of NFTs associated with unique pieces of digital art has exponentially grown and it is predicted to reach 20 billion USD by 2028 [Jen22].

Because tokens are a fundamental feature of Ethereum, the Ethereum community is constantly working to define and improve different 'standards' for the Ethereum tokens. Similar to an interface in an object-oriented programming language, an Ethereum token standard defines the functions that a token of a certain class must implement. To conclude this section, we briefly review two of the most popular Ethereum token standards: the ERC-20, which is the standard for private cryptocurrencies (i.e., fungible tokens) and the ERC-721, which is a popular standard for the implementation of non-fungible tokens.

6.5.2.1 The ERC-20 Ethereum standard

The ERC-20 is one of the most established and used Ethereum standards. A smart contract implementing the ERC-20 standard must provide the functions and events listed in Table 6.3.

Table 6.3 The Ethereum ERC-20 standard

Function	Normal expected behavior
name()	Returns the name of this token, e.g. the 'Comuzzi-Grefen-Meroni Token'
symbol()	Returns a short name of this token. This is normally used in asset exchange markets to identify the token, e.g. 'CGM'
totalSupply()	Returns the number of units of this token created from its creation
balanceOf(address_owner)	Returns the number of units of this token owned by the node address–owner
transfer(address_to, value)	Allows the caller (i.e., the node issuing a transaction invoking this function of the token smart contract) to transfer a certain amount of tokens that they own (value) to a recipient node (address_to)

The expected behavior of a fungible token is not surprising: tokens can be transferred between nodes and it should be possible to query the balance of a token's units of any node. The standard also defines other functions (not shown in Table 6.3) through which a node can delegate another node to spend tokens on their behalf.

The behavior described in the second column of Table 6.3 is, indeed, the one 'expected' from a fungible token. However, whenever the business circumstances require it, fungible tokens can be programmed to behave in a different or more nuanced way. Even if the behavior of each function is not the one described in Table 6.3, the applications using the token would still be able to use it as long as the standard interface remains the same, i.e., the smart contract exposes functions named as in Table 6.3. For instance, a token can be programmed such that transfers lower than 5 or higher than 30 token units are prohibited – this logic would be programmed into the transfer() function – or that nodes in a specific list are banned from receiving transfers higher than 20 token units. The standard interface of Table 6.3 can also be extended by a token smart contract with additional functions. For instance, a function may be implemented to provide the average token balance of all nodes owning at least 1 (or 5, 10) tokens. Adding such a 'programmable' layer to digital assets is the most prominent features of Ethereum tokens.

Generally, with the example provided above we hope to have convinced you that Ethereum tokens are an extremely flexible way to implement the logic controlling the life cycle of digital assets. Because they 'live' within the Ethereum blockchain, Ethereum tokens obviously inherit all the benefits characterizing information exchange among nodes on the Ethereum blockchain. For instance, every interaction (through transactions) of the nodes with the tokens remains stored immutably and forever in the Ethereum ledger, and it can be queried at any time if needed (e.g., for auditing purposes). The flexibility provided by smart contracts, allows tokens to become fully 'programmable' digital assets.

6.5.2.2 The ERC-721 Ethereum standard

The ERC-721 is the minimal standard for non-fungible Ethereum tokens (a more advanced one, which we do not discuss in this book, is ERC-1155). Some simple functions in this standard are similar to the ERC-20 ones, e.g., name() and totalSupply()

return the name of the NFT and the number of its tokens that exist, e.g., the number of collectible digital sports cards available in a given collection. The main differences between ERC-721 and ERC-20 are the following:

• Tokens in ERC-721 are non-fungible and, therefore, unique. So, each one of them is identified by a unique token_id.
• ERC-721 tokens cannot be split among owners, so each one of them is owned by a node.
• The standard defines a set of functions to control the ownership of individual tokens.

Table 6.4 shows the functions in the ERC-721 standard that control the ownership of tokens. Simply, the function transferFrom () allows a node to transfer the ownership of a token that it owns to another node. The function ownerOf () returns the address of the owner of a token identified by token_id. Like for ERC-20 tokens, the behavior of an ERC-721 token is programmable. The internal implementation of every function can in fact be customized to specific business needs. Additional functions can also be defined if necessary.

Table 6.4 The Ethereum ERC-721 standard (selected functions)

Function	Normal expected behavior
balanceOf(address_owner)	Returns the count of the number of unique tokens by the account address_owner
ownerOf(token_id)	Returns the owner of the asset associated with token_id
transferFrom(address_from, address_to, tokenId)	Transfer the asset identified by token_id from the account address_from to the aaccount address_to. The account address_from must be the originator of the transaction calling this function

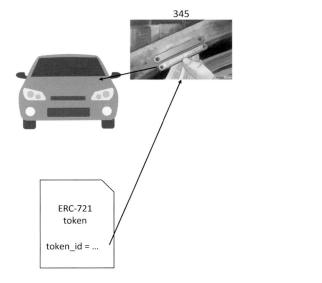
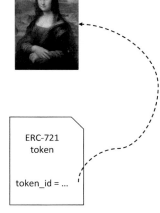

Figure 6.11 Counter-party risk and Ethereum tokens.

One fundamental problem characterizing tokens that represent digital identifiers of physical assets in the real world is the one of the so-called 'counter-party risks' (see Figure 6.11). This is the problem of the reliability of the association between the digital tokens in the blockchain and the assets that they represent in the real world. Figure 6.11 depicts the example of tokens associated with motor vehicles and (valuable) paintings. Now, the counter-party risk is the risk of failing to guarantee that, once a digital token associated with one specific physical asset is created, the association between the two will never be broken. In the case of digital tokens associated with motor vehicles, the problem may be solved by the VIN (Vehicle Identification Number). The VIN is a unique serial number of a motor vehicle generated according to the ISO 3778 standard. It has been used worldwide for a long time. Every motor vehicle in the world, no matter where it is circulating and by whom it was manufactured, has a unique VIN. Obviously, the VIN can be used to establish a precise and reliable association between a motor vehicle and a digital token representing it. What we need to do is to include the VIN as a variable in the token associated with a motor vehicle. There is still of course a risk that a vehicle's VIN may be altered or removed at some point in time (like a killer would do to the registration number of the gun that he or she used in a gangster movie). However, in many business applications, this risk may be considered negligible.

In the case of digital tokens associated with paintings, unfortunately, we do not have an equivalent of a VIN. The authenticity of a painting, which is highly correlated with its value in the real world, is often established through a complex process that requires specialized expertise. There is no unique identifier that we could simply embed into a token's smart contract code to solve the counter-party risk problem. In other words, Ethereum tokens for (valuable) paintings suffer from a high counter-party risk. As we discuss at the end of this chapter in the case study, providing a solution to mitigate the counter-party risk in applications that use Ethereum tokens is a crucial aspect for the Ethereum blockchain adoption.

6.6 Ethereum distributed applications (DApps)

With smart contracts, a blockchain system like Ethereum can be programmed to execute arbitrary business logic that manipulates the input given by the users and the state of the blockchain system. Therefore, smart contracts turn blockchain systems into full-fledged 'distributed information systems'.

A distributed information system used by a network of users and that uses a blockchain at its backbone is normally referred to as a 'Distributed Application', or in short, a 'DApp'. While the term DApp was initially coined for distributed applications that use the Ethereum blockchain, today it is commonly used for distributed applications that use any smart contract-enabled blockchain system.

An information system (see Figure 6.12) can be simply modelled as the interaction of three layers:

- The data storage layer, in which the data used by an application reside.
- The application logic layer, which contains the business logic that manipulates the data based on the user input.
- The presentation layer, which captures the user input and presents the result of the execution of the application logic to the user.

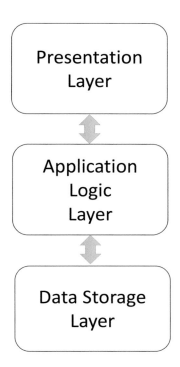

Figure 6.12 Traditional three-layered information systems.

For example, in an e-voting application, the data storage layer contains the data about registered voters and the votes cast by them; the application logic layer contains the logic that verifies whether a user asking to vote is registered, and allows users to cast a vote (usually no more than once!); the presentation layer can be a Web site, or a mobile phone app, through which users can cast their votes and receive a confirmation that their vote has been recorded.

Now, a DApp can be defined more specifically as an information system where at least one of the architectural layers presented above is implemented in a distributed way using blockchain. The most common cases are the ones in which the application logic layer and the data storage layer are distributed. In a DApp, the application logic layer is implemented by smart contracts of a blockchain system. The data storage layer is represented by the distributed ledger of a blockchain system: every node maintains a consistent copy of the data required by the DApp in an immutable database.

Ethereum-based DApps represent the most prominent example of DApp. They are DApps in which the application logic layer is implemented using Ethereum smart contracts. Web applications or mobile app through which users can manage Ethereum tokens are a typical example of Ethereum DApps.

To get a glimpse of how a DApp works, let us consider an example in which the CGM token, introduced in the first part of the book, is now implemented as an Ethereum ERC-20 fungible token. Figure 6.13 sketches the functioning of a DApp that manages the CGM token, i.e., a 'wallet' for CGM tokens. The presentation layer of this DApp

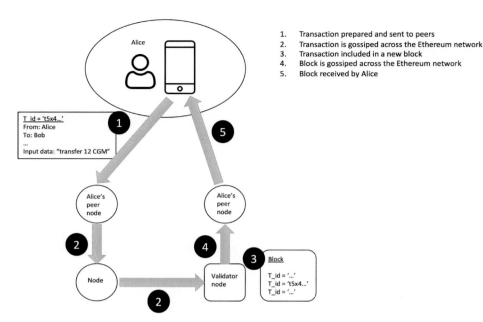

1. Transaction prepared and sent to peers
2. Transaction is gossiped across the Ethereum network
3. Transaction included in a new block
4. Block is gossiped across the Ethereum network
5. Block received by Alice

Figure 6.13 Example of a DApp.

is a mobile app. Through this app, the users can issue a transfer of CGM tokens. For instance, the chess players of the BC4C-CGM blockchain use this app to transfer the deposits of their games. The application logic is implemented by an Ethereum smart contract. This smart contract implements the ERC-20 token standard. The data layer is also implemented by the Ethereum blockchain. Since the smart contract complies with the ERC-20 standard, the balance of CGM tokens of every node are state variables of Ethereum.

Figure 6.13 also sketches a typical usage scenario of this DApp. When Alice transfers CGM tokens to Bob, for instance, she does that through the mobile app. Under the hood, the mobile app packs the information regarding the transfer (like the recipient node, the amount of token, the function invoked in the smart contract, the gas, etc.) in an Ethereum transaction (Step 1 in Figure 6.13. Then, the transaction is issued to the Ethereum network. The transaction, if valid, is gossiped across nodes (Step 2). It also reaches Bob, but Bob, like any other Ethereum node, cannot trust that the tokens have been transferred to him until the transaction is included into a new block. The transaction at some point is picked up by a validator node to be included in a block (Step 3). The new block (approved by other validators in the same epoch) is gossiped across the network, reaching all the nodes, including Bob and Alice (Step 4). When the nodes receive this new block, they execute all the transactions in it, including the one concerning the transfer made by Alice to Bob. At this point, Bob finally has a confirmation that the CGM tokens have been transferred by Alice on his mobile App. Similarly, the mobile app can notify Alice that the transfer has been completed (Step 5).

From a business standpoint, it is crucial to understand the benefits and drawbacks of using an Ethereum DApp to implement the functionality of an information system. These are summarized in Table 6.5.

Table 6.5 Pros and cons of DApps

Pros

Deterministic and verifiable business logic execution	A smart contract code is received and can be inspected by every node. Therefore, the application logic of a DApp is verifiable by any user. Also, smart contracts only allow the execution of deterministic logic (no random numbers allowed!), which means that by inspecting the code users know exactly how the DApp is going to behave.
Zero downtime (decentralization)	The execution of the application logic is decentralized across the Ethereum network. Users do not have to wait for a server somewhere (which may become unavailable) to execute their input. Practically, this means that a DApp has no downtime: a transaction invoking a DApp's smart contract is sooner or later picked up by a miner to be included in a block.
Resistance to censorship	Because it relies on the decentralized paradigm of the Ethereum blockchain, a DApp is highly resistant to censorship. While a DApp hosted on a (cloud) server may be taken down by a hostile government, it is virtually impossible that a single institution could take down the whole Ethereum network. An Ethereum DApp stays alive as long as there is still at least one node somewhere in the world running the Ethereum protocol and connected to the Internet.
Immutability of data	All the interactions between the users and a DApp (i.e., transactions) and the data that they generate (i.e., changes of the Ethereum state) are immutably recorded on the Ethereum blockchain. As such, they remain available forever to be consulted, for instance for auditing reasons or to resolve disputes or, simply, to verify their existence.

Cons

Cost	Issuing transactions on the Ethereum network is not free of charge. Every time users invoke a function of a DApp, they have to pay a fee in ETH. The price of ETH in fiat currencies is extremely volatile and, depending on the current exchange rates, the fees may not be negligible in many business settings. To solve the cost issues, DApps often choose to store only the most important data on the Ethereum blockchain. Other data can be stored off-chain on distributed file system solutions, such as IFPS (discussed late in Chapter 9).
Performance	Every interaction of the users with a DApp cannot be trusted until it is stored in a block deep enough in the Ethereum main chain. Even though Ethereum is quicker than Bitcoin from this point of view, the time required to complete the invocation of a DApp's function may exceed the limits considered acceptable in many business settings. Moreover, the performance of the Ethereum blockchain is not particularly reliable. The time it takes for a transaction to be included in a block may fluctuate unpredictably depending on the network load condition and the location or time zone of the nodes issuing the transactions.
Maintenance and regression to centralization	From a technical standpoint, the tools provided by the Ethereum protocol to manage the evolution of smart contracts are very limited. Basically, once a smart contract is deployed, it cannot be modified. A new version of it, where even only one small instruction is updated, must be deployed as a new smart contract. These may create enormous maintenance problems for DApps. To overcome this issue, often a DApp delegates to a smart contract only the core part of its application logic, which is not likely to change in the near future. The remaining application logic can be delegated to other (non-DApp) applications, such as other Web applications. This, however, means moving away from the blockchain paradigm: any other traditional application, in fact, may be seen as a centralized intermediary.

With the discussion of the benefits and drawbacks of DApps of Table 6.5, for the first time in this book we have focused on understanding the suitability of blockchain for a specific business scenario. For instance, it seems like DApps are not a good choice for implementing applications that require a predictable and reliable level of performance, or that have to manage large data and frequent interactions with their users (the cost of using a DApp in this case may explode). On the other hand, a DApp is a good choice for applications that require a high level of transparency and reliable access to historical data. Understanding the suitability of different business scenarios for blockchain is the focus of Chapter 9.

6.7 Case study – Everledger: secure provenance in supply chains over Ethereum

In this chapter, we have discussed the challenge of the counter-party risk when creating Ethereum NFTs and, more generally, Ethereum-based DApps that handle physical assets in the real world. In the business world, however, every challenge is also an opportunity. Everledger is an Australian technology company that has leveraged the counter-party risk in blockchain applications as a business opportunity.

Everledger promises to help their customer to surface and connect asset-related information in markets where transparency is imperative with the help of a combination of technology, like AI, IoT and, obviously, blockchain (more specifically Ethereum). In other words, Everledger provides solutions to improve collecting, verifying, and managing the provenance information of the assets exchanged in different markets. There are in fact many markets in which obtaining provenance information about the assets that they are about to buy is not straightforward for the customers. Long and complex supply chains are typical examples, particularly when customers also require information regarding product sustainability and ethical responsibility. For instance, it could be extremely hard for a producer of steel parts to demonstrate a sustainability record for its product, particularly when these undergo several refinement steps at different manufacturers, possibly in different countries. Similarly, it may be impossible for a clothes retailer to provide reliable evidence that all the clothes on the shelves at their stores are manufactured in locations following high ethical standards for local workers. Generally, the combination of blockchain and other technologies may come to help in these situations: technologies like AI and IoT may be used to capture the evidence of the provenance information required by the customers, whereas a blockchain can be used to immutably and reliably store and make available this information forever.

There is one industry in which provenance information of retail products is particularly important. By no coincidence, this is also the industry for which Everledger developed their first solution as a start-up company a few years ago: the diamond trade. Diamonds are extremely valuable physical assets. Unfortunately, their provenance and use are often associated with illicit and unethical operations. Diamonds are sometimes still extracted by workers in exploitative conditions in remote regions with dismal human rights records. Because they concentrate enormous value into a tiny physical space, they are also used as a means of value exchange in illicit trades, such as narcotics or weaponry illegal trafficking. When buying a diamond ring for their partner, one would obviously welcome safe and reliable information ensuring that what they are about to buy has never been involved in illicit activities, nor has it been extracted by exploited workers.

The solution proposed by Everledger to address this problem relies on associating individual diamonds with an Ethereum NFT. In this way, all the information regarding the trades in which a diamond has been involved could be stored reliably and immutably on the Ethereum blockchain. There it will remain forever, to be available for customers in the future. As we discussed earlier, however, the use of NFTs introduced the issue of counter-part risk. How can it be possible to create a reliable association between the physical diamonds and their counter-part digital tokens in the blockchain world?

The solution developed by Everledger relied on exploiting the physical properties of diamonds when hit by a light source. Basically, the shape of every diamond is somehow unique. Therefore, the light projected on a diamond is uniquely reflected by it. A combination of information regarding how sources of light are reflected by it, combined with other physical properties of a diamond such as its size, weight, and brightness, can then be used to create a unique fingerprint for each individual diamond. Such a fingerprint has three important properties:

- It is unique for each diamond on the market.
- It can be easily captured as digital data.
- It can be easily calculated at any time. The physical properties of a diamond, including the light reflection properties, in fact, can be assessed by any diamond shop lab using industry-standard machinery and procedures.

From a technical standpoint, the solution provided by Everledger used a cryptographic hash of the diamond fingerprint introduced above to link the physical diamonds and the Ethereum NFTs representing them. This solution clearly minimizes the counter-party

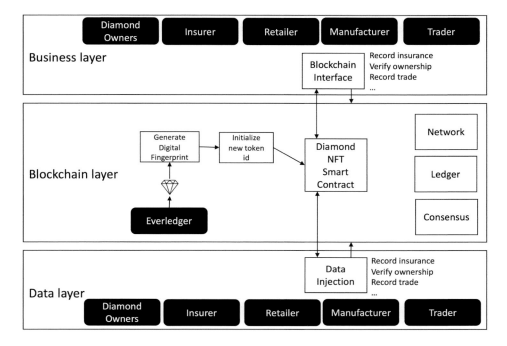

Figure 6.14 Reducing counter-party risk in the diamond trade.

risk. The procedures applied to create (and re-create, whenever needed) the digital fingerprint are schematized in Figure 6.14, using the blockchain reference architecture introduced in Chapter 4. The diamond fingerprint and its related NFT are created as early as possible after a diamond is extracted. From then on, the NFT is used to track any step of the diamond supply chain, by bulk traders, insurers, jewelry manufacturer, or retail shops. Note that the schema reported in Figure 6.14 can be replicated for any highly valuable physical asset. The real challenge is to figure out a way to create a simple, repeatable, and reliable mechanism to generate a unique identifier for each asset available on the market.

6.8 Conclusions

This chapter has presented the Ethereum blockchain. Ethereum is a cryptocurrency, like Bitcoin, but unlike Bitcoin it also provides the possibility to deploy smart contracts. This has huge implications on the design of Ethereum. For instance, the fee mechanism of Ethereum (gas) is more complex than Bitcoin's to account for the fact that a transaction may invoke a smart contract, besides simply transferring ETH between two accounts. We also discussed how the consensus mechanism of Ethereum differs from Bitcoin's. They both used to be designed as PoW mechanisms, but Ethereum has recently switched to a mechanism based on PoS.

We then looked specifically at a class of Ethereum smart contracts: tokens. Specifically, we discussed how ERC-20 tokens can be used to create private cryptocurrencies, whereas ERC-721 tokens are the basis of the so-called NFTs. The chapter was concluded by discussing the concept of DApps. These are distributed applications in which the application logic is implemented by Ethereum smart contracts. DApps can represent the backbone or resilient and transparent applications that are censorship-proof, i.e., they cannot be shut down by any institution.

This chapter concludes our discussion of public blockchain systems. In the next chapter, we will consider private blockchains. These are systems where the identity of the user is known and, usually, the number of users is limited. They are usually developed to support asset and information exchange in business scenarios that, unlike cryptocurrencies, do not require universal access, like supply chains or private healthcare networks.

6.9 Questions and exercises

1 Using any online Ethereum blockchain explorer, find transactions issued on the main Ethereum network with the following characteristics:
   a One transaction transferring ETH between two EOAs
   b One transaction invoking a smart contract. Indicate also which is the contract that was invoked and which is the function of this contract that was invoked by this transaction
   c One transaction deploying a new smart contract
   d One transaction in which more than 80% of the gas was used
2 Consider the Ethereum transactions of Figure 6.15, received by a validator node in the same order as their numbering (T1 received before T2, etc.). Assume that the nonce of the latest transactions received before T1 by this node from Jin, Min, and Hyun are 763, 8, and 765, respectively.

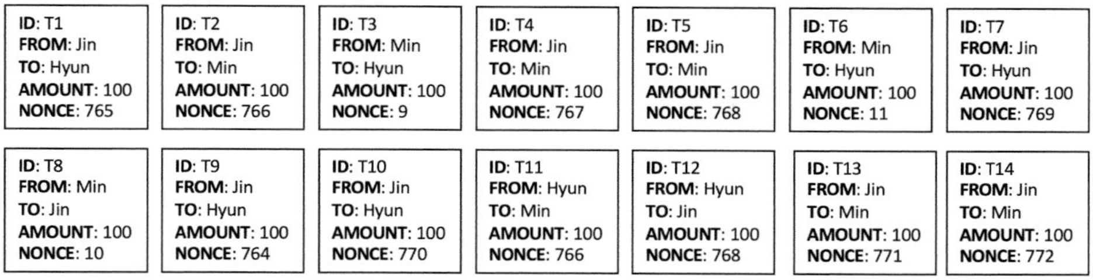

ID: T1	ID: T2	ID: T3	ID: T4	ID: T5	ID: T6	ID: T7
FROM: Jin	FROM: Jin	FROM: Min	FROM: Jin	FROM: Jin	FROM: Min	FROM: Jin
TO: Hyun	TO: Min	TO: Hyun	TO: Min	TO: Min	TO: Hyun	TO: Hyun
AMOUNT: 100	AMOUNT: 100	AMOUNT: 100	AMOUNT: 100	AMOUNT: 100	AMOUNT: 100	AMOUNT: 100
NONCE: 765	NONCE: 766	NONCE: 9	NONCE: 767	NONCE: 768	NONCE: 11	NONCE: 769

ID: T8	ID: T9	ID: T10	ID: T11	ID: T12	ID: T13	ID: T14
FROM: Min	FROM: Jin	FROM: Jin	FROM: Hyun	FROM: Hyun	FROM: Jin	FROM: Jin
TO: Jin	TO: Hyun	TO: Hyun	TO: Min	TO: Jin	TO: Min	TO: Min
AMOUNT: 100	AMOUNT: 100	AMOUNT: 100	AMOUNT: 100	AMOUNT: 100	AMOUNT: 100	AMOUNT: 100
NONCE: 10	NONCE: 764	NONCE: 770	NONCE: 766	NONCE: 768	NONCE: 771	NONCE: 772

Figure 6.15 Transactions received by an Ethereum node.

In which order will the transactions be included in a block by the validator?

There is one transaction that will not be processed by the node. Which one? What must happen in order for this transaction to be processed?

3 Propose and discuss one application in the real world of Ethereum fungible and non-fungible tokens. In your discussion, consider the following questions: What is the reason to develop the token? What is the behavior of the token that should be coded into the smart contract? How does the token extend/modify the ERC-20 or ERC-721 interfaces? How would you propose to solve, if relevant, the counter-party risk problem in the case of the non-fungible token?

4 Consider the case of an e-voting DApp, i.e., an application based on Ethereum smart contracts to support the voting of users. Assume for simplicity that the users can cast only yes/no votes and that it is not necessary to ensure the anonymity of the votes. For instance, this DApp may allow members of a parliament to cast their votes from home during the Covid-19 pandemic (votes in favor/against a bill, in most cases, are indeed not anonymous). Based on what is discussed in Section 6.3, show a typical usage scenario of this DApp, describing also the functions of the smart contract that implements its application logic and providing examples of the content of the transactions that invoke this smart contract.

Notes

1 Unlike EOA, the acronym SCA is not universally accepted, but it helps to be concise and precise in the context of this book.

2 In Figure 6.2, the prefix 0x is used to signal that what follows is encoded using Base-16 or Base-64. This is a common practice for computer scientists.

3 The 'wei' is the smallest Ether denomination, with 1 ETH = 10^{18} wei. Transaction fees are often denominated in Gwei, with 1 Gwei = 10^9 wei.

4 Accessed as of late June 2022, during the writing of this book. Note that this information may change in the future (however, information about this SCA cannot be deleted from the Ethereum ledger!).

7 Private blockchain

Learning goals

7.A   The reader can define private blockchain and discuss its benefits and draw-backs in respect of public blockchain.

7.B   The reader can explain how Ethereum can be used for the implementation of private blockchains.

7.C   The reader can describe the characteristics of a Corda-based system and can explain how the ledger, the transactions, and the consensus mechanism are implemented in such a system.

7.D   The reader can describe the characteristics of a system implemented using Hyperledger Fabric and can explain how the ledger, the transactions, and the consensus mechanism are implemented in such a system.

7.E   The reader can sketch how Corda or Hyperledger Fabric can be used to implement concrete blockchain systems in specific business scenarios.

7.1 Characterizing the private blockchain

In Part 2 of this book, we have considered, until now, only public blockchain technology, i.e., Bitcoin and Ethereum. As we have seen in Chapter 3, however, blockchain can also be applied by a private network of business partners. From a design standpoint, building a private blockchain can be less challenging than a public one. For instance, because the identity of the nodes is known, the nodes can be trusted to a higher degree. Moreover, in a private blockchain, we can design finer-grained data visibility policies. Every node need not have access to the entire ledger of transactions. A transaction may be visible only to the nodes for which it has a business meaning. In this section, we first discuss the need for private blockchains, stemming from the limitations of public blockchains. Based on this discussion, we then derive a set of general features that characterize private blockchains.

Public blockchains, like Bitcoin and Ethereum, enable the implementation of decentralized asset exchange systems, like cryptocurrencies, open to anybody. While public blockchains are particularly well-suited for the implementation of digital currencies used worldwide, they are also unsuitable in many more traditional business domains.

First, public blockchains are normally secured through highly resource-consuming consensus protocols, like PoW. Other types of consensus mechanisms that have been

DOI: 10.4324/9781003321187-9

touted to solve the hunger for resources of PoW rely on the use of other resources of the nodes to establish consensus. The Proof-of-Stake (PoS) consensus mechanisms, for instance, require the nodes to use their own cryptocurrency to gain the right to propose new blocks. In many traditional business settings, this type of consensus mechanisms is not a viable solution. In fact, running a PoW consensus requires that at least some of the nodes implement the miner functionality. Miner nodes basically accept to be rewarded using a blockchain's cryptocurrency for the resources (i.e., electricity) that they employ to mine new blocks. In many practical scenarios, there is no need for a cryptocurrency at all. That is, all the economic exchanges in most practical scenarios are handled using traditional fiat currencies. The absence of a business case to introduce a cryptocurrency clearly makes it practically impossible to use the PoW consensus mechanism, or any other consensus mechanism that relies on the ownership of cryptocurrency by the nodes of a blockchain.

A second shortcoming of public blockchains concerns the availability and transparency of the blockchain data. The data in a public blockchain ledger, like the transactions and/or the variables describing the blockchain state, are usually public. This means that anybody, even possibly outside the blockchain, can get access to these data. In the previous chapters, we have seen that anybody can access the information regarding all the transactions ever issued in the Bitcoin and Ethereum blockchains using an 'explorer', i.e., a public Web site. Consequently, anybody can reconstruct the amount of BTC or ETH (or any other ERC-20 Ethereum token) owned by any node of the Bitcoin or Ethereum blockchain. The transparency of public blockchains is welcome in many application scenarios, like cryptocurrencies or the track and tracing of valuable digital and physical assets. However, we must also realize that transparency is not at all welcome in most business scenarios. For instance, a private equity fund investing in real estate does not want to make public the price at which it purchased new real estate. Similarly, a network of regional hospitals would be firmly against making public the data about patient treatments. By analyzing these data, in fact, competing suppliers may reconstruct important information that may become a source of competitive advantage, such as detailed information regarding delivery times in different regions, or the prices applied. In most traditional businesses, the information regarding the business operations must remain privy to a usually limited number of business actors.

To conclude, we can summarize here the three main characteristics of private blockchain systems:

A   In a private blockchain system, the nodes must be vetted before being admitted to a private blockchain and, as a consequence, the identity of the nodes of a private blockchain must be known.
B   The information stored in the ledger of a private blockchain must remain private to the nodes of the blockchain. Moreover, it should be possible to segregate the information stored in the ledger of a private blockchain among different groups of nodes as required by the specific business settings.
C   The consensus mechanism in a private blockchain system need not be based on highly resource-consuming algorithms, but, exploiting the usually limited size of the network and the fact the identity of the nodes is known, it can rely on more lightweight solutions that would speed up the overall system performance while not compromising its security.

7.2 Ethereum as a private blockchain

In Chapter 6 we have presented Ethereum as a public blockchain. The nodes of the Ethereum blockchain can own and exchange Ether (ETH). Ether is used by the nodes to pay the transaction fees and to reward the miner of new blocks (through the coinbase transaction included in every new block).

Ethereum can also be used as a framework to create private blockchain networks. The Ethereum client, in fact, could be downloaded and installed on a set of nodes belonging to a private Internet network. This can be, for instance, a set of desktop computers connected to a private Local Area Network (LAN) or a Virtual Private Network (VPN). By definition, in this case, the identity of the node is known, since we must know which nodes belong to this private network and on which nodes the Ethereum client must be installed. At the same time, this network is private, i.e., it cannot be accessed by any other computational node. In principle, the LAN or VPN connecting the nodes could be completely disconnected from the Internet. That is, the other nodes physically would be unable to reach the nodes on the private network.

Since an Ethereum client is installed on every node, a private Ethereum network behaves like the public Ethereum network. For example, the format of the transactions is the same, the nodes can issue transactions that deploy new smart contracts, and at least one of the nodes should also implement the functionality to propose new blocks. However, there are also many differences between a private and a public Ethereum network. First, the Ether in a private Ethereum network is basically 'fake', i.e., it does not have value outside the private network. Most importantly, it does not have a price in fiat currencies. As such, the nodes can be created with an ETH balance as high as we want or, alternatively, the transaction fees (gas price) can be made so low that a fraction of an Ether would be sufficient for a node to issue billions of transactions. Second, the design of the consensus protocol can be parameterized to fit the need of the specific business scenario for which the private Ethereum network was created.

There are numerous examples of private Ethereum blockchains that can be mentioned. For instance, it is common for academic researchers interested in blockchain to develop and test new ideas on private Ethereum blockchains, e.g., [XHL+18] [SMJ21]. A private Ethereum blockchain, in fact, provides researchers with a feature-rich blockchain (which may include the option of deploying smart contracts) in a completely controlled environment that can be used free of charge. This is often a good alternative to the public Ethereum test network, whose performance is often unpredictable and unreliable [CCM21]. The prototype of the case study of Chapter 8 (Artefact-based business process monitoring), for example, is implemented as an open-source private Ethereum blockchain [MPV19].

7.3 Corda: private blockchain based on a need-to-know ledger

Corda is a framework for developing private blockchain networks created by R3 and available open source since 2016 (https://www.r3.com/products/corda/) [Bro18]. It has gained remarkable traction, particularly in the financial sector, in recent years. Note that, unlike Bitcoin or Ethereum, Corda is not a blockchain system by itself, but it is a development framework that is used to create private blockchain systems for specific business scenarios. Based on this premise, in the remainder of this section, we use for brevity 'Corda system' to refer to a 'private blockchain system developed using the Corda framework'.

The Corda framework aims at overcoming two specific limitations of public blockchain:

1 In a public blockchain, each node maintains a local copy of the ledger data. In other words, the same data in the ledger are replicated at every node. While this can be fundamental to avoid introducing a central authority to determine the content of the ledger, generally this implies massive data replication, which is highly inefficient.
2 Since each node has a copy of the ledger data, every node has visibility over all the transactions issued by any other node. As we mentioned earlier in this chapter, this may not be an issue in public blockchains where the identity of the nodes remains unknown. When the identity of the node is known, and the transactions can contain sensible information about one's own business, making all the ledger data known to every node may not be the best choice.

Corda addresses these two limitations by proposing the idea of a so-called 'need-to-know' ledger. That is, the main innovation of Corda is the way in which the blockchain data are stored and managed. The next section focuses on this aspect, i.e., the data structure of Corda, whereas Section 7.3.2 briefly discusses the other aspects of Corda, such as the structure of the network in a Corda system and the consensus mechanism.

7.3.1 Corda data structure

The ledger of a Corda system is structured on a need-to-know basis. The nodes store in their local ledger only the data that are relevant for them, that is, the data that concern their own private business and not the private business of other nodes. This derives from the necessity of many business scenarios. Even in scenarios characterized by a network of several partners working together to achieve a common business goal, each individual party may still not be willing to share all the information regarding the business operations with all the other partners. In practice, in most scenarios a party would like to share with other parties only the minimal amount of information necessary to keep the business operating well [RTK+16]. For instance, cross-nation real estate management often involves several parties besides the buyer and the seller of real estate, like financial intermediaries (at least a bank in the country of the buyer and one in the country of the seller, and possibly additional international intermediaries), and real estate management agencies to which a foreign buyer delegates, for example, the renting and maintenance of the property. The banks and the financial intermediaries need to know only about the financial details of the property purchase. They need not know whether a property is being rented to somebody or how much it costs the buyer to maintain it. Similarly, the real estate managers need not know about every detail of the financial transactions between the buyer and the seller, such as whether the buyer has contracted a mortgage to finance the purchase. They only need to be assured that the buyer is the legal owner of the property.

The ledger of a Corda system is exemplified in Figure 7.1. It stores 'states', rather than transactions. As explained in detail later in this section, a state is an immutable piece of information, or a 'fact', known by two or more nodes. Not all the facts stored in a Corda

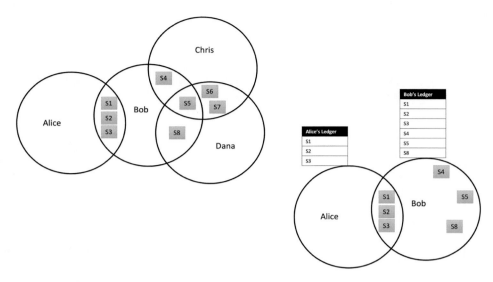

Figure 7.1 The Corda ledger built on a 'need-to-know' basis.

ledger are known to all the nodes. Instead, facts are distributed across nodes according to the 'need-to-know' basis: nodes have access in their local ledger only to the facts that are relevant for them. This principle creates the multi-lateral ledger that we see in Figure 7.1. For example, the fact S1 belongs only to the ledger of Alice and Bob, meaning that it is relevant only for those two nodes of the network. In the real estate scenario that we mentioned earlier, Alice and Bob may be the banks used by the buyer and the seller, respectively. The fact S1 may be some detail regarding the money transferred for the purchase of some real state made by the buyer to the seller. The ledger of a Corda system is made immutable by the traditional chaining of cryptographic hashes described in Chapter 3. Each state stored by a node contains its own hash and the hash of the state that precedes it in the same ledger.

The states stored in a Corda ledger evolve over time thanks to the transactions. A transaction in Corda is issued by one node, i.e. the originator. The originator also digitally signs the transaction. The transactions in Corda, and the state evolution mechanism that they entail, generalize the mechanism of UTXOs that we described in Chapter 5 for the Bitcoin blockchain. A transaction 'consumes' states as input and 'produces' new states as output. Therefore, the states in a Corda ledger can be 'historic' (i.e., consumed) or 'unconsumed'. A transaction can use only unconsumed states as input. The execution of a transaction makes the input states 'historic' and may produce new 'unconsumed' states as output.

An example of the state evolution mechanism described above is provided in Figure 7.2. It concerns the facts describing a debt that the node Alice has toward the node Bob. The first state shared by Alice and Bob captures the fact that Alice owes 20$ to Bob (created by the transaction T1). At time $t = t_1$ this state is 'unconsumed'. Then, at time $t = t_2$ Alice repays a part of his debt (7$) to Bob. This is captured by the transaction T2, which turns the state S1 into 'historic' and creates a new 'unconsumed' state S2. The

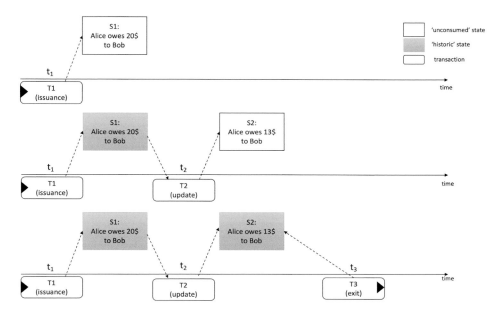

Figure 7.2 Types of states and their evolution through transactions in Corda.

state S2 captures the fact that now Alice owes only 13$ to Bob. Eventually, at time t = t₃ Alice repays its outstanding debt to Bob. This is captured by the transaction T3, which turns the state S2 into 'historic', without producing any new states.

To sum up, the states in Corda are modified by the transactions. A transaction may have zero or more states as input and may produce zero or more new states as output. A transaction can only use 'unconsumed' states. The execution of a transaction turns the input state into 'historic' and may produce new 'unconsumed' states. Hence, at any point in time, the ledger maintained by a Corda node contains a set of historic states and a set of unconsumed states. The latter are the only ones that can be the input of new transactions. Finally, as shown in Figure 7.2, there are three types of transactions in Corda:

- 'Issuance' transactions, which have no input and create new states (e.g., transaction T1 in Figure 7.2)
- 'Update' transactions, which have at least one state in input and produce at least one output state (T2 in Figure 7.2)
- 'Exit' transactions, which have at least one input state, but no output states (T3 in Figure 7.2)

As we mentioned earlier, the mechanism described above can be seen as an extension of Bitcoin's UTXOs mechanism. The historic states are in fact like the transaction outputs that have already been used as input of other Bitcoin transactions and, therefore, cannot be used any more by new transactions. The unconsumed states are like the unspent transaction outputs (UTXOs) of Bitcoin. They can be used as input by new transactions. At the same time, while the state of the Bitcoin blockchain (i.e., the balance of all the users)

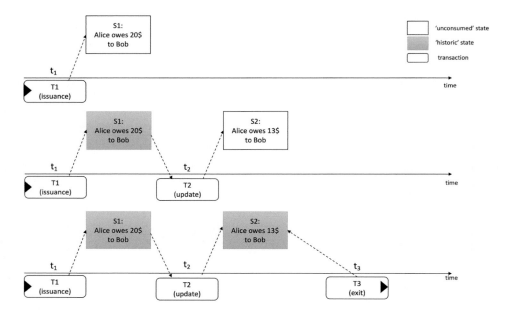

Figure 7.3 Example of contract in Corda.

can be reconstructed using the collection of UTXOs, the current state of a Corda system is constituted by the collection of its 'unconsumed' states in the multi-lateral ledger.

Other important elements of a Corda system are the so-called 'contracts', which we touch only briefly in this book. A contract in Corda must not be confused with the blockchain 'smart contract' discussed earlier in this book. In Corda, a 'contract' specifies the rules that a transaction must satisfy to be valid. In other words, a contract contains the instructions for the nodes to determine whether a transaction must be stored in the ledger or not. For example, a real estate purchase 'contract' in Corda may specify that a purchase transaction must contain specific information regarding the buyer and the seller (e.g., their legal denomination and address), and the property that is purchased (e.g., its registration number in a public registry). Any purchase transaction that does not contain this information in its input facts must not be considered valid. A contract in Corda can also contain 'legal prose' describing the terms of the contract. For instance, a real estate purchase contract may also contain some legal text describing the information required about the buyer, the seller, and the purchased property. Including the legal prose may help resolve contract disputes.

7.3.2 Corda network and consensus mechanism

In the previous section, we have described how the data are stored in the ledger of a Corda system and how the nodes of such a system can modify these data by issuing transactions. In this section we focus on how the nodes of a Corda system can agree on which transactions are valid and, therefore, on the state of a Corda system at any point in time. In other words, we focus here on the consensus mechanism in a Corda system. After having introduced the consensus mechanism, we conclude this section by briefly discussing the different types of nodes that can exist in a Corda system network.

When a new transaction is issued by a node in a Corda system, the nodes of the system must agree on the following two issues:

- Is this new transaction valid?
- Is the state update (or creation) entailed by this transaction unique?

We have already touched briefly on aspects concerned with the validity of a transaction in a Corda system in the previous section. A transaction is valid if it consumes only states that are 'unconsumed' and if it satisfies all the conditions specified by the relevant contracts. Additionally, similarly to any other blockchain system, a node validates a transaction by verifying that is well-formed and it is digitally signed by its originator.

The second issue listed above, i.e., the uniqueness of state updates entailed by a transaction, is the one requiring a longer discussion. This issue can be seen as a generalization of the double spending problem in public blockchains. The problem that we must solve, in fact, is ensuring that an unconsumed state cannot be used twice in two different transactions. Figure 7.4 exemplifies this issue. Alice may issue two transactions, T1 and T2, close in time and consuming the same input state (i.e., the fact that her balance is 50$). The transactions T1 and T2 are used to clear outstanding debts that Alice has with Chris and Bob, respectively. This would be possible if Bob and Chris receive these transactions in a different order. Specifically, if each of them receives first the transactions that repays Alice's debt with them. In other words, Figure 7.4 depicts a situation in which Alice has managed to 'consume' a state of a Corda system twice. However, at the same time the execution of T1 and T2 also created two states (S4 and S5) that are inconsistent.

In a public blockchain, the problem of double spending is prevented by the PoW consensus mechanism, which is embodied by the computational work of the miner nodes. In a private blockchain system, it would be desirable to solve this problem is a

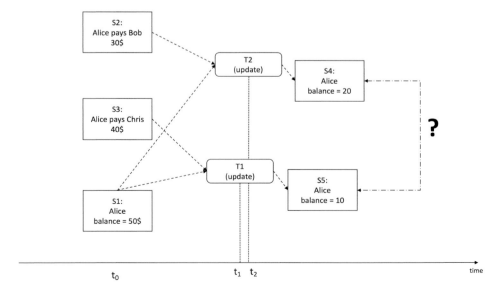

Figure 7.4 Uniqueness of state updates in Corda.

simpler way, avoiding (i) the high energy consumption that typically comes with the execution of PoW and (ii) the delays in the confirmation of transactions typically introduced by PoW.

In a Corda system, the uniqueness of state updates is guaranteed by the so-called 'notary' nodes. A notary in a Corda system is a node that does not participate in the business operations. It is more like a 'service' node contributing to the smooth operation of a Corda system. A notary in a Corda system has only one role: it monitors the usage of one or more states. When a new 'unconsumed' state is produced by a transaction, it is assigned to one notary node. A notary monitors continuously whether new transactions are using this state as input. As soon one transaction does that, the notary turns the 'unconsumed' state into a 'historic' one. For example, in Figure 7.4, if T1 is validated by Chris before T2 is validated by Bob, the notary monitoring the state S1 will turn S1

Computer Science Focus: consensus mechanisms in private blockchains

Since a node cannot freely join a private blockchain, and it is always associated with a specific individual or organization, the risk of malicious actions in a private blockchain is much lower than in public blockchains. Consequently, consensus mechanisms in private blockchains tend to maximize performance rather than resisting adversarial control. Currently, two families of consensus mechanisms are adopted:

- **Crash Fault Tolerant (CFT)** consensus mechanisms offer a high protection against failures, but no protection against malicious actions. Firstly, a node is elected as 'leader' and, for the election to be valid, a quorum must be reached. In particular, given N nodes, at least $N/2 + 1$ (i.e., the majority of the nodes) must be online to cast their vote. Once the leader has been elected, it will be in charge of validating the information (e.g., by acting as a notary in Corda). The other nodes will act as 'followers' by keeping track of the operations carried out by the leader. Also, the followers will constantly check if the leader is still online. If that is no longer the case, the followers will elect a new leader. It is worth noting that, since only one node is in charge of validating the information at a specific point in time, CFT provides no way to detect if that node has been compromised and is providing misleading information.
- **Practical Byzantine Fault Tolerant (PBFT)** consensus mechanisms offer a fair protection against both failures and malicious actions. Firstly, a 'client' node makes a request to one of the nodes responsible for the consensus (e.g., one of the notaries in Corda), which acts as 'master'. Then, the master forwards the request to the other nodes responsible for the consensus, which act as 'masons' receiving orders from the masters. After that, both the master and the masons inspect the request, compute the reply, and send it to the client. Finally, the client checks the replies and, given N nodes responsible for the consensus, as soon as the client receives $N/3 + 1$ identical replies, it can trust the outcome. It is worth noting that, since a subset of the nodes must agree on the outcome, PBFT can tolerate nodes being compromised as long as they are slightly less than $N/3$.

into 'historic'. In this way, Bob would fail to validate T2 – because it uses a historic state as input – thus preventing Alice to consume a state twice.

A single notary, as in the example made above, while solving the problem of double spending, may also create a more general issue concerned with the inner essence of blockchain systems. A single notary, in fact, can act as a central authority and a single point of failure. Blockchain was invented precisely to avoid these in the first place. In other words, in the example made above, the notary monitoring S1 may collude with Alice and allow her to use the state S1 twice. This can be done by a notary simply by delaying its actions, i.e., turning S1 into 'historic' only after Bob has validated T2. If the same notary then monitors also S5 and S4, then the notary may immediately turn S5 into 'historic', such that the state S4 (assigning a higher balance to Alice) is the only one that can be used in the future. This problem is solved in Corda systems by considering multiple notaries for the same state. Practically, instead of a single notary, every new state can be monitored by a network of notary nodes. When a state is used in a transaction, the notaries monitoring this state must reach an agreement on turning this state 'historic'. Practically, this is done through a consensus mechanism. Consensus mechanism in private networks can be much more lightweight than the PoW mechanism. More about consensus mechanism in private blockchain networks is given in the Computer Science Focus.

An important limitation of Corda is that it lacks the support to smart contracts. In a Corda system, it is not possible to define arbitrary business logic to manipulate the state of the system based on the input provided by the transactions. The so-called 'contracts' in a Corda system, as mentioned earlier, are simply a way to bundle together the transaction validation rules. Smart contract-enabled private blockchain systems can be implemented using Hyperledger Fabric, which we discuss in the next section.

7.4 Hyperledger Fabric: smart contract–enabled private blockchain

Hyperledger Fabric [ABB+18] is a framework for developing private blockchain networks developed by the Hyperledger Foundation since 2016. Hyperledger Fabric (HLF in brief in the remainder of this chapter) has been primarily designed to support business transactions between technological, financial, and supply chain companies. Similar to Corda, HLF aims at disclosing information in the blockchain with the participants on a need-to-know basis. To do so, it relies on two elements, named channels and private data collections, which we present in Section 7.4.1. In addition, HLF also supports smart contracts. Smart contracts in HLF are named 'chaincode'. Compared to Ethereum smart contracts, chaincode allows to process transactions also involving private off-chain data. Finally, HLF allows to designate specific participants for executing smart contracts and for creating new blocks. Such details are discussed in Section 7.4.2.

7.4.1 Hyperledger Fabric data structures

Due to its focus on business transactions, information in HLF is represented by business objects. A business object is a factual representation of a physical or virtual object (e.g., a package, a quote, or an invoice) manipulated and exchanged by the organizations in a private network. Each business object is composed of multiple attributes. The values of these attributes represent the state of a business object. For example, a business object 'invoice' may contain the VAT number of the customer, the items purchased and, for each of them, the quantity and the unit price, the total amount to be paid, the discount applied to the customer and whether the payment has been received from the customer.

To keep track of the business objects and their evolution over time, HLF relies on two data structures:

1   The 'world state': this is a key-value database that maintains the most up-to-date information for each business object. Its main purpose is to make business objects and their state quickly accessible by the nodes.
2   The 'blockchain': this is an ordered collection of transactions grouped inside cryptographically linked blocks. Its main purpose is to maintain an immutable history of how the business objects changed over time.

In HLF, only the chaincode is responsible for creating, updating, and deleting business objects. With respect to Ethereum, where transactions are not required to invoke smart contracts to store new information in the blockchain (e.g., one can add new information simply as transaction data, or a transaction can record an exchange of Ether, with no smart contracts invoked), HLF requires each transaction to invoke a chaincode. Moreover, update and delete operations in a chaincode simply modify the business objects in the world state. They cannot change the blockchain.

To address the need-to-know principle, HLF allows to partition the network of nodes into so-called 'channels'. From a conceptual standpoint, a channel can be seen as a single ledger, completely independent from the other channels, with its own world state and blockchain. Consequently, transactions are confined within the channel where they were issued. Therefore, nodes that do not have access rights to that channel cannot see the transactions issued on it, nor can they access its business objects.

This feature can be particularly useful in scenarios such as a supply chain. For instance, one customer C may want to keep track of the business relations with the dealers D1, D2, and D3, with D1 affiliated to supplier S1, and D2 and D3 affiliated to supplier S2. However, the suppliers are not willing to share this information with their competitors.

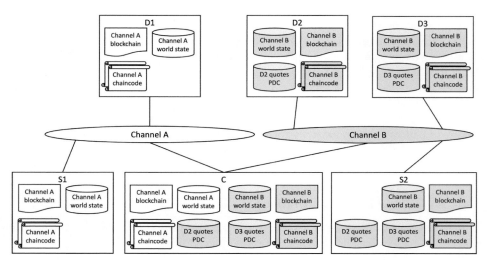

Figure 7.5 HLF deployment example with channels and private data collections.

As shown in Figure 7.5, this issue can be solved by creating two channels A and B. The supplier S1 and the dealer D1 are granted access to channel A, whereas the supplier S2 and the dealers D2 and D3 get to access channel B. The customer C is granted access to both channels A and B. In this way, S1 can only see the transactions issued by itself, D1 and C, but not S2, D2, or D3. Similarly, S2 can see the transactions issued by itself, D2, D3, and C, but not S1 or D1. Conversely, being part of both channels, C can access the transactions issued by all the nodes.

Channels still present some limitations. Firstly, for a transaction to be visible by the nodes belonging to different channels, it must be issued once in each channel. For example, if C wants to make the same request for quotation accessible to D1 and D2, it must create two business objects by issuing a transaction twice, firstly on channel A, then on B. Secondly, the only way to restrict a subset of the nodes in a channel from accessing a transaction is to create a new channel and issue the transaction there. For example, to prevent D3 from seeing the quotes sent by D2 and exploiting this information to get a better deal (e.g., deliberately applying a discount higher than the one applied by D2), a solution relying on channels requires D2 to set up a new channel including only itself, C, and S2.

To achieve finer-grained access control over private information, as well as to support the deletion of sensitive information once it is no longer needed, HLF introduced 'private data collections'. In a nutshell, a private data collection is a set of business objects that are kept in a side database and replicated to specific nodes via off-chain mechanisms. Whenever a business object is added to, modified, or removed from a private data collection, its digest (i.e., hash) is computed and stored in the blockchain of the corresponding channel. In this way, authorized nodes can know if their copy of that data object is up-to-date and, if not, they can retrieve the most recent one. Access control policies can be defined to specify which nodes are allowed to read from and/or write to a private data collection. Policies also allow to specify an expiry date to business objects, after which they will be automatically purged from the collection.

Thank to these capabilities, private data collections are more flexible than channels. In particular, they are indicated whenever there is a need for short-term collaborations between nodes, or when a channel-based solution would require to define several channels. In the supply chain example, the problem of making quotes sent from D2 inaccessible to D3 could be solved by storing the quotes inside private data collections. More in detail, D2 can create a private data collection for its own quotes. Then, it can define a new access control policy allowing only S2 and C to replicate the information on that collection. The same can be done by D3 for its own quotes.

7.4.2 Hyperledger Fabric network and consensus mechanism

In Chapter 6, we have discussed how smart contracts are executed in Ethereum. Whenever a new transaction invoking a smart contract is issued in Ethereum, it is first included in a new block. Then, when they receive this new block, all the nodes must replay the transaction by executing the smart contract inside their own EVM. Such an approach is named 'order-execute', because the transactions must be first ordered inside a new block before being executed.

To work, this approach requires that smart contracts running on different nodes, given the same transaction history, must provide the same output. Thus, only specialized programming languages that are guaranteed to be deterministic (e.g., they cannot use random numbers) can be used to implement smart contracts. For the same reasons, the information required to execute a smart contract must be made available to all the nodes, either in the form of input parameters or as the internal state of the smart contract. In both cases, it is eventually stored in the blockchain, thus becoming immutable and accessible by all nodes. This approach also requires transactions to be processed sequentially. Indeed, when a new block is received, the nodes must execute the transactions in it one by one, thus potentially limiting the scalability and throughput of the blockchain network.

To overcome these limitations, HLF relies on a different approach to execute smart contracts, named 'execute-order-validate'. As the name suggests, the transactions are firstly processed by a subset of the nodes, who 'execute' the smart contracts invoked by them. Then, the transactions are ordered inside blocks. These are created and validated by another subset of the nodes. Finally, the transactions inside a block are validated by all the nodes and, upon a successful validation, the nodes update their own copy of the ledger. In the following subsections, we discuss in detail how each of these steps is performed.

7.4.2.1 Execution

To issue a new transaction in HLF, a node must first create a 'proposal'. Inside the proposal, the node must specify the chaincode function to invoke and the input parameters. Optionally, a node can also declare some input parameters as transient. In this case, the values related to such parameters will not be stored in the proposal itself, nor will they be included in the transaction. Instead, they will be retrieved from a private data collection and, as such, kept off-chain. Then, the node that created the proposal, which is named 'target peer', digitally signs the proposal and forwards it to a subset of the nodes in a channel, who are responsible for checking its correctness. Such nodes are named 'endorsing peers', and they are selected based on an endorsement policy.

When it receives the proposal, each endorsing peer checks its local copy of the ledger and identifies the business objects manipulated by the chaincode being invoked. Then, it computes the so-called 'input set', that is, the values of the attributes of such business objects before the chaincode is executed. Then, the endorsing peer executes the chaincode and computes the output set, that is, the values of the attributes of the previously identified business objects after the chaincode has been executed.

Based on the outcome of the chaincode, the endorsing peer decides whether to endorse the proposal or not (hence the name endorsing peer). If it decides to endorse the proposal, the endorsing peer creates a proposal response containing the endorsement decision and the input and output sets, signs it, and sends it to the target peer. It is worth noting that, at this stage, the changes to the business objects made by the chaincode invocation are neither persisted by the target peer nor by the endorsing peer.

Figure 7.6 shows an example of the execution phase carried out by the nodes in the HLF deployment for the logistics scenario outlined Section 7.4.1 (Figure 7.5). To accept the request for a quote with ID 'R1', D2 creates a proposal invoking the *AcceptReq* function of the chaincode *QuoteH*, passing *R1* as input parameter. Once it receives the proposal, the endorsing peer C identifies the data object *R1* with value *Sent* as the input set, executes the *AcceptReq* function of *QuoteH*, and identifies the data object *R1* with

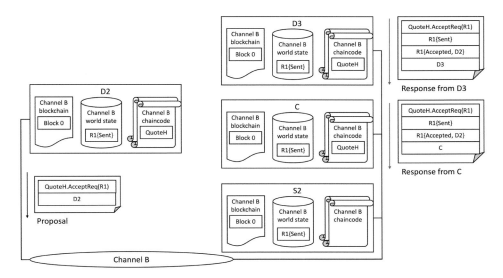

Figure 7.6 Execution phase. D2 acts as a target peer, whereas C and D3 as endorsing peers.

value *Accepted* as the output set. Then, C creates the proposal response, by combining the request with the input and output sets, signs the response, and sends it back to D2. The same is done by D3, whereas S2 does not take part to the ordering phase as it lacks the *QuoteH* chaincode. Note that at this stage the world state remains unchanged for all the peers.

The introduction of endorsing peers, who are the only one in charge of executing a chaincode, brings several advantages. Firstly, there are no restrictions on the complexity of a chaincode, as well as no requirement for determinism. Thus, chaincode can be written in any general-purpose programming language, such as Java or Python. Secondly, a chaincode can predicate on data that is accessible only by the endorsing peers, such as business objects in a private data collection. Also, once the chaincode has been executed and the proposal invoking it has been endorsed, private data can be safely deleted. Finally, as chaincode is executed only by a subset of the nodes, it is possible to run multiple chaincodes in parallel, thus increasing the overall performance of the blockchain network.

7.4.2.2 *Ordering*

Once the target peer has collected enough endorsements for a proposal, it checks whether the endorsing peers agree on the outcome of the proposal. In particular, the number of endorsing peers that must agree with the proposal is also specified in the endorsement policy. If the endorsement policy is satisfied, the target peer creates a transaction containing the proposal and all the proposal responses sent by the endorsing peers. Then, it sends the transaction to another subset of the nodes, named 'ordering service'.

As the name suggests, the nodes in the ordering service are responsible for specifying in which order the transactions should be included in a new block. To this aim, a node is selected to create the next block. Once the node has determined the ordering of the proposals, it creates a new block including the associated transactions, and forwards the new block to all the other nodes in the channel. It is worth noting that the ordering service neither validates the transactions, nor executes any chaincode.

Figure 7.7 shows an example of an ordering phase that is the logical continuation of the example discussed in the previous section. Firstly, the ordering service selects S2 for ordering the transactions. Then, D2, D3, and S send the transactions T1, T2, T3 to S2, which orders them, creates Block 1 and forwards it to all the peers in Channel B. Note that, although all the transactions invoke functions of the *QuoteH* chaincode, and S2 lacks that chaincode, it has no effect on the ability for S2 to order the transactions. Also note that at this stage the world state still remains unchanged for all the peers.

One of the main advantages brought by the ordering service is that it prevents to introduce forks in the blockchain. Indeed, since only one node oversees the creation of a new block, it is impossible for 2 blocks to link to the same previous block. Another advantage of the ordering service is that it is not bound to a specific consensus mechanism. Indeed, HLF supports out-of-the-box three implementations of the ordering service: Raft, Kafka, and Solo. Raft and Kafka are Crash-Fault-Tolerant (CFT) implementations where one node is dynamically elected as leader, and the others as followers. The leader oversees the creation of the new blocks, whereas the followers keep track of the transactions being issued and of the blocks being created. If the leader goes off-line, a new leader is elected among the followers. In addition, Raft is specifically designed to be easily distributed among multiple organizations, and implementations supporting the Byzantine-Fault-Tolerant (BFT) consensus mechanisms are planned to be developed. Conversely, Solo consists of a single node and, therefore, offers no redundancy and is mainly used for testing purposes. It is worth noting that other, custom implementations of the ordering service can be deployed in HLF without having to change the other nodes. Additionally, multiple ordering service implementations can exist in a single HLF deployment.

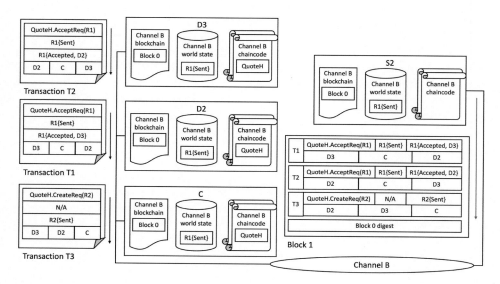

Figure 7.7 Ordering phase in HLF. D2, D3, and C act as target peers, whereas S2 is selected to order transactions and create the new block.

7.4.2.3 Validation

When a node receives a new block from the ordering service, either directly or through other nodes via gossiping, it inspects the transactions in the block following the same order as the one specified by the ordering service. For each transaction, the node checks if it satisfies the corresponding endorsement policy. In addition, the node verifies if the transaction has not been invalidated by the other transactions in the block. In particular, it inspects the input set to determine if it is consistent with its own copy of the world state.

If the validation check succeeds, the node marks the transaction as valid. In addition, the node updates its own copy of the world state with the output set of that transaction. If the validation check fails, the node marks the transaction as invalid, leaving the world state unchanged. This approach prevents the occurrence of the double spending issue. Indeed, if two concurrent transactions try to change the same attribute of a business object, they will have the same input set but different output sets. Thus, only the first transaction – that is, the one that is listed first in the block – will have an input set consistent with the world state. Thus, the transaction will be marked as valid, and it will update the world state. Conversely, the other transaction will have an input state inconsistent with the updated world state. Thus, the transaction will be marked as invalid, and no change to the world state will be made.

Figure 7.8 shows an example of validation that is the logical continuation of the example discussed in the previous section. Once it receives a copy of Block 1, a peer of Channel B adds it to its own copy of the blockchain. Then, it starts inspecting the transactions in it (left). When it inspects T1 (the first transaction), the peer detects that the input set requires business object *R1* to have value *Sent*, which is consistent with the world state. Then, it marks T1 as *valid* and updates the world state by assigning to *R1* the value *Accepted*, according to the output set of T1 (center). Then, the peer inspects T2 (the next transaction) and detects that the input set requires *R1* to have value *Sent*. However, in the world state *R1* now has value *Accepted*, as it was updated by T1, which happened concurrently to T2. Therefore, T2 is marked as *invalid*, and its output set is ignored. Finally, the peer inspects T3 (the last transaction) and detects that no input set has been defined. Therefore, it marks T3 as *valid* and applies the output set to the world

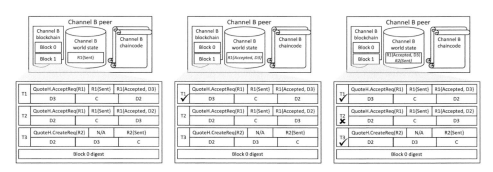

Figure 7.8 Validation phase in HLF. In the left part, Block 1 has not yet been inspected. In the central part, Block 1 has been partially inspected (only T1 has been processed). In the right part, the inspection of Block 1 has been completed (all its transactions have been processed).

state, which creates a new business object *R2* with value *Sent* (right). Note that, since the order of inspection of the transactions in Block 1 has been defined by the ordering service, all peers of channel B perform this operation in the same way. Also note that, although all the transactions invoke functions of the *QuoteH* chaincode, that chaincode is not required for peers to process the transactions.

It is worth noting that, although each node independently updates its own copy of the world state, the process is consistent through all the nodes. In particular, since the order in which the transactions should be applied is decided by the ordering service, it is impossible for two nodes to have discrepancies in their own copy of the world state. This clearly prevents the double spending problem. It is also worth noting that, to update the world state, only the output set is required. Therefore, nodes do not need to execute any chaincode at this stage.

To conclude, the execute-order-validate approach followed by HLF is effective to achieve scalability, to manage private data, and not to incur in the limitations imposed by specialized smart contracts, such as Solidity smart contracts in Ethereum. However, this approach is applicable only because HLF is a private blockchain, where the nodes are identifiable and associated with specific organizations. In a public blockchain, where any node can anonymously join, it would be impossible to define effective endorsement policies, as there would be no way to determine if the majority of the endorsing peers and the target peer are controlled by the same entity. Similarly, if the ordering service makes use of a CFT consensus mechanism, a malicious user could take control of it, and consequently prevent transactions from being included into a block or cause transactions to follow an order where they are invalid. Finally, the chaincode based on general-purpose programming languages could be exploited by a malicious user to cause deadlocks and other performance issues in the blockchain network.

7.5 Case study: real world applications that use Corda and Hyperledger Fabric

Both Corda and HLF are at the core of the implementation of many private blockchains currently live and running in different business contexts. In this section, we discuss briefly two of them: the Spunta Banca project, based on Corda, and IBM FoodTrust, based on HLF.

7.5.1 *Spunta Banca*

Spunta Banca distributed ledger technology (https://www.r3.com/case-studies/spunta/) is a project promoted by the Italian Banking Association (ABI) and coordinated by its research and development division (ABI Lab) focusing on the process of reconciliating bilateral interbank transactions. The problem that it aims at solving sounds simple: every time a transaction involving two commercial banks is executed, these two banks must agree precisely on every aspect that characterize it, ranging from the identity of the owners of the accounts involved to the exact amount that was transferred. This process is called 'spunta' in Italian, and historically has been based on piecemeal solutions, involving possibly different IT systems at each end of the transaction, but also the exchange of multiple phone calls and fax messages to reconcile even a single transaction.

In the project, a blockchain system based on Corda has been developed. The problem of running correctly the 'spunta' process, in fact, clearly matches the characteristics of a Corda system. Specifically, in the system developed the transactions are recorded in a need-to-know-based ledger. Usually, in fact, most transactions concern only two banks. Only in some cases other banks or financial institutions may be involved. For instance, a third bank may guarantee a collateral of a large financial transaction between two other banks. Moreover, all the rules concerning the reconciliation of transactions, such as a detailed specification of all the data that must be reconciliated for each transaction type, are coded into the system as Corda's 'contracts'. Therefore, they are checked in real time when the nodes validate transactions. Additionally, a Corda-based system brings the typical benefits of blockchain to the problem of reconciliating interbank transactions, like an immutable record of all transactions that can be consulted whenever a dispute over a transaction occurs.

The Corda-based Spunta Banca system has launched in October 2020 and it is processing millions of transactions daily for a network of more than 100 Italian banks. In a nutshell, it allows to run in almost real time and with extremely high reliability a process in a trustless network of banks that historically has been highly time consuming and prone to errors.

7.5.1.1 IBM FoodTrust

FoodTrust (https://www.ibm.com/blockchain/solutions/food-trust) is a private blockchain system developed by IBM and that uses HLF at its core. In a nutshell, FoodTrust is a solution that connects the participants in a food supply to create a private, immutable, and shared record of food data. For instance, in the supply chain of a certain brand of coffee, FoodTrust can be used to collect all the data that are generated from harvesting the beans until the coffee ends up in our home in a fancy-colored package.

FoodTrust is highly customizable and it is normally part of a broader 'solution' that IBM brings to customers in one of the following 7 use cases: supply chain efficiency, brand trust, food safety, sustainability, food freshness, food fraud, and food waste. The supply chain efficiency and food waste use cases, for instance, leverage the transparency and real-time information sharing of private blockchain to distribute the data across the supply chain. Supply chain data can then be analyzed in real time to identify and reduce bottlenecks or to identify critical parts of the supply chain where food gets wasted in large amounts. Other cases of FoodTrust being used leverage other benefits of a blockchain-based solution. For instance, in the brand trust and food safety use cases, the objective is to build a detailed and, most importantly, immutable account of the provenance of all the ingredients of a specific product that customers find in a supermarket. This can be used either for marketing purposes or to address food safety emergencies. For instance, if a batch of contaminated products is found (this happens not so rarely, for instance, for frozen food products), the information regarding where the products in this batch have been delivered and where the ingredients used in this batch have come from is available in the system. Most importantly, it can be trusted because by design it cannot have been tampered with by any node, since it is stored on a HLF world state and blockchain. Finally, the food freshness use case leverages a private blockchain system in combination with IoT technology. For instance, IoT sensors can be deployed along a food supply chain, and the data produced by them can be stored in a private blockchain ledger, to create a reliable record that demonstrates the freshness of a product. For instance, it could be possible to demonstrate that some fish that we find in a supermarket was caught no later than 24 hours before and, since then, has always been stored or transported at a temperature comprised between one and four degrees. The potential of combining blockchain and IoT technology is discussed in depth in the next chapter.

7.6 Conclusions

This chapter has discussed how we can build private blockchain systems. We started by considering Ethereum, discussing how the same implementation running the public Ethereum network can also run on a network of private nodes. Then, we looked in depth at two frameworks for developing private blockchain systems: Corda and HLF. For each of them, we focused on specific design features that are possible only due to their 'private' nature, specifically because the identity of the nodes in a private blockchain is known. In Corda, we have seen how the ledger can be designed on a need-to-know basis and how the states stored in it can evolve based on a transaction validation that generalizes the UTXO mechanism introduced for Bitcoin in Chapter 5. For HLF, we have discussed how channels and private data collections can be used to implement a need-to-know ledger. Then, we focused on presenting the way in which transactions are validated, distributed, and executed in HLF, which differs substantially from what we have seen for the public blockchain, like Bitcoin or Ethereum.

The next chapter focuses on understanding the synergy between blockchain and the IoT. In recent times, the IoT has powered the so-called 'smart' revolution, allowing organizations to generate and collect massive amount of data regarding their business. Blockchain obviously can play a key role in the management of such data, particularly in scenarios where IoT data must be collected and stored to improve the trust among a network of collaborating business parties.

7.7 Questions and exercises

1   Consider the business scenario of a private network of universities, like the network of public universities in a US state. These universities must share student data (regarding academics, but also payment of fees, dormitory occupancy, etc.). At the same time, however, they also have to protect the more sensitive student data, which can be shared with other institutions only if strictly necessary. This network of universities also would need to automate the processing of student information, like generating automatically student offers or transcripts. Based on these considerations, and other assumptions that you may want to make, discuss which type of private blockchain system you would suggest using (Ethereum, Corda or HLF).
2   Consider the BC4C and BC4C-CGM systems introduced in the Part 1 of this book. For each of them, discuss whether it would be possible to implement them using Corda and HLF, and, if so, whether it would be advisable (in particular, what would be the main benefits and drawbacks of using a private blockchain to implement these systems?)
3   Discuss a business scenario and a specific application in it that can be supported successfully by a private blockchain implemented using Ethereum, Corda, or HLF.
4   A corporate travel agency wants to deploy a private blockchain to track the deals and reservations with affiliated customers, airlines, and hotels. In particular, airlines and hotels can offer special deals to the agency, which in turn can offer them to its customers, which can place reservations. However, airlines and hotels want their

deals to be visible only to the travel agency and the customers, and not to their competitors. Discuss to which extent the private blockchains presented in this chapter can fulfill these requirements, and which blockchain-specific features could be used.

5 Consider a node A in HLF that has the copy of the world state shown in Table 7.1:

A then receives a new block containing the transaction listed in Table 7.2:

Indicate which transactions should the node consider valid, which ones should it consider invalid (and therefore discarded), and how the world state would look after the block has been processed.

Table 7.1 World state of HLF node

Business object	Attribute	Value
R1	Status	Sent
R2	Status	Approved
R3	Status	Rejected
R4	Status	Sent

Table 7.2 Transactions received by HLF node

Transaction	Chaincode function	Input set	Output set
T1	Approve(R1)	R1{Status: Sent}	R1{Status: Approved}
T2	Reject(R4)	R4{Status: Sent}	R4{Status: Rejected}
T3	Approve(R3)	R3{Status: Sent}	R4{Status: Approved}
T4	Create(R5)	N/A	R5{Status: Sent}
T5	Reject(R2)	R2{Status: Sent}	R2{Status: Rejected}
T6	Reissue(R3)	R3{Status: Rejected}	R3{Status: Sent}
T7	Create(R6)	N/A	R6{Status: Sent}

8   Blockchain and the Internet of Things

8.1 What is the IoT?

If you have recently looked in a shop for a lightbulb or a thermostat, you may have found products advertised as *smart* or *IoT-enabled*. By a further inspection of the product packaging, you may have read that the product can connect to the Internet and be remotely controlled using a Web application or an app on your smartphone. Also, some products may advertise that they can learn your habits and, based on their learning, update their functionality autonomously. For instance, a lightbulb may automatically dim itself at a certain time of the day, or a thermostat may decrease a room's temperature when you are not in it.

Such products are good examples of consumer-oriented IoT applications. More precisely, the term Internet of Things (IoT) was coined to describe physical objects equipped with sensors, a computing device such as a microprocessor, and some sort of network connectivity (e.g., Bluetooth, 4G mobile Internet, etc.) [AIM10]. These features enable objects to become 'smart', that is, they can be aware of their own conditions and of the conditions of the environment around them, and autonomously react to changes in these conditions. In addition, smart objects are meant to interact with each other and with traditional computer applications through the Internet. For example, a smart thermostat can sense the room temperature, and a smart lightbulb the light in the room. Together they can infer that the sun is setting, and therefore activate the heating

DOI: 10.4324/9781003321187-10

and lighting. Also, they can use other information available on the Internet, such as online weather forecasts, to determine how to act.

8.2 Foundations of the IoT

Although the IoT is a relatively new paradigm, some of its elements are not entirely brand-new. Indeed, the IoT bases its foundations on pre-existing concepts and technologies. These already existed before the term IoT was even coined and they were in some cases extended to better meet the needs of IoT. We discuss these technologies briefly in this section.

8.2.1 Radio Frequency Identification (RFID)

If you have visited a departmental store and bought some clothes, you may have noticed a small, usually squared, microchip-like adhesive paper attached to the clothes or their price tag. That item is a 'Radio Frequency Identification' (RFID) tag. It is a low-cost disposable piece of electronics used to track the object to which it is attached (e.g., a pair of trousers). More in detail, an RFID tag can react to a radio-frequency message sent by a transmitter. In this way, the transmitter can know which tags are close to its proximity and, if the tag is equipped with additional sensors, the transmitter also senses their conditions. RFID tags can be active or passive. The 'passive' RFID tags require no power source and operate only with the energy emitted by the transmitter. For this reason, they are typically not equipped with sensors, and are used to transmit only a unique ID that identifies the object to which they are attached. Conversely, the 'active' RFID tags operate on batteries or other types of power source (e.g., a solar panel), and are often equipped with sensors to provide information on the conditions of the attached object.

As in the example of the department store, RFID tags are often used for asset management. As shown in Figure 8.1, by placing transmitters close to the exit door of the store, on the store shelves and in the warehouse, the department store can know which clothes are available in the warehouse, which ones are exposed in the storefront, and which ones have been bought. Also, RFID tags provide effective anti-theft protection.

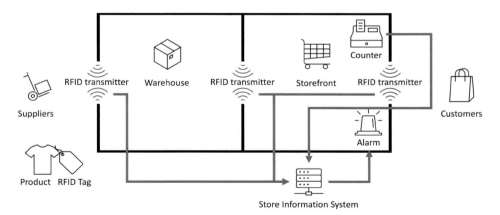

Figure 8.1 Example of an RFID infrastructure in a retail store.

If somebody steals a pair of trousers, the transmitter at the exit door can detect that the clothes are leaving the store and report it to the store information system. In turn, the information system can check the list of sold items and, if the clothes are not on the list, will then trigger an alarm.

Originally, RFID tags were meant to be used within the boundary of an organization. There were in fact no standards to uniquely name the tags, which prevented querying external organizations on information about a specific tag. To solve this issue, allowing for instance RFID tags to be used through a whole supply chain, the EPCglobal standard was created [SAB07]. Specifically, the EPCglobal standardizes the messages sent by an RFID tag. It also specifies how different organizations should interact with the tags and exchange information regarding them.

Despite the many similarities with the IoT, it is worth noting that the RFID is not an IoT solution 'per se'. Until the advent of active RFID tags, the only information on the attached physical objects that a RFID tag could produce was a fixed identification string. Also, RFID tags are not capable of autonomously communicating with each other. Instead, it is up to the transmitter to periodically query the tags in its proximity. Finally, although the EPCglobal standardizes how to make tags interoperable among different organizations, it does not specify that the communication should happen over the Internet.

8.2.2 Wireless sensor and actuator network (WSAN)

If you stayed in a hotel or worked in an office built during this century, it is likely that the heating, ventilation, and air conditioning (HVAC) in that building was controlled by a wireless sensor and actuator network (WSAN), such as the one shown in Figure 8.2. As the name suggests, a WSAN is made up of several small-scale sensing devices, which are responsible for collecting information on the environment where they are located (e.g., temperature sensors in the rooms and shared spaces). Such information is then forwarded by the sensing devices to a central computational node, named 'sink', via wireless communications, e.g., a Wi-Fi or Bluetooth connection. In turn, the sink aggregates the information and, potentially interacting with other information systems, determines if actions must be taken (e.g., switch on the heating system to raise the temperature of a room to 20°C). If so, the sink communicates with the devices controlling the machines that can change the environment where they are located, named 'actuators'. Once instructed by the sink, the actuators activate the machines to take the desired action (e.g., switching on the furnace or a heat pump).

With respect to a traditional control system, a WSAN offers several advantages. Firstly, it does not require any wiring and, more importantly, it allows to easily reconfigure the sensors and actuators. Indeed, the sink can discover new sensors and actuators that are added to the network. Similarly, it can detect when existing sensors and actuators are malfunctioning or no longer active and exclude them from the network. Also, the sink can detect if the sensors and the actuators are repositioned (e.g., the temperature sensor in a storage room is moved to a corridor) and reconfigure the network accordingly.

When compared to the IoT, its main difference with WSANs lies in the way in which the computation is performed and messages are exchanged. Indeed, sensors and actuators have very limited computational power, which is often sacrificed to achieve lower energy consumption. Therefore, the operations that they can execute on the

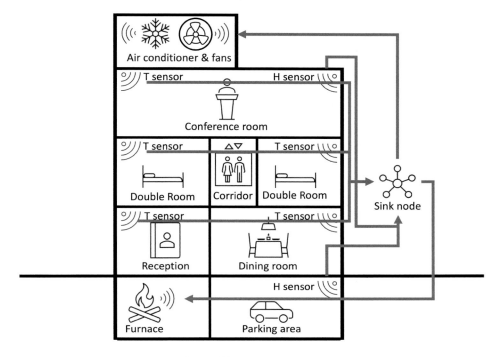

Figure 8.2 WSAN components (example).

sensor data are limited to filtering out incorrect sensor readings and performing simple aggregations. For the same reason, they are rarely capable of directly communicating with each other. Therefore, it is up to the sink to discover and coordinate the sensors and the actuators, as well as analyzing sensor data and interacting with other computer systems.

8.3 Applications for the IoT

At the beginning of this chapter, we have already mentioned one of the IoT potential applications, that is, smart buildings. However, this is only one possible application for the IoT. In this section, we provide a (non-exhaustive) list of applications where the IoT has been successfully exploited.

8.3.1 Logistics

When applied to the logistics domain, the IoT is used to monitor the conditions and the position of the goods that must be delivered [SYZ+21]. In this application, the IOT not only allows to track where the goods are located and to estimate how long the delivery process will take, but it is also used to react to failures. For instance, a smart shipping container can detect if its content has been spoiled (e.g., because, while its content needed to be kept at a low temperature, by mistake the container has remained for an entire day under the hot sun on a docked ship) and alert, for instance, the manufacturer of the goods. The manufacturer, in turn, can contact the shipper, asking to discard the content of the container, while in the meantime organizing a new delivery. Further details on how the IoT can be coupled with the blockchain in the logistics industry are provided later in this chapter in the case study on artifact-driven process monitoring.

8.3.2 Healthcare

By relying on smart medical equipment and smart rooms, a hospital can easily keep track of the conditions of the patients, as well as their treatment [DF19]. For example, the IoT technology allows to know if a patient was moved to a different room, and if the patient has taken all the drugs prescribed to him or her. All this can be done without doctors having to manually enter this information in the patient's health record. Additionally, IoT technology can also allow us to keep track of the inventory of the hospital and restock drugs and medications automatically.

In the case of assisted living, the advantages that the IoT paradigm brings to patient management are even more noticeable. Firstly, the IoT makes it possible for a general practitioner to remotely monitor chronically ill patients and patients that were recently dismissed from a hospital. In addition, it can even allow to remotely perform medical treatments, such as administering insulin to patients affected by diabetes.

8.3.3 Manufacturing

The IoT is a central paradigm of the so-called Industry 4.0 revolution [ZXK+17]. Indeed, by making manufactured products smart, it is possible to keep track of their usage after they have left the factory. This allows to predict potential product failures due to wear and tear, and to schedule preventive maintenance accordingly. Also, the IoT allows to detect issues that were not foreseen when the product was initially designed, but that emerge during the product usage. This information can be then used to selectively recall defective products, or to improve future versions of a product.

When applied to machines on a manufacturing production line, the IoT makes them self-reconfigurable, so as to increase the agility of the shop floor. Also, the IoT allows to dynamically keep track of the level of wear and tear of the machines, and to perform corrective actions to minimize the machine downtime.

8.3.4 Smart cities

By making street furniture smart, the IoT can significantly simplify the management of cities in which we live [AHL+16]. For example, street lamps can automatically adjust their brightness depending on the traffic or weather conditions. Similarly, traffic lights and signs can be made aware of accidents and traffic conditions, so as to automatically reroute the traffic. The same devices that we mentioned earlier when presenting smart home applications can be used for public buildings, such as university campuses and shopping malls. In addition, smart devices can be used to monitor the level of air, noise, and light pollution. IoT systems coupled with deep learning-enabled image recognition systems may even provide evidence that a crime is occurring in the city streets.

8.3.5 Sustainable energy

By making energy meters smart, the IoT enables utility companies to know in real time the power consumption of their customers. In this way, it is possible to predict with greater accuracy when a surge in energy utilization is going to happen and take countermeasures [Sal20]. Smart energy meters are also an enabling technology for the so-called microgrids. In a microgrid, users who have installed on their site alternative energy sources, such as solar panels, can inject into a local power grid the energy that they are producing in excess and be rewarded. Finally, when deployed at power stations, smart energy meters simplify tracking the provenance of the energy being produced. Therefore, they can be used to apply different prices depending on the energy source, for instance incentivizing renewable energy, and penalizing energy obtained from burning carbon fuels.

8.4 Combining the IoT with blockchain

Until now in this chapter, we have focused on the general advantages that the IoT paradigm brings. However, it is worth noting that the adoption of the IoT also presents several open issues [MSD+12]. Some of these are related to the hardware nature of smart objects, such as reducing energy consumption and increasing computational power. Other issues are instead focused on the communication and interaction among smart objects.

Among these issues, the need for a common communications channel to allow smart objects to interact with each other, and to uniquely identify each of them, has arisen. Another relevant issue is how to make the IoT 'trusted'. In particular, smart objects often run unattended, they potentially have a long life, and they are usually always connected to the public Internet. These characteristics advocate for adequate security measures to be deployed, such as:

- **Access control:** Smart objects should be controlled only by trusted parties. Also, in some cases, the data collected by smart objects should be accessible only to specific subjects.
- **Secure data provenance:** The origin of the data collected and exchanged by smart objects should always be known. No subject should be allowed to alter the data produced by a smart object.
- **Identity management:** Each smart object should be uniquely identifiable. No subject should be able to impersonate a smart object and, for instance, generate data on its behalf.

To address these issues, recent research efforts have been made to combine the IoT with blockchain. In particular, as shown in Figure 8.3, the blockchain can be seen as a trusted communication channel, which allows different untrusted smart objects to communicate with each other. Using a blockchain, smart objects can submit their sensor readings and commands for other devices such as blockchain transactions, which can then be accessed by the devices that need this information. On top of that, business applications can trust the data and events coming from smart objects through the blockchain-trusted communication channel. Depending on the capabilities of the blockchain

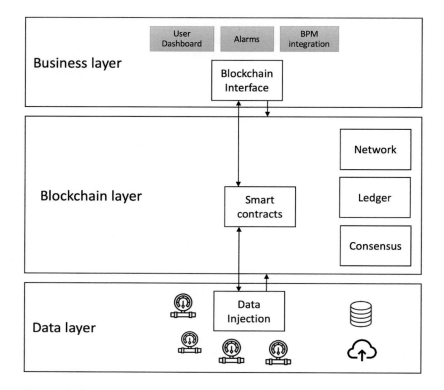

Figure 8.3 Conceptual architecture of a blockchain-based IoT application.

and of the smart objects, the aggregation of sensor data can be performed by the smart objects themselves, by the blockchain with the use of smart contracts, or by the business applications.

As we have learnt in this book, whenever new data have to be stored in a blockchain, a transaction must be issued. Transactions contain, beside the data, the address of the sender node, which is unique. In addition, since the transactions are digitally signed using the private key of the sender, it is impossible for an attacker to impersonate the sender. Therefore, by keeping track of the accounts associated to the smart objects, it is possible to address the issues of 'secure data provenance' and 'identity management' mentioned above.

Blockchains equipped with smart contracts in IoT applications can also address the issue of 'access control'. Indeed, smart contracts allow to define access control rules based on the address of the node that invokes them. In this way, it is possible to allow an actuator to react only to commands sent by trusted devices. For example, a smart light-bulb may refuse requests to switch on or off coming from unauthorized devices. Only when a new device (e.g., the smartphone of the owner of an apartment) is registered, such requests can be accepted. Smart contracts can also be used to discard sensor readings coming from untrusted devices. For example, let us suppose that a specific batch of smart thermostats is found to be faulty, causing a furnace on which they are installed to be always on. The manufacturer could recall the faulty batch and, while waiting for the thermostats to be replaced, notify a smart contract to discard transactions coming from those devices. It is worth noting that, in most blockchain implementations, all the data sent through transactions are accessible to all the nodes of that blockchain. In that case, if one wants read access control on sensor readings, it is necessary to either store the data off chain or to rely on a private blockchain that supports read access control mechanisms, such as channels and private data collections in Hyperledger Fabric (as seen in Chapter 7).

There is also a clear synergy between the IoT and blockchain. On the one hand, in fact, we already discussed how the IoT can exploit the blockchain to address some of its current issues. On the other hand, by relying on smart objects, the blockchain can also benefit from adopting IoT technology. Specifically, the IoT can be used to bridge the gap between the on-chain and off-chain worlds.

To this aim, the sensor readings can be used by a smart contract to receive information from the off-chain world. For example, considering the BC4C-CGM system of Chapter 4, one may wish to extend it to also support chess tournaments held in person. In this case, the players may use a smart chessboard that can detect the position of each chess piece. In this scenario, the smart contract of BC4C-CGM can receive information from the smart chessboard and use this information to infer the status of a game. In this way, the BC4C-CGM blockchain can automatically detect checkmate, and then transfer the deposit to the winner of a game. In addition, it could also detect when an incorrect move is performed and potentially disqualify the player who tried to execute it.

Alternatively, the events generated by a smart contract can drive the actuators to make 'trusted changes' in the off-chain world. For example, a delivery company may use a blockchain to keep track of its shipment orders and integrate them with smart lockers in convenient locations where the customers can pick up the goods that they ordered. When a shipment has been paid and the goods have been delivered to the desired locker, a smart contract may wait for the customer to send a transaction once he or she is in front of the locker. If the address of the account from which such a transaction is originated matches the one of the recipient indicated in the shipment order, then the smart contract may command the smart locker to open its door, allowing the customer to pick up the goods.

8.5 Challenges in blockchain-based IoT platforms

Several open issues in the IoT can be addressed with the blockchain. At the same time, the blockchain can rely on the IoT as a mean to interact with the off-chain world. However, building a blockchain-based IoT platform is not straightforward. The challenges of combining blockchain and IoT are discussed in detail in this section. Most of these challenges already exists for 'non-IoT' blockchain-based applications. However, they become even more relevant when the IoT is adopted, especially considering the power consumption and communications requirements that smart objects are expected to have.

8.5.1 Latency

Latency in a computer system can be defined as the difference between the time at which a command is issued and the time at which its execution actually begins. Latency is relevant for instance when transferring information: as an example, depending on the connection speed and the Internet traffic conditions, it may take a while between the time at which we enter a URL in a Web browser and the time at which the Web page that we requested is sent to us and shown by the browser. As we know, before a transaction is included in the blockchain, it must be selected by a miner or a validator and included in a new block. This process is usually quite lengthy, particularly when the blockchain adopts a consensus protocol based on proof-of-work. Therefore, depending on the type of blockchain used and on how many transactions are simultaneously submitted, it can take from a few seconds up to several minutes for a transaction to be included into a block. Consequently, if smart objects communicate frequently with each other, and especially if they have to react to information sent by other nodes, the blockchain alone may not meet the latency requirements to be used as a communication channel.

8.5.2 Volume

Most blockchains limit the amount of information that can be included into a transaction, typically in the order of tens to hundreds of kilobytes. This limit is adequate for most IoT applications. However, if sensor readings are sent in bulk (for instance to overcome the latency mentioned above), or if large data must be sent (e.g., audio, images, or videos), then the blockchain transactions alone may no longer be sufficient for exchanging this type of information.

8.5.3 Computing power

Mining a new block, as we learned, is a computationally intensive process. Indeed, when a consensus protocol based on proof-of-work is adopted, the miners must race with each other to be the first in creating a new block. Thus, they must be equipped with very powerful and power-hungry computing devices. This strongly conflicts with the low-power requirements that smart objects are expected to meet. Even when consensus protocols based on other mechanisms – such as proof-of-stake or voting – are adopted, the computational power required to assemble a new block may still be too high for most smart objects.

8.5.4 Storage requirements

As the blockchain involves an append-only ledger, old data stored in the ledger will never be deleted. Therefore, storage requirements for a blockchain are expected to grow forever at a pace determined by the number of transactions issued. In particular, the size of the ledger of most public blockchains has now exceeded hundreds of gigabytes, which is well beyond the storage capacity of IoT smart objects.

8.6 IOTA: a DLT for the IoT

IOTA is a blockchain specifically designed with IoT applications in mind, which aims at overcoming the challenges discussed earlier in this chapter. It features fast transaction processing time, low computational power required by the nodes, and no processing fee for transactions [SM20].

Instead of requiring multiple transactions to be stored in a block referencing its predecessor – as it is usually done in blockchains – IOTA relies on a completely different data structure, called the 'Tangle'.[1] Figure 8.4 shows the main differences between a blockchain structure and Tangle. In particular, each transaction in IOTA is included in an individual block, named tip, which has to reference from 2 to 8 other existing blocks at any point in time in order to be valid. Therefore, rather than resembling a chain, the Tangle has a grid-like structure. More properly, the Tangle is a direct acyclic graph, i.e., a graph with no loops (acyclic) and in which edges have a direction (from a source node to a sink node).

In addition, the IOTA network is constituted of nodes, but none of these nodes are required to act as 'miners' of new blocks. A node that submits a transaction is responsible for creating the associated block (i.e., connecting the new tip to up to eight preceding transactions in the Tangle) and forwarding it to its neighbor nodes via a gossip protocol. The neighbors then validate the block and, if valid, forward it to their neighbors, and so on. However, to prevent spam transactions, a node must provide a lightweight proof-of-work when creating a new block. If a node lacks computational resources, it is possible for that node to delegate the proof-of-work to a remote node.

Since no miners are required, IOTA applies no processing fee to transactions. However, IOTA also provides its own cryptocurrency, named 'Iota', which can be optionally used by nodes to transfer value. Unlike other blockchains, like Bitcoin or Ethereum, in which new cryptocurrency units are produced through mining, IOTA has a finite number of cryptocurrency units (2,779,530,283,277,761 units to be precise)

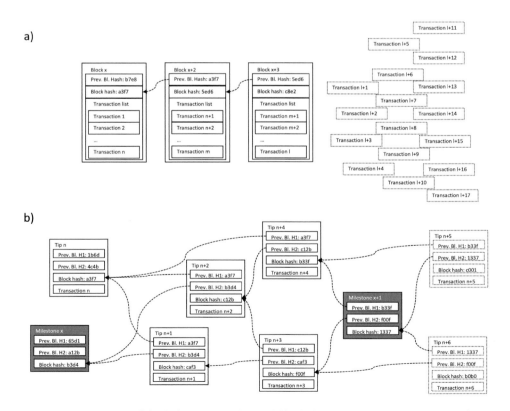

Figure 8.4 Structure of the ledger in a traditional blockchain (a) and in IOTA Tangle (b).

that were created when the IOTA blockchain was launched and distributed among its investors.

To ensure that a block is valid, each IOTA node must perform the following steps:

- Verify that the block is well-formed, that is, all the required fields are populated, and the size of the transaction data does not exceed 32KB.
- Verify that the signature of the block is valid, that is, that a block has been digitally signed by the sender.
- Verify that the block references valid blocks, that is, it contains their hash.
- Verify that the result of the lightweight proof-of-work is correct.
- If Iotas are exchanged, verify that the balance of the sender account is not negative after the transaction is processed.

If any of these validation steps fails, the node discards the block and does not forward it to its neighbors. Additionally, to handle double-spending issues, a node verifies if two or more pending transactions would lead to a negative balance of the sender node. In this case, the node identifies the blocks containing such transactions as conflicting and forwards this information to its neighbors. Nodes then resort to voting to determine which blocks among the conflicting ones should be accepted, and which ones should be discarded.

To ensure that the Tangle is consistent throughout all the nodes, special blocks named 'milestones' are periodically issued by a central client, named 'coordinator'. A milestone is subject to the same validation process as the other blocks. Therefore, it must reference from 2 to 8 previous blocks. In this way, nodes can be certain that a transaction has been confirmed if its block has been directly or indirectly referenced by a milestone. Note that the presence of the 'coordinator' appears to violate the principles of blockchain that we introduced in Part 1. The coordinator, in fact, can be seen as an intermediary that all nodes of an IOTA network must trust. The designers of IOTA are aware of this problem. The coordinator was introduced as a 'temporary' design feature that could be removed once the Tangle reaches a sufficient size. However, real-world IOTA implementations seem to maintain the coordinator as a permanent feature.

Thanks to the Tangle and its transaction validation mechanisms, IOTA allows for multiple branches to co-exist and, at the same time, be valid. Indeed, only branches containing invalid transactions are discarded. Also, a node can issue new transactions and create the corresponding blocks while being disconnected from the network. Once it is back online, it forwards these blocks to its neighbors. These blocks eventually are added by all the nodes and confirmed by a milestone, provided that they do not cause any double-spending issue.

The aforementioned characteristics make IOTA particularly suited for IoT applications. By not requiring miners, transactions can be validated in a very short time, thus overcoming 'latency' issues. By relying on a consensus protocol more lightweight than, for instance, proof-of-work, IOTA makes it possible for 'low-powered' smart objects to actively take part as nodes. Finally, by not needing nodes to be always online or to use a reliable network, IOTA can be used as a primary communication channel for smart objects.

However, there are still two main issues that IOTA needs to address. Firstly, IOTA was originally not designed to support smart contracts. Therefore, on-chain validation mechanism on transaction data cannot be implemented in IOTA. In addition, as discussed before, IOTA still relies on a centralized entity, i.e., the coordinator, to confirm transactions. Secondly, IOTA lacks access control mechanisms on transaction data. This makes it possible for any node to access all transactions issued, as well as their contents.

To address these issues, two parallel projects have been initiated by the consortium behind IOTA: IOTA 2.0 and IOTA Streams.

8.6.1 IOTA 2.0

IOTA 2.0 aims at overcoming several of the limitations that were found in the current implementation of IOTA [PMC+20]. In early 2022, a test network has been made available for developers to start experimenting with IOTA 2.0.

One of the key changes in IOTA 2.0 is the introduction of 'mana', a value characterizing each node independent from the Iota cryptocurrency, which is used to determine the extent to which each account can be trusted. When a new transaction exchanging Iotas is issued, a quantity of mana proportional to the number of Iotas specified in the transaction is 'pledged' to an account chosen by the account that owns the Iotas. The 'mana' is then used to control how new transactions are handled by nodes. Firstly, the mana value determines how many transactions can be issued by a node, thus limiting the throughput. In addition, nodes can issue new transactions only if they have enough mana, thus reducing the risk of spam. Secondly, the neighbor nodes are determined by the amount of mana that they own (IOTA calls this feature 'Autopeering'). In particular, the gossip protocol forwards newly created blocks to nodes with a similar amount of mana. In this way, multiple malicious nodes are not able to become neighbors of an honest node with higher mana and corrupt it, for instance by sending fake transactions.

Another relevant change in IOTA 2.0 is the need to include an accurate timestamp, that is, an absolute date and time reference, when a new block is issued. This is addressed by a mechanism through which a timestamp is validated by the other nodes to ensure it reflects reality. If this is too far off from the current time, the associated block is discarded. In this way, transactions can be ordered based on the timestamp, and milestone blocks are no longer required. This allows IOTA 2.0 to remove the coordinator, thus becoming fully decentralized.

In addition, IOTA 2.0 introduces support for smart contracts by making two different execution environments available. A 'native' environment, based on the WebAssembly (WASM) virtual machine [RTH+18], allows to develop smart contracts that exploit all the native functionality of IOTA. In addition, an environment that mimics the Ethereum EVM is also available. In this way, smart contracts built in Solidity can be easily ported to IOTA, and developers acquainted with Ethereum can easily start coding smart contracts for IOTA.

Other enhancements offered by IOTA 2.0 are a faster transaction processing time, the possibility to mine custom tokens, and the use of dynamic proof-of-work algorithms. Custom tokens allow IOTA to support NFTs and private cryptocurrencies. Since proof-of-work in IOTA is required only to counter spam, dynamic algorithms allow to adjust the complexity depending on the number of spam transactions being submitted.

8.6.2 *IOTA streams*

Being designed as a public blockchain, IOTA assumes that all the transactions are accessible by all the nodes. However, when confidential data must be exchanged among specific users, this behavior becomes undesirable. We have already seen in Chapter 6 how this problem is addressed, for instance, by Corda (through the need-to-know ledger) and Hyperledger Fabric (through channels). To address this issue, the IOTA Streams project introduces support for private branches. Like in Hyperledger Fabric, these are also named 'channels'.[2]

To access a channel, an account must subscribe to it by sending a request to the 'author', i.e., the account that created the channel. To allow that account to issue new transactions in the channel, the author must grant access to it. Transactions in a channel can be either sent in plain text or be encrypted. The transactions in plain text are accessible and can be validated by all the subscribers of a channel. Conversely, the encrypted transactions are accessible only to specific subscribers, and they can be encrypted with either the public key of the recipient or with a pre-shared key.

Public keys are effective when the transaction is addressed only to one specific recipient. Conversely, as shown in Figure 8.5, if multiple recipients must receive the same transaction, it requires multiple copies of it to be sent, each one encrypted with the public key of that specific recipient. To solve this issue, the sender and the recipient can agree on a common pre-shared key to be used to encrypt transactions. In this way, only a single copy of the transaction encrypted with the pre-shared key is required, since all the authorized recipients will have that key and use it to decrypt the transaction. However, IOTA Streams provides no mechanisms for subscribers to agree on and to distribute the pre-shared keys.

Thank to channels and encryption, IOTA Streams allow to implement access control mechanisms on transaction data. In this way, IOTA can be used to also send confidential information.

8.6.3 *IOTA applications in the IoT*

Several prototypical projects exploiting IOTA for IoT applications exist. Among these, the most mature applications are the IOTA Mobility and the IOTA Industry Marketplace initiatives.

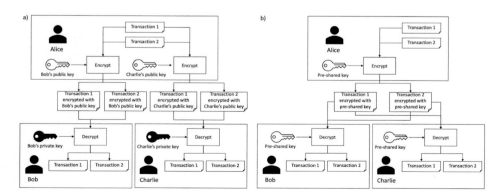

Figure 8.5 Managing encrypted transactions in IOTA Streams through (a) public key encryption or (b) pre-shared key encryption.

8.6.3.1 IOTA Mobility

Following the IoT paradigm, IOTA Mobility aims at turning electric vehicles into smart objects. Thanks to the many sensors that are installed in a modern vehicle, it is possible to collect information on the driving style of the owner, the level of wear and tear of its components, the faults it developed, and the parts that were replaced. This information is particularly useful to car manufacturers to improve the design of their own products.

Thanks to IOTA, it is possible to store this information on the blockchain, making it immutable and persistent. Also, since IOTA supports cryptocurrency payments, the owner of a vehicle can use IOTA also to sell the information collected on his/her own vehicle. In addition, IOTA allows electric vehicles and charging stations to have their own wallet, and to automatically negotiate payments whenever the users must recharge their own vehicle. When no charging stations are available, IOTA also opens the possibility for an electric vehicle to be recharged by another one, paying back the energy consumed with Iota cryptocurrency units. Finally, IOTA allows vehicles to automatically pay parking and tolls, making the driving experience entirely cashless.

The IOTA Mobility initiative has been embraced by the car manufacturer Jaguar Land Rover, which is testing IOTA as a means for sharing data and paying tolls and parking on its cars [IOT22a].

8.6.3.2 IOTA Industry Marketplace

The IOTA Industry Marketplace [IOT22] is a vendor- and industry-neutral platform to facilitate machine-to-machine communications and order processing in the context of Industry 4.0. Thanks to the IoT, this platform allows smart objects to directly issue, negotiate, and process orders and payments, without relying on traditional information systems, such as a Manufacturing Execution System (MES) or an Enterprise Resource Planner (ERP). In this context, IOTA is used to certify the information exchanged and to handle payments.

Participants in the IOTA Industry Marketplace play two different roles. Service providers offer data, products, and services for a fee. Service requesters search for service meeting-specific criteria. A single participant, like a smart object or a human being, can impersonate both roles. All steps in the negotiation process are traced with IOTA. IOTA is also responsible for collecting the fees paid by the service requester to the service provider when a negotiation succeeds. To this aim, a software component, named 'Market Manager', acts as a bridge between IOTA and the associated participant. Whenever a new message is issued by the participant, the Market Manager translates it into an IOTA transaction, which is then submitted.

To demonstrate the advantages brought by the IOTA Industry Marketplace, a prototypical deployment with actual tooling machines has been deployed at the Otto-von-Guericke University (OVGU) in Magdeburg. In addition, experiments are currently carried out by WeWash shared laundry services.

8.7 Implementing IoT applications with existing blockchains

In the previous section, we discussed how IOTA can overcome most of the challenges of blockchain-based IoT platforms. However, it is worth noting that it is still possible to build an effective IoT platform with the other blockchains that we presented earlier in this book. While doing that, however, we must be careful when defining which components of the platform run on the blockchain, and how the aforementioned challenges of IoT can be mitigated with a proper design. In this section, we discuss which considerations should be made when building an IoT platform using the Bitcoin, Ethereum, and Hyperledger Fabric blockchains.

8.7.1 Bitcoin

As we have learned in Chapter 5, Bitcoin is primarily designed to exchange cryptocurrency units. It does not support smart contracts, the time required to validate a transaction is significantly high, and the amount of off-chain data that can be attached to a transaction is very limited. Nevertheless, an IoT platform based on Bitcoin can still be implemented.

To address the low volume of data, Bitcoin should be sided by an off-chain communication channel, as shown in Figure 8.6. In this setting, the actual data is sent through the off-chain channel, while their digest (hash) is sent in a Bitcoin transaction. In this way, the IoT platform can still provide information on the provenance of sensor readings. In addition, it can guarantee the immutability of those data. By computing the digest of the data being received and comparing it with the one on the blockchain, nodes can detect if the data have been tampered with. Finally, as it is virtually impossible to reconstruct the data from the digest, the IoT platform can guarantee the confidentiality of the sensor readings, provided that proper access control mechanisms are implemented on the other communication channel. However, by having the data effectively off chain, the blockchain can no longer be used to enforce the persistence of the data.

To address the high computing power and storage requirements, Bitcoin allows to create and deploy light nodes. Light nodes do not take part in the mining process and are only responsible for submitting transactions and receiving new blocks. Thus, they

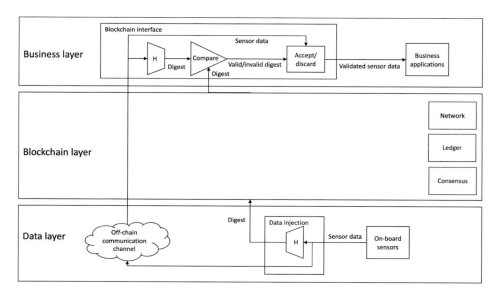

Figure 8.6 Architecture of a blockchain-based IoT application with an off-chain communication channel.

do not have to perform the proof-of-work, which is the most computationally inten-sive task in Bitcoin. In addition, light nodes do not have to store every block locally. Conversely, they store only the information on which transactions are stored in each block. Thus, they can retrieve only the transactions that they need by querying a full node (i.e., a node that has a copy of the whole ledger) in the blockchain. Thus, by deploying light nodes on IoT devices, it is possible for them to take part in the Bitcoin network.

It is worth noting that all IoT platforms based on Bitcoin must deal with Bitcoin's high latency. Indeed, a transaction can take on average ten minutes to be mined into a block. Also, since Bitcoin is prone to forks, nodes must wait for a block to be followed by at least 6 blocks before considering the enclosed transactions as valid. Therefore, the platform is not able to assess the authenticity and provenance of sensor readings for at least one hour. Another disadvantage of Bitcoin is the lack of support for smart contracts. Therefore, all validation mechanisms and access control policies for sensor readings cannot be executed on-chain. Finally, although light nodes have very limited computing power and storage requirements compared to full nodes, their requirements may still be too high for low-powered smart objects (e.g., most smart lightbulbs).

8.7.2 *Ethereum*

Compared to Bitcoin, Ethereum offers smart contracts. Smart contracts allow to imple-ment access control policies when writing information in the blockchain, as well as data validation mechanisms. However, Ethereum smart contracts require a fee to be paid proportional to their complexity and to the amount of information stored.

Therefore, the amount of information and logic that IoT platforms based on Ethereum should store in the blockchain must be carefully planned. One possibility is to store only the digest of the sensor readings in the blockchain, similarly to what is done in IoT systems that use Bitcoin. However, in this case it is only possible to deploy smart contracts that validate the identity of the device submitting the digest. The actual data must be processed off-chain.

Another possibility is to keep sensor readings, as well as the analysis and aggregation tools, entirely off-chain, and to store only the results of the analysis and aggregation in the Ethereum blockchain. By doing so, smart contracts can also be used to validate the information submitted by nodes by performing simple quality checks. In addition, smart contracts can implement part of the business logic of the applications that run on top of the IoT infrastructure. For example, it is possible to execute business processes that depend on IoT events, as well as remuneration schemes for the participants. More about this aspect is discussed in the case study at the end of this chapter.

Like IoT platforms based on Bitcoin, platforms based on Ethereum also have to deal with the high latency. Therefore, if the business logic is implemented as smart contracts, business decisions cannot be taken in real time, which can be unacceptable in some settings. Also, despite Ethereum also offering light nodes, the computing and storage requirements can still be too high for some smart objects.

8.7.3 *Hyperledger Fabric*

Thanks to its private permissioned nature, Hyperledger Fabric allows to address some of the limitations of Bitcoin and Ethereum in IoT scenarios. Since the transactions that are included in a new block are decided by 'orderer' nodes, it is not possible by design in Hyperledger Fabric to have forks. Bear in mind that forks in the blockchain are the main reason behind the high latency of Bitcoin and Ethereum. Also, the consensus protocol adopted by Hyperledger Fabric is not based on proof-of-work. This makes the creation of new blocks fast. These two features allow Hyperledger Fabric to achieve a transaction latency much lower than Bitcoin and Ethereum.

Regarding access control mechanisms, the channels allow Hyperledger Fabric to make part of the blockchain visible only to specific accounts. In addition, private data collections allow Hyperledger Fabric to automatically handle the management and replication of off-chain data among the accounts authorized to access it. At the same time, this allows to store such data on the blockchain whenever they are manipulated. Finally, Hyperledger Fabric supports arbitrarily complex chaincode, which can also process information without disclosing it to unauthorized accounts. These two features allow to achieve fine-grained access control mechanisms for sensor readings.

However, the private nature of Hyperledger Fabric is also a limiting factor for the interoperability of an IoT platform with other systems. Indeed, when a new device must be integrated into the platform, the organizations that control the platform must explicitly grant access to that device. Similarly, if the device needs to communicate to organizations belonging to different channels, it must send transactions multiple times, one per each channel.

8.8 Case study: secure artifact–driven process monitoring

In this chapter, we have learned what the IoT is and how it may benefit from using blockchain. To provide a concrete example of how the blockchain can be helpful in building trust among heterogeneous smart objects, in this section we present the results of an academic project about secure artifact-driven business process monitoring.

8.8.1 Artifact-driven process monitoring

Business Process Management (BPM) is the discipline devoted to the discovery, modeling, automation, monitoring, analysis, and optimization of business process [DLM+18]. The term 'business process' refers to a set of interrelated operations, named business activities, whose aim is to provide value by turning input resources into a value-added product or service. Examples of business processes are the production of a car, the delivery of a shipping container, or the assessment of a mortgage application.

Process monitoring is a specialization of BPM that aims at collecting information on how business processes are executed. This information is then analyzed to determine how well the process is performing. This becomes particularly relevant for business processes that span among multiple independent organizations – potentially competing – and that are composed of tasks that cannot be automated. For example, the delivery of a shipping container is often organized along multiple legs, each one carried out by a different organization using different means of transport. In addition, it is composed of several activities that require manual labor to be performed. For instance, in the first leg a truck driver must drive to the manufacturer's premises, pick up a container, and then drive to an inland terminal. Since nobody has full control on the execution of the whole process, monitoring how the process is executed becomes critical to promptly react to issues that could arise and to take countermeasures to address them. For example, when realizing that a container and its content were damaged, a manufacturer may choose to organize a new shipment to the customer, who might otherwise complain when receiving damaged goods. By knowing in which leg of the delivery process a container was damaged, the manufacturer may also charge a penalty to the organization in charge of that leg.

Collecting monitoring data for inter-organizational processes involving manual activities is quite challenging. As shown in Figure 8.7a, the organizations involved must agree on which information should be collected and made available to the other participants. This often requires a lot of effort – both from a technical, organizational, and security viewpoint – to make information inside corporate information systems accessible to the other participants and it may become infeasible for short-term collaborations. In addition, the users responsible for executing tasks must manually send notifications regarding when the tasks started and when they were completed. The users, unfortunately, are human beings. As such, they may forget to send such notifications, or they may intentionally delay or alter them to achieve a malicious objective.

To solve these issues, artifact-driven process monitoring [Mer19] has been proposed. The key assumption behind this novel approach is that, when executed, activities change the conditions of one or more objects involved in a process. For example, the first-mile

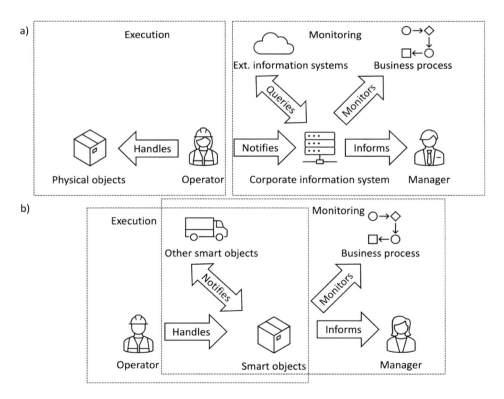

Figure 8.7 Comparison of traditional process monitoring techniques (a) and artifact-driven monitoring (b).

delivery of a container would change its location from the manufacturer's premises to the ones of the inland terminal. Thanks to the IoT, it is possible to make these objects smart. Smart objects can then be aware of their own conditions and of the process in which they are participating. They can also exchange this information with other smart objects in the process. Thus, smart objects can autonomously determine when activities are executed and if they violate the execution order agreed upon by all participants.

Thanks to artifact-driven process monitoring, organizations no longer need to open their information systems to external participants. As shown in Figure 8.7b, it is sufficient for them to receive notifications sent by smart objects to be informed on how the business processes are executed. Users no longer need to explicitly notify when activities are carried out by them. Instead, they only can focus on doing their work right. The smart objects will take care of notifying on their behalf when the tasks are started or completed.

8.8.1.1 Exploiting Ethereum as a trusted communication channel

As discussed before, artifact-driven process monitoring is an effective technique to monitor business processes involving multiple organizations. However, its first implementation presented the same security issues as other IoT applications. When the value of the goods or services handled and produced by a process is high, when the competition among participants is fierce, or when violations in the process execution can cause significant damages, a malicious participant may exploit the IoT smart objects in the process to inject misleading monitoring information. For example, if a violation causing damages occurred, the organization responsible for that action may alter the monitoring information collected by its smart object to cover its tracks. Additionally, it may impersonate another smart object and send forged monitoring information, so as to prove that someone else was responsible for that damage.

To address these issues, mechanisms to enforce access control, to track the provenance of monitoring information, and to securely manage the identity of smart objects are required. As we learned in this chapter, the blockchain is an effective technology to address these issues. For this reason, to achieve trust in artifact-driven process monitoring, the current implementation relies on Ethereum for the exchange of information among smart objects [MPV19]. Ethereum was selected because, at the time, it was one of the few blockchains supporting smart contracts. Also, as a public blockchain, Ethereum makes it easy for smart objects belonging to different organizations to exchange information, opening the way to short-term collaborations among organizations. Finally, at the time it was selected, Ethereum was one of the few blockchains already providing a mature ecosystem, being adopted in several projects, and offering advanced programming tools, libraries, and testing environments.

Each smart object in the system implemented is associated with a unique Ethereum account. In this way, it is not possible for a smart contract to send information on behalf of another one. Thanks to smart contracts, it is possible to deploy access control policies that allow smart objects to send information only if they are authorized to do so (i.e., they take part in the same process execution). Finally, the blockchain guarantees that monitoring information cannot be altered by the participants, and that the identity of the sensors that provided the information is always known.

To counter the limitations that blockchains have in terms of volume and latency of transactions, the architecture of Figure 8.8 has been adopted. Monitoring information

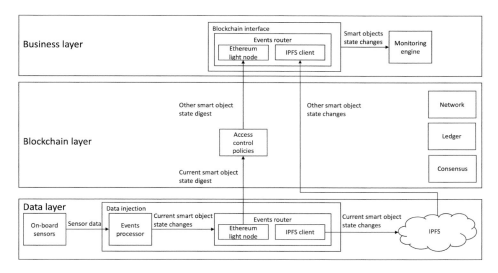

Figure 8.8 Architecture of trusted artifact-driven process monitoring implementation.

is generated when the conditions of the associated smart object change are written in the InterPlanetary File System (IPFS).[3] This is a peer-to-peer distributed file system. Then, the digest of the file containing this information is computed and stored inside an Ethereum transaction. This approach allows to significantly reduce the number of Ethereum transactions issued and their sizes. It also helps to significantly reduce the cost of a transaction in terms of cryptocurrency, i.e., gas required to be executed. Thus, trusted artifact-driven monitoring can be sustainable also from the economic point of view.

The main downside of this approach is that the blockchain cannot guarantee that data are persistently stored, as this task is delegated to the distributed filesystem IFPS. However, if the distributed filesystem is configured to keep multiple replicas of the same file at different locations, and not to accept update or delete operations, the risk that a malicious participant manages to delete or alter monitoring information is almost null. Also, should that participant manage to do so, the digest would no longer match the one in the Ethereum blockchain, and the data could be clearly identified as forged.

This system has been tested with six different types of delivery processes provided by a European logistics company. In total, 53 process executions were monitored, and the average cost for monitoring a single process execution ranged from 787424 to 1538362 gas units (amounting from 0.50€ to 1.00€ given the gas price and conversion rate of March 2019, when the tests were carried out). To further lower the cost of trusted arti-fact-driven monitoring, and to overcome the few limitations in the current implementation, future work in this project aims at replacing Ethereum with IOTA 2.0.

8.9 Conclusions

This chapter has discussed how blockchain can be beneficial for IoT applications. We started by explaining what the IoT paradigm is, and which technologies provide the foundations for it. We also presented some of the applications that benefit from the IoT. Then, we have discussed to which extent blockchain can address some of the open issues in IoT applications. To this aim, we showed how the reference architecture introduced in Chapter 4 can be adopted to build blockchain-based IoT applications. After that, we pointed out which new challenges arise from blockchain-based IoT applications. We also introduced IOTA, a blockchain specifically designed to address such challenges. Finally, we discussed how the blockchain technologies introduced in Chapters 5, 6 and 7 can be adopted to implement IoT applications.

This chapter concludes the second part of the book, devoted to blockchain technology and applications. The third part of the book focuses on assessing whether and how to apply blockchain to specific business scenarios. In particular, we provide a set of decision-making tools to determine if a specific scenario would benefit from a blockchain, and to determine which type of blockchain to adopt. We also explain how the blockchain can play a key role to transform organizations by enabling innovative business models. Finally, we discuss how the blockchain can support the emerging outcome management business scenarios.

8.10 Questions and exercises

1 In Section 8.3, we have discussed some of the most prominent application domains for the IoTs. Can you think of another application domain where IoT could be beneficial? (Hint: there are many!) The criterion is that the domain requires organizations and/or people to interact with physical objects, potentially interacting with each other and with information systems.

2 In Section 8.7, we have discussed which Bitcoin, Ethereum, and Hyperledger Fabric can address the challenges that blockchain presents when combined with the IoT. Can you do a similar comparison for Corda? To do so, you need to remember that Corda offers access control mechanisms at the transaction level, relies on lightweight consensus mechanisms, and does not support smart contracts.

3 You are an electricity distributor and, to address the need for sustainable energy production, you are considering adopting blockchain-based smart meters. In particular, you are interested in having certified information on the provenance of the energy in your grid.

Based on such requirements, discuss the strengths and weaknesses of a solution relying on IOTA, Bitcoin, Ethereum, or Hyperledger Fabric.

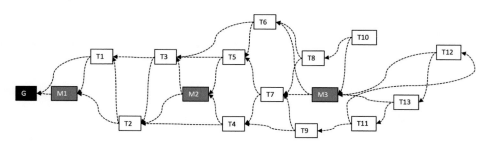

Figure 8.9 An IOTA tangle.

4 Consider the IOTA tangle of Figure 8.9. G represents the genesis block. Tx represents a tip. My represents a milestone. The dashed arrow represents a reference among blocks (for instance, the dashed arrow from T3 to T1 indicates that T3 references T1).

Indicate which transactions have been confirmed, and which ones are still unconfirmed, motivating your answer. Also state if, among the unconfirmed transactions, there are any malformed transactions and, if that is the case, motivate your answer.

Notes

1 For this reason and as advertised by the vendor, IOTA is technically a DLT but not a blockchain. However, given the broader definition of blockchain we provided in this book, we will refer to IOTA as a blockchain.
2 See https://www.iota.org/solutions/streams.
3 See http://ipfs.io.

Part III

Blockchain in business – the ways to use blockchain in practice

The first two parts of this book have focused on blockchain as a mechanism and a technology. In Part 1, we have discussed blockchain conceptually as a mechanism. The blockchain mechanism can be exploited to create the trust required to exchange valuable information and assets in a trustless network of business partners. In Part 2, we have presented different types of blockchain technology that implement the mechanisms introduced in Part 1. In doing so, we have also introduced many concrete applications of blockchain in the real world.

In the discussions in the book so far, we have seen that blockchain is a technology that can support a wide range of business scenarios, but certainly not all of them. So, in which situations or under which conditions does the use of blockchain make sense? And if it makes sense, what would a blockchain application look like from the business perspective? Answering these questions is the focus of Part 3. We begin in Chapter 9 by presenting a set of decision-making tools that help structuring the decision on whether to use blockchain in a given business scenario. In Chapter 10, we look at blockchain from the standpoint of business models, with the aim of understanding how blockchain can transform existing business models and even enable new ones. Finally, Chapter 11 discusses the application of blockchain in a novel class of business scenarios, i.e., outcome management-based business.

Note that the three chapters of Part 3 are infused with the discussion of several business applications of blockchain. Hence, in this last part of the book we part ways with the habit of concluding each chapter with a case study. As you will see, several case studies are introduced; some of these are discussed in depth in the main body of each of the next three chapters.

DOI: 10.4324/9781003321187-11

9 Suitability of business scenarios for blockchain

Learning goals

9.A The reader can explain which aspects should be considered when assessing the suitability of blockchain adoption in specific business scenarios.

9.B The reader can explain how the characteristics of a business scenario and the technical characteristics of blockchain contribute to the assessment of the fit between blockchain and a given business scenario.

9.C The reader can appraise the fit between a business scenario and blockchain using the decision-making tools provided in this chapter.

9.D The reader can defend or critique, depending on the context, a decision to apply blockchain in a given business scenario.

9.E The reader can discuss the suitability of blockchain for hazardous waste management, electronic health records management, and self-sovereign identity management.

9.1 Structuring the decision of adopting blockchain

In the past chapters, we have discussed the foundational mechanisms of blockchain, focusing also on the technological aspects. Given this background, our objective in this chapter is to address the suitability of blockchain for a business scenario. In simpler words, in which business scenarios is it a good idea to use blockchain?

The approach that we take in answering this question is shown in Figure 9.1. The ultimate objective is, given a business scenario, to decide what technology to use: a traditional (centralized) database, a public blockchain, or a private blockchain. Blockchain, in fact, can be seen, at least at a first glance, as a data storage system with peculiar characteristics: distributed across a network, immutable, consistently updated without the need of a central authority, but, at the same time, costly to use and usually slow. As such, it is not surprising that we take traditional database technology as the principal technological 'competitor' of blockchain.

The approach is split into two steps. Step 1 (discussed in the next section) concerns an analysis of the characteristic of a business scenario. Step 2 (discussed in Section 9.2) concerns a more detailed technical analysis of the type of support required from an IT system in the business scenario under consideration. For each step, we propose a specific decision-making tool that practitioners, like business analysts or IT experts, can use to

DOI: 10.4324/9781003321187-12

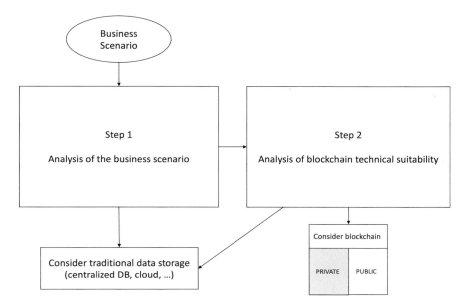

Figure 9.1 A decision-making approach to assess the fit between a business scenario and blockchain.

take a decision. The same tools can also help in defending the decisions that have been taken or criticizing the ones taken by others on solid theoretical and practical grounds.

9.2 Business suitability of blockchain

It should be clear to us by now that there are many scenarios in which the use of blockchain simply does not make sense. For instance, from the very beginning of this book, we have stressed that blockchain is fundamental when a trusted authority does not exist. If such a trusted authority already exists or can be designated, then it does not make much sense to use blockchain. Blockchain may also be pushed in scenarios where a trusted central authority already exists. However, any new solution based on blockchain in these scenarios is likely to be a very disruptive one. An example is the one of national banking systems. In the current systems, national central banks are clearly a trusted central authority. Blockchain can be pushed into this scenario, in the form of cryptocurrencies. Even though a future in which cryptocurrencies will completely replace the existing fiat currency systems is envisioned by many, its actual implementation will be extremely disruptive and seems infeasible for now, at least in the short-to-medium term.

In Step 1 of Figure 9.1, a business scenario is assessed using four aspects[1] for its suitability for blockchain:

- multi-party,
- trusted authority,
- centralized operations, and
- immutability.

These criteria are evaluated sequentially. The output of Step 1 is either the decision to discard the idea of using blockchain, opting for a more traditional centralized database solution, or to continue the process to Step 2. In the remainder of this section, we discuss in depth the rationale behind the assessment of a business scenario in respect of each of the four criteria listed above.

9.2.1 *Multi-party*

The first aspect to assess is whether a business scenario implies a multi-party collaboration. A business scenario is multi-party if it cannot exist without the presence of two or more collaborating business actors. Table 9.1 lists a few typical examples of multi-party business scenarios. Business scenarios that involve only one business actor are becoming increasingly rarer. However, they still exist. An extreme example is a craft artist transforming cheap raw wood into beautiful interior design decoration objects sold by the artist directly. The craft artist, in this case, is responsible for all the value-adding operations turning wood into decoration objects. There is no need for the artist to collaborate with other business actors.

Blockchain clearly makes sense only in multi-party scenarios. In fact, blockchain involves a network of nodes. In a multi-party business scenario, each business actor involved runs at least one node of the blockchain network. If only one business actor is involved, then a traditional database can be adopted. The craft artist, for instance, does not need to store data about her business, like client data, invoices, or raw material inventory, on a blockchain. These data can be stored in a centralized database owned and managed by the craft artist. She is the only source of such data and the only one who will ever need them.

9.2.2 *Trusted authority*

The second aspect to assess is whether, in the given business scenario, a trusted authority exists or can be created/designated. As we mentioned already, the use of blockchain makes sense only when such a central authority cannot be identified.

For instance, national banking systems hold a nation's central bank as the central authority. Every retail and investment bank operating in a country holds in fact an account at the central bank. Every non-cash transaction that occurs in a country between different banks triggers an update of the account balances of the banks held at the central bank. As such, the central bank always holds the 'golden ledger' with the

Table 9.1 Examples of multi-party business scenarios

Business scenario type	Actors involved
Global supply chain management	Clients, suppliers, logistic service providers, transportation companies, port and custom authorities, insurers, banks and credit providers.
Healthcare	Patients, private clinics, public hospitals, government agencies, and private insurers.
Credit card operations	Credit card issuers, client banks, merchant banks, high street merchants, and insurers.

list of correct transactions. Another example is the one of casinos and gambling houses. Gambling is normally strictly regulated, with casinos licensed by the authority of a state. The state of Nevada in the US, for instance, monitors closely every casino in Las Vegas on aspects ranging from budget and cash flow to employees and policing records. The state is clearly the trusted authority in this case. The state in fact issues the licenses to operate a casino, establishes the veracity of the information collected regarding a casino's operation, and exerts control of its operations whenever required, i.e., removing employees who do not comply with the state laws on gambling.

A good way to find business scenarios where a trusted authority cannot be identified or designated is to look for scenarios that match at least one of the following three criteria:

- *The scenario is international.* It is usually hard to designate trusted authorities when a business crosses the boundaries of nation-states. For instance, it is impossible to identify a central authority in currency remittance between banks in different countries or in transnational real estate markets. These markets are usually regulated nationally by a state authority. However, states usually have power only within their national boundaries. Other intermediaries, like international arbitrators, must be considered to manage the relation between local banking and real estate authorities of different countries.
- *The scenario is very new.* New businesses usually are not born with trusted third parties. Trusted third parties usually emerge later when a business grows in size, e.g., the market value or the number of participants. For instance, the market of NFTs has become known worldwide only in 2021. With the number of NFT creators and marketplaces rapidly increasing, customers and investors are increasingly calling for regulations to be established (and regulators be designated to enforce them) to protect their rights, e.g., avoiding scams.
- *The scenario is very closed.* There are many scenarios where new participants cannot be easily admitted or created. In these cases, the participants may fail to identify a trusted third party. For instance, for reasons of national security, national nuclear programs are kept strictly private. They may involve different national agencies, each one regulating and overseeing a different aspect, like nuclear energy production, nuclear waste disposal, atomic military programs, and nuclear research and development. It is unlikely however that one single agency could be designated to regulate and oversee every aspect related to the generation, use, and management of nuclear energy, even within the boundaries of an individual state.

If a trusted authority exists that decides which information regarding the value exchange among the business partners is correct, then a blockchain is not needed. In this case, every business partner should trust this authority and the information regarding the operations of a business can be stored in a traditional database. Cryptocurrency systems, like Bitcoin, have been created precisely as alternative systems for regulating cash payments among people bypassing a nation's banking system.

9.2.3 Centralized operation

The third aspect to be considered is whether the operations in the business scenario are centralized or not. Centralized operations in this context mean that, even though different actors can be involved in the operations of a business, the execution of the business is fully controlled by one of these business actors. The more the operations in a business scenario are decentralized, the more blockchain is likely to be a good fit for that business scenario. Decentralization in fact increases the number of collaborating parties. In turn, the higher the number of parties involved, the more complex it becomes to establish their reliability and trustworthiness.

As an example, we can consider the business scenario of energy (i.e., electricity) generation and distribution (see Figure 9.2). This business scenario has been historically characterized by centralized operations (see Figure 9.2a): the electricity generation and distribution were controlled by a national company, usually owned by the state. This company was the only one allowed to produce and distribute electricity to the households of a country. In many countries, however, energy markets have been deregulated in more recent times (see Figure 9.2b). Deregulated energy markets establish a marketplace between energy producers and energy resellers to private households. Energy resellers purchase the energy needed to suit the demand that they predict, and then set the best rate for their customers. The energy is then delivered through the existing utility infrastructure. The utility companies that own the infrastructure are responsible for transmitting energy, but not for setting the rate at which the users pay the energy. Deregulation in principle allows customers to receive the same service as the centralized solution, but at a rate that better fits their needs.

The advancement of digital technologies enables to push decentralization even further, thereby requiring new forms of trusted coordination. In the case of energy markets, modern technological advances in IoT, such as smart energy meters, have enabled the creation of microgrids [LR11] (see Figure 9.2c). Microgrids (briefly mentioned already in Chapter 8) are small networks of energy users. Each user in a microgrid can be a

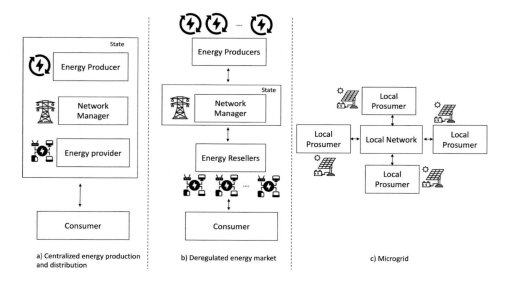

Figure 9.2 Energy markets: from centralized to fully decentralized. (a) A centralized energy production and distribution scenario. (b) A deregulated energy market scenario. (c) A microgrid scenario.

'prosumer', i.e., a consumer of energy, but also a producer of it. Nowadays, in fact, energy can be produced by any household, for instance by installing solar panels. In a microgrid, users may sell to other users the energy that they are generating and that they do not need, thus creating a dynamic energy market within the microgrid.

In this context, blockchain can become the mechanism that creates trust among the actors of a decentralized operation. Powerledger (https://www.powerledger.io), for instance, is an Australian company providing blockchain-based solutions for distributed energy production and distributions, e.g., microgrids (see Figure 9.2c). The solutions offered by Powerledger are used to establish a reliable and immutable record of energy production and consumption by individual prosumers. In Powerledger, cryptocurrencies and smart contracts can also be used to clear the energy exchange among the nodes of a microgrid. In this way, even the economic transactions related with energy exchange remain (immutably and reliably) stored 'on-chain'.

9.2.4 Immutability

The final aspect to be evaluated in Step 1 of our decision-making approach is whether a business scenario requires, or at least can tolerate, the immutability of information typical of blockchain. The transactions issued on a blockchain, in fact, by design cannot be deleted. Hence, any data stored in a blockchain system remains available to every node of a blockchain network forever. Consequently, blockchain is suitable for business scenarios where the immutability of data is welcome.

The immutability of data is welcome in most 'track and tracing' of valuable assets scenarios. If the objective is to build a reliable record of what happened to a certain asset across its history, a system simply becomes more reliable if, once stored, the data in it can never be deleted. The case study of Everledger (Chapter 6) is exemplary in this context: Everledger creates value for its customers by building an immutable record of what happens to diamonds from their extraction to the retail markets. The suitability of blockchain in complex supply chains is also conceptually linked to the data immutability criterion. Supply chain data are immensely valuable to run a smooth business. They also allow to resolve conflicts among business actors emerging from delays or errors in the goods delivery process. Obviously, supply chain data can be trusted to a higher degree if they are stored on a system from which, by design, they cannot be deleted or altered. This reduces the chances for malicious business actors of being able to hide supply chain data that would make them liable for delays or errors along the supply chain. The supply chain business models that can be enabled by blockchain are discussed in depth in Chapter 10.

There are also many business scenarios, however, for which data immutability is not a good property. In some scenarios, data immutability may not even be legal. Many business scenarios require that data can be removed by business actors with the authority to do so, because of important business reasons or by law. For instance, in the criminal justice system of most countries, judges have the authority to expunge (a part of) the criminal record of a citizen. Expunged criminal records are no longer accessible by other courts or state authorities. Basically, they have been deleted forever by the criminal justice system. Similarly, companies may be required to delete, after a certain amount of time, all the data that they collect from applicants to the job positions that they advertise. If job applications are stored on a blockchain, it may be simply impossible to delete these data.

Recently, several countries have devised national regulations regarding the management and privacy of personal data by public and private companies. For instance, the EU has introduced in 2016 the General Data Protection and Regulation (GDPR, https://gdpr.eu). In the US, the California Consumer Privacy Act (CCPA, https://oag. ca.gov/privacy/ccpa) has similar provisions to the EU GDPR. These regulations usually have provisions for the customers' 'right to be forgotten'. Companies complying with these regulations are not allowed to store customer data forever. Customers must have the guarantee that their data will be deleted by a company that has collected them within a certain timeframe, e.g., a few years.

Now, regulations like the EU GDPR or the expunging of criminal records are clearly at odds, at least at a first glance, with blockchain. By design, in fact, the data stored in a blockchain can never be deleted or altered. Private blockchain systems, such as Hyperledger Fabric or Corda, may provide mechanism to address the privacy requirements imposed by regulations such as the EU GDPR, even without allowing to physically delete the transactions issued in the past. For instance, in Hyperledger Fabric the visibility of channels can be adjusted to prevent specific nodes to access the data belonging to that channel. Mechanisms of this type, however, are often a workaround to address legally binding requirements on data management and privacy. They should always be designed and implemented very carefully.

To sum up, Figure 9.3 summarizes Step 1 in our decision process. When appraising the suitability of blockchain for a business scenario, the four criteria discussed in this section are evaluated sequentially. At each step, a decision can be made to consider a traditional database instead of blockchain. If a business scenario is found suitable for blockchain along all the four criteria, then we can move to Step 2. In Step 2, more technical issues related with the suitability of blockchain are considered. These are discussed in the next section.

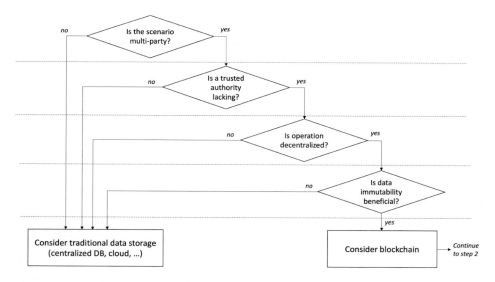

Figure 9.3 Step 1 decision of whether to consider blockchain for a business scenario.

9.3 Technical suitability of blockchain

After having appraised the suitability of blockchain for a business scenario, a final decision regarding whether to use blockchain (and what type of blockchain) must consider more technical aspects of the IT solution that must be implemented. The outcome of Step 2 (see Figure 9.1) is a decision regarding whether to use a public blockchain, a private blockchain, or a traditional centralized database. Even though a business scenario has been appraised to possibly benefit from blockchain, the technical considerations made in Step 2 may still advise us to choose a traditional database solution.

The four criteria that we consider for assessing the technical suitability of blockchain for a business scenario are the following:

1   The size of the data that must be stored.
2   The level of performance, e.g., response time and throughput, required by a system to operate effectively.
3   The maximum cost that is considered acceptable to run the system.
4   The level of transparency of the data, required or tolerated.

The possible outcomes of the decisions of Step 2 are summarized in Figure 9.4. For each aspect, we consider one or more questions. Next, we discuss in detail the four aspects and the related questions to be considered for the decision.

9.3.1 Data size

In this book, we have highlighted several times that the size of the data that blockchain can handle is usually limited. Bitcoin and Ethereum have strict limitations on the size of the transactions. Moreover, the transaction fees usually increase with the size of the

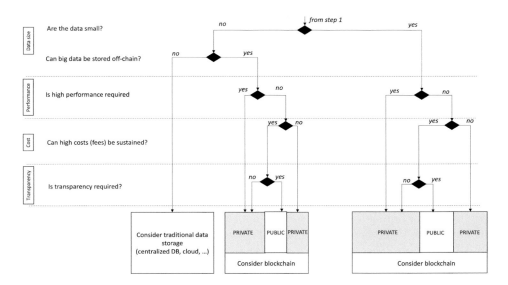

Figure 9.4 Step 2 decision of whether to consider blockchain for a business scenario.

transactions. This creates an incentive for nodes to keep the size of the transactions limited. Moreover, the blocks generated in a public blockchain are replicated in the ledger of every node of the network. This means that, on the one hand, a node receives all the data generated in a blockchain, while, on the other hand, a node is interested only in a subset (often small) of them. This calls for limiting the size of transactions and/ or the extent to which the ledger data are replicated across the nodes. Private block-chains can do at least the latter. For instance, we have seen in Chapter 7 that Corda's ledger is built on a need-to-know basis: nodes receive only the data in the ledger that concerns them.

The evaluation of the 'data size' aspect in the decision model of Figure 9.4 is split into the following sub-steps:

1   Evaluating the actual size of the data, i.e., whether the business scenario is charac-terized by 'small' or 'big' data.
2   When a business scenario is characterized by 'big' data, evaluating whether such data can be stored off chain, having only a small 'digest' of the data stored in the blockchain.

Characterizing the size of the data required by a business scenario in absolute terms, i.e., 'small' versus 'big', is always challenging. Data, in fact, can be 'small' or 'big' depending on many aspects, like the computational power available to process them or the physical storage capacity available to store them. In a machine learning application, a dataset of a few GB may be considered 'small' when compared to the Terabytes (TBs) required to train a neural network to self-drive a car. A few hundreds MB of data may be 'small' for modern desktop computers, but they could be very 'big' when processed by an IoT device with limited storage and computational capabilities, or when transmitted using expensive long-distance wireless networks (as in the case study presented later in Chapter 11).

Since the size of data is always relative, how do we evaluate the size of the data when assessing the suitability of blockchain for a business scenario? The answer that we can give in this book is not based on hard science, but it is rather based on common sense considerations derived from the analysis of the blockchain technology discussed in this book.

For a blockchain, 'small' data must be limited in size in absolute terms, i.e., a few hundred KB of data. The only data contained in a Bitcoin transaction, for instance, are basically the list of UTXOs used and the list of transaction outputs produced. These are likely to occupy only a few KB on any storage unit. In Ethereum, a cryptocurrency exchange requires to specify only the amount of ETH transferred from the originator to the recipient. When an Ethereum transaction invokes a smart contract, the data field contains the values of the invocation parameters. These are usually primitive data types, such as integer numbers or small strings, which would not occupy more than a few KB on a hard disk. All other data that exceed a few hundred KB should be considered 'big' for a blockchain. This applies typically to all types of multimedia data, e.g., images, videos, or scanned documents. Note that 'big' data to store in a blockchain may also be generated by high-frequency 'small' transactions. A typical case is the one of blockchain for IoT applications, which we discussed in Chapter 8.

As mentioned above, from the point of view of the data size, cryptocurrencies are business scenarios characterized by 'small' data. Similarly, the BC4C blockchain and its evolutions presented in Part 1 of the book are also dealing with 'small' data. Basically, these data are the moves in a chess game and cryptocurrency transfers. Individual readings of an IoT device, like the temperature of a room at a given point in time, a timestamp, or the id of an item on sale in a shop, are also 'small' data.

Data, however, can easily become 'big' from a blockchain standpoint. In IoT scenarios, like a retail clothing shop, data become big if, for instance, for every order from a supplier we are also required to store a scanned version of an invoice or a signed delivery receipt. Similarly, in a supply chain scenario, data become 'big' if we are required to store electronic versions of every document, such as bills of lading, invoices, delivery receipts, or custom stamps. In a healthcare scenario, data become 'big' when we are required to store, for instance, radiography images or other forms of multimedia output of diagnostic exams.

When 'big' data are generated, these may be stored on a traditional database solution, such as on the cloud or on a database hosted by the nodes of the network. This solution is feasible, but it clearly violates the principle of decentralization of blockchain. The cloud provider or the node(s) hosting the data become 'de facto' a centralized authority controlling the data. Nevertheless, some business scenarios may still tolerate such a lack of decentralization in data storage. They may in fact trade off the decentralization of data for other benefits typical of the blockchain, such as the immutability of the transaction record or smart contracts.

There is an alternative solution, however, that allows to handle 'big' data using blockchain, preserving most of the benefits of blockchain data storage. This solution is depicted in Figure 9.5. No matter where the 'big' data are stored, a unique digest of the data, usually generated using a cryptographic hashing algorithm, can be stored immutably in the blockchain. Every time a node wants to use the off-chain data, a node downloads the data, calculates the digest, and verifies whether this digest matches the one stored in the blockchain. If that happens, then the node has the guarantee of having downloaded the correct version of data. Otherwise, the node has the certainty that the data downloaded are not correct and, therefore, they should not be used. Not that this is a typical application of cryptographic hashing, which was already discussed in Chapter 2.

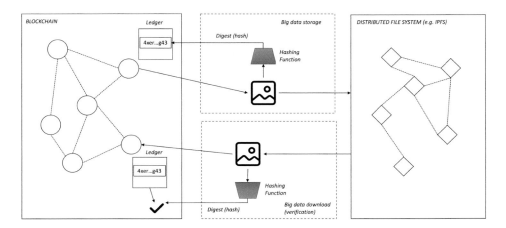

Figure 9.5 How to handle 'big' data in a blockchain.

In more technical terms, storing the digests of the data of the blockchain guarantees their integrity in use, i.e., the nodes can verify effectively if they are using the correct data. It does not guarantee data availability and immutability, i.e., the data can still be tampered with or be lost while stored off-chain. As far as the 'database' where the off-chain data are stored, there can be different solutions. As we said earlier, this database can be hosted by one of the nodes of the blockchain or by a cloud provider. Alternatively, the nodes could decide to use a so-called 'distributed file system'. This is a file system in which the data to be stored are divided into smaller 'units' and these units are distributed (and even replicated to improve performance) across the nodes of the network. When a node needs certain data, the distributed file system protocol allows a node to retrieve all the 'units' required from the other nodes. The IPFS (InterPlanetary File System,) is a publicly distributed file system that is commonly used by Ethereum-based applications. The IPFS can also be deployed in a private network, e.g., allowing the data to be distributed only among the nodes of a private blockchain. Solutions like IPFS fit well with the distributed nature of blockchain. The off-chain 'big' data in fact are never stored entirely by one node only (which may act as a central authority).

Another aspect that must be considered is the encryption of off-chain data. For a network of collaborating business partners, in fact, storing 'plain text' business data on a cloud or on a distributed file system, may not be the optimal solution. They may have a strong incentive to keep these data private. This requirement can be addressed by extending the scenario of Figure 9.5 with public key encryption. The data can be stored off-chain in an encrypted form, i.e., encrypted before being stored using the private key of one of the nodes. The public key to decrypt the data after the download can be stored, together with the hash of the data, on the blockchain, or may be provided 'on-demand' by the node who encrypted the data to the other nodes of the blockchain.

The suitability of the different forms of data storage discussed above depends on the type of business scenario under consideration. For instance, a supply chain where scanned copies of every document must be stored fits well the scenario in which the scanned copies are stored off-chain and a digest of them in the blockchain. Conversely, we must be very careful when storing the data off-chain in the healthcare scenario mentioned earlier. The results of diagnostic exams are sensitive information. They cannot be simply stored on the cloud or on the public IPFS, unless they are first encrypted. Encryption, however, works only in private blockchain settings, where the nodes encrypting the data can share their public key to decrypt data with other nodes that they trust. Alternatively, sensitive information can be stored by a trusted node of the healthcare network, like the hospital where the exam has been administered. On the one hand, this violates the decentralization principle of the blockchain. On the other hand, however, the blockchain can still provide unique features in this scenario, like a reliable and immutable record of which nodes have accessed the data, or a means to verify whether the data downloaded from the trusted node are the correct ones.

9.3.2 *Performance*

The performance of an information system is roughly indicated by the time that it takes to reply to a request (i.e., the 'response time') or the number of requests that it can serve in a fixed amount of time (i.e., the 'throughput'). In blockchain, we can consider the transactions as the 'requests' made to the system, i.e., requests to change the state of the system (possibly through the execution of smart contracts). Therefore, the performance of a blockchain system is indicated by the time required to process a transaction (response time) and the number of transactions that a blockchain can process in a fixed amount of time, e.g., a minute (throughput).

As already mentioned several times in this book, the performance of a blockchain is usually low when compared to traditional, centralized systems. For instance, due to the proof-of-work consensus mechanism, we must wait at least a few seconds (sometimes much more) to know that a Bitcoin transaction has been included into a valid block by some miner and up to one hour to be sure that this block will remain on the main chain forever. This yields that the Bitcoin's throughput is orders of magnitude lower than the one of traditional banking systems or of the worldwide credit card systems (a few transactions per second in Bitcoin vs. a few thousand transactions per second in the other systems). Ethereum is quicker than Bitcoin, yet its throughput remains much lower than the one of traditional banking systems. Due to the need of digitally signing and validating every transaction and of executing the consensus mechanism, even the performance of private blockchain systems remains much lower than the one, for instance, of traditional IT systems, such as the relational databases storing the data used by the ERP or CRM systems in large companies.

Because of its relatively poor performance, blockchain obviously only suits business scenarios where high performance is not a primary requirement. Global supply chains often fit the low performance of blockchain systems. A supply chain process is often by definition 'long-lived'. For instance, it takes a few months for a container to ship from Rotterdam in the Netherlands to Tokyo in Japan, or a few weeks from Hong Kong to the US West coast. Therefore, particularly from the point of view of response time, the performance required is not particularly extreme. Not all supply chains fit this scenario, however. The supply chain transaction throughput required by a large retailer may indeed be very high (Amazon, for instance, ships millions of packages per day).

The IoT scenario is one in which performance may become an issue and where the design of blockchain can be tweaked to fit a specific business scenario. For instance, IoT sensors and RFID tags placed on the items on the shelves of a large retailer, like Walmart in the US, may generate an enormous amount of data to be processed. Consider, for instance, tags placed on each single box of fresh produce, like fruits or salads, handled by every single Walmart in the US, sending a signal whenever a box is moved to/from a warehouse and to/from the shelves. Assuming that every sensor reading generates a new blockchain transaction, such a scenario is likely to generate thousands of blockchain transactions every second. Instead of completely giving up on using blockchain in this type of scenario, a design choice could be made to issue transactions bundling together multiple sensor readings. For instance, bundling together 100 readings in one transaction would roughly improve the throughput of the system by two orders of magnitude. This choice trades off the timeliness in storing the readings for the possibility of exploiting the typical performance range of blockchain. In other words, we could tolerate some delay while storing the readings to allow them to be reliably and immutably stored on a blockchain. This issue is considered also by the case study of Chapter 11, in the context of outcome management business.

9.3.3 Cost

The next aspect to be considered when assessing the suitability of blockchain for a business scenario is the cost. The costs of using a blockchain can be divided into 'infrastructure' and 'transaction' costs. Infrastructure costs concern the setup, operation and maintenance of the blockchain. Transactions costs concern the cost of using the blockchain for executing transactions. Since public blockchains already exist and can be used by anybody, in a public blockchain (see Table 9.2), one must worry only about the latter. Transaction costs in public blockchains can be high and volatile, particularly when transaction fees are paid in a cryptocurrency like Bitcoin or Ethereum. In a private blockchain, there are normally no transaction costs. That is, the nodes of a private blockchain do not pay a fee to submit transactions. However, a private blockchain must be created from scratch, operated, and maintained. Therefore, the infrastructure costs can be high. In the context of this chapter, however, we argue that the cost of setting up and maintaining a private blockchain is comparable with the infrastructure costs that the network of nodes will incur implementing any other technological solution to support their collaboration, i.e., implementing a (non blockchain-based) cross-organizational information system [Gref15]. Hence, in the remainder, we focus on the blockchain transaction costs, which are typical of public blockchain.

Obviously, the higher the throughput of transactions issued on a public blockchain, the higher the total amount of fees that must be paid in a fixed time period by the nodes of a system. When considering using a public blockchain for a business scenario, it becomes fundamental (i) to establish whether the fees to be paid are reasonable, and (ii) to determine who should contribute to the payment of fees.

A business scenario like Everledger (see Chapter 6) is one where the fees to be paid for using the Ethereum public blockchain do not appear to be critical. In Everledger, in fact, blockchain is used to create a reliable and immutable record of the change of ownership of very valuable physical assets, i.e., diamonds. The throughput of transactions required by such a system is normally very low. Diamonds in fact do not change ownership frequently. Moreover, given the high value associated with the assets that are tracked, it is reasonable to assume that the nodes taking the ownership of such assets would be willing to pay a small fee to register a change of ownership in Everledger. Conversely, the IoT-based case study of Chapter 8 is one where specific design choices had been made to reduce the number of transactions issued to the public Ethereum network. While improving the performance of the system, this also reduces the cost associated with its operation. In fact, if the system would have been designed to issue a single transaction for each sensor reading, then the cost of operating the system would be dominated by the fees required to issue the transactions to Ethereum. We will see that similar considerations also hold for the case study presented in Chapter 11.

9.3.4 *Transparency*

The final aspect to be evaluated concerns the level of transparency that characterizes the system that we plan to build. Generally, blockchain is a very transparent technology.

Table 9.2 Classification of the costs associated with using blockchain

	Infrastructure costs	Transaction costs
Public blockchain	Usually none	Transaction fees
Private blockchain	Blockchain setup, operation, and maintenance (comparable, however, with similar costs of similar non-blockchain solutions)	Usually none

In a public blockchain, every node maintains a copy of the ledger, which contains all the transactions issued at any point in time by the nodes of the network. In other words, every node has full access to all the data stored in the system. This is a fundamental property of public blockchains. It ensures that every node has access to the correct state of the blockchain ledger at any point in time. In the private blockchain, the mechanism can be devised to limit the transparency of the system. Hyperledger Fabric, for instance, allows to define separate channels. Each channel has a separate ledger and can be accessed only by a restricted set of nodes. Corda limits transparency by building the ledger on a need-to-know basis: the nodes have access only to the facts that are relevant for their own business.

The issue of limiting transparency in a blockchain is directly linked to the issue of node identification. In a public blockchain, the nodes are anonymous. Therefore, the nodes can tolerate that all the transactions issued can be accessed by every other node. In Bitcoin or Ethereum, for instance, anybody can access the BTC or ETH balance of every node of the network. This is not a problem, because a Bitcoin or Ethereum account cannot be linked to the actual owner (for instance a physical person or a business). Conversely, in a private blockchain, the identity of the nodes is known. This allows the implementation of mechanisms to restrict the access of certain nodes to specific transactions. For instance, nodes without a given clearance level may be prevented to access transactions containing classified information, or nodes from a certain geographical area may be prevented to access transactions originated by nodes outside that area.

Based on these considerations (see Figure 9.4), scenarios that require a high level of transparency of the data recorded on the blockchain should opt for a public blockchain solution. Conversely, when transparency of the data must be limited or it is not desirable at all, a private blockchain should be considered.

9.4 Applying the decision-making tools

In this section, we show how to use the tools presented in the previous sections to appraise three different classes of business scenarios:

1   Safe disposal of industrial waste (Section 9.4.1)
2   Management of electronic health records (Section 9.4.2)
3   Self-sovereign identity management (Section 9.4.3)

9.4.1 Safe disposal of industrial waste

Hazardous industrial waste must be disposed of properly, to avoid natural disasters and, more generally, to avoid dissatisfaction in the public opinion. For instance, highly polluting liquid waste of chemical processes should be appropriately treated before it is disposed of in the public sewage system; hazardous solid wastes, like batteries and other vehicle parts, should also be disposed of following specific procedures.

Unfortunately, proper disposal procedures are often not followed when dealing with hazardous waste. This is mainly due to profit-related reasons. The treatment of hazardous waste costs (a lot of) money. The hazardous wastes may need to be processed using several different expensive treatments. They may also need to be stored, in some cases even for long periods, before they can be finally disposed of in more traditional ways.

Companies therefore may have an incentive in skipping such treatments, relying for instance on organized crime for dumping liquid waste directly into the sea or burying hazardous wastes in public grounds. An extreme case is the one of radioactive waste disposal. Radioactive waste is extremely dangerous for both the environment and human beings. After being properly packed, radioactive waste drums must be securely stored in concrete-reinforced structures for several decades before their radioactivity level would become safe. Additionally, radioactive waste may be stolen to be used as a source of nuclear material by countries excluded, e.g., by sanctions, from global markets, or to achieve alternative ends, such as weaponry building.

Monitoring the execution of the appropriate procedures required to dispose of specific types of hazardous waste is thus an important application for improving social and environmental welfare. Different monitoring data can be produced by different business partners during the disposal process. These data include, for instance, records of waste packaging, transportation of packaged waste at different sites, and execution of waste treatment activities. Concretely, these data may range from small data, like the id of a technician in charge of a certain waste treatment activity or the id of waste packaging drums, to big data, like scanned copies of transportation bills or digital photos of disposed waste. The question that we ask in this section is whether blockchain is a good idea to support this kind of business scenario.

Figure 9.6 shows the application of the decision process presented earlier in this chapter to this scenario (HWD – Hazardous Waste Disposal). In Step 1, it appears clear that blockchain could be a suitable technology for HWD:

- The HWD scenario is multi-party. There can be in fact multiple organizations in need of disposing the same type of hazardous materials. There are likely to be multiple organizations providing the types of treatments for hazardous wastes. Additionally, several government agencies may have a clear interest in monitoring the execution of these procedures.

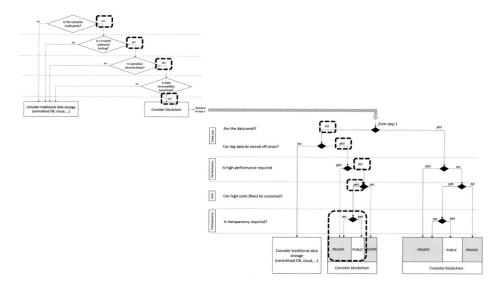

Figure 9.6 Blockchain and hazardous waste disposal (HWD).

- In the HWD scenario, it is not possible to elect a trusted authority. While the industry is strictly regulated, the enforcement of the correct procedures is normally left to different public safety agencies, like government agencies, state departments and, eventually, police forces.
- The operations in the HWD scenario are decentralized. The producers of hazardous waste, the companies providing appropriate treatments, and the monitoring agencies are likely to be independent organizations. There is no clear leader in such a scenario that can coordinate the operations in a centralized way.
- The HWD scenario can be classified as a 'track and tracing' of valuable assets scenarios. Here, however, the value of the assets to be tracked should be intended as an opportunity cost: companies have an incentive to save money by not engaging in proper disposal procedure, and an effective monitoring system allows to neutralize this incentive. As such, the HWD scenario clearly benefits from the data immutability property. The objective is in fact to build reliable records of the execution of hazardous waste disposal procedures that cannot be tampered with by malicious users.

In Step 2, we dive deeper into assessing the suitability of blockchain for the HWD scenario from a more technical standpoint. The data to be stored in the HWD scenario may be 'big'. On the one hand, most monitoring data in this scenario concern small information tokens, like ids of the procedures that were administered, of the human operators in charge, or timestamps. However, better evidence of the execution of the procedure may require additional evidence captured by 'big' data. Scanned copies of official documents produced along the process, like waste delivery receipts, or multimedia content demonstrating the actual execution of treatments, may increase the reliability of the monitoring data, lowering the chance that this could be forged or tampered with. These additional 'big' data to be stored, however, are not likely to contain particularly sensitive information. Therefore, in principle they could be stored on distributed file system solutions that could be accessed by all the nodes of a blockchain network.

The HWD scenario does not seem to need particularly high performance. The disposal of hazardous waste is likely to be a long-lived process, which produces data along an extended time span. These monitoring data usually are not consulted extremely frequently and/or in real time. Hence, this scenario can tolerate the reduced performance typical of blockchain. Regarding the sustainability of costs related with the transaction fees, we argue that registering the hazardous waste process monitoring data on a public blockchain may help companies increase their level of transparency and, more generally, positively contribute to creating improved corporate social responsibility. Along this line of reasoning, we assume that the producers of hazardous waste would be willing to pay the fees required to adopt a public blockchain. Note that such fees are most likely to be negligible when compared to the huge costs of hazardous waste disposal (and the benefits derived from promoting a clean and responsible image of a company).

The last aspect concerns the transparency of the data. As mentioned above, it is reasonable to assume that the producers of hazardous waste would have no problem in publishing their waste monitoring data on a public blockchain. This may in fact increase their perceived transparency and social responsibility image. At the same time, the data to be published do not appear to be core business data that should remain protected. There are, however, instantiations of the HWD scenario where transparency of data may become a concern. One such example is the one of the disposal of radioactive waste mentioned earlier. Nuclear energy production is usually an extremely regulated business, managed to the highest safety and security standards. The location and size of radioactive waste disposal site or the type and quantity of disposed radioactive waste is information that national governments are likely to maintain a secret, owing mainly to national security. As such, in this case we would argue for a solution in which a private blockchain is adopted.

9.4.2 Management of electronic health records

We are all likely to receive different forms of medical treatment from several healthcare providers in our life. Cancer patients, for instance, may visit different hospitals and private clinics to receive treatments and consultations regarding their condition. During their life, people simply move to various cities or even countries, thus possibly receiving treatment from different healthcare providers in different locations. In recent times, caregivers have also realized the importance of having access to the entire medical history of patients to take better-informed decisions [VC14]. This is especially critical in the case of chronic conditions, like diabetes or hypertension, for which a timely diagnosis may require detailed knowledge of a patient's medical history.

The medical history of a patient is captured in the so-called Electronic Health Records (EHRs). Ideally, the EHRs of a patient should integrate seamlessly the data regarding all the treatments, medications, surgeries, etc. that a patient has received during their lifetime from any healthcare provider [KT16]. In this way, patients can easily reproduce their medical history whenever necessary. In practice, however, each healthcare provider, like hospitals, private clinics, or even general practitioners, maintain separate EHRs of their patients. While there may be some integration efforts at the national or regional level, integrating information from different EHRs is normally challenging. Practically, it is often impossible for anybody to reproduce their entire medical history

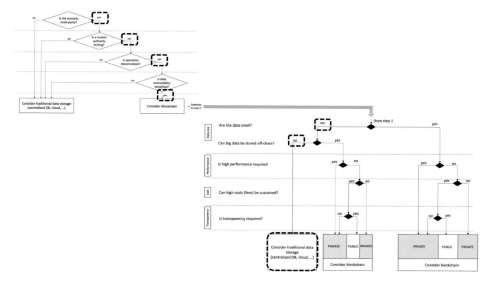

Figure 9.7 Blockchain for electronic health records (HER)?

in an integrated medical record. Our medical history is scattered among the EHRs of all the institutions from which we received treatments. There are various reasons why integrating EHR is often impossible, like technical difficulties, e.g., different data formats adopted by different applications and/or countries, different and/or conflicting national and international regulations, or even reluctance from healthcare providers to shift ownership of the medical data to the patients.

We can now ask ourselves whether blockchain could be a viable solution for overcoming these challenges, enabling the development of fully integrated EHRs. More than an EHR, the vision that we have in mind is the one of a Personal Health Record (PHR) [VC14]: an integrated record of the personal medical history owned by an individual, which could be shown whenever necessary to support diagnosis and/or treatment anywhere in the world.

Figure 9.7 depicts the application of the tools that we discussed in this chapter to the PHR case. Focusing on Step 1, the PHR scenario appears to potentially benefit from being approached using blockchain:

- The PHR scenario is multi-party, since during our life we are likely to receive treatment from multiple healthcare providers. Besides the healthcare providers, there are other relevant partners in this scenario, like government and private insurance supporting payments, or employers who may need to consult our medical records as a standard check during a hiring process.
- The PHR scenario does not have a clearly identifiable central trusted authority. As mentioned earlier, there may be some efforts to standardize healthcare records at a national or regional level, usually imposed by government agencies. However, particularly when crossing the boundaries of individual nations, it is impossible to designate a trusted authority.
- The PHR scenario is also clearly decentralized. Treatments can be provided by different independent healthcare providers. These have no particular reason to trust each other and often compete to acquire customers on the basis of the quality of care and price.
- Finally, the immutability of data fits well with the PHR scenario. The objective of a PHR is indeed to build a reliable record of all medical data regarding an individual. A guarantee that such data, once stored in a PHR, cannot be tampered with is obviously welcome. There is a concern related to the visibility of such data to different types of stakeholders. We may require the employers, for instance, to have access only to a limited subset of our medical history. In this case, appropriate mechanism should be implemented to prevent employers accessing the medical data that they are not entitled to.

The analysis of the PHR business scenario in Step 2, however, reveals the unsuitability of blockchain in this business scenario. The main concern in this context is the size of the data. Besides even worrying about the potential issues related with the transparency of the medical data or the cost of storing them, we need to consider that medical data are usually 'big'. Medical treatment outcomes in fact are often captured in large files, like high-quality images. As such, they cannot be stored directly using a blockchain system. Moreover, medical data are also particularly sensitive. Therefore, storing them on a distributed file system to which any node of a blockchain network has access does not appear to be a viable option. In the end, based on the analysis supported by the tools presented in this chapter, we would advise against using blockchain for the implementation of PHRs.

Should this decision outcome put a definite end to any effort to exploit blockchain for the management of medical records? The answer is no. In fact, if you are a blockchain enthusiast, you might have often read in the news about different types of blockchain technology applied in the healthcare, even in the management of medical records.

There are indeed multiple applications in the healthcare in which blockchain makes perfect sense [HKG+20]. Many of these potential applications are currently explored by multiple start-ups and even more established large organizations. In the specific context of medical records, one such application is the track and tracing of the 'access' to medical records. While above we have demonstrated that blockchain is not appropriate to store and distribute the actual medical data, blockchain can still be used to create a reliable record of who has accessed our medical records and when it was done. As we have now learnt from several examples discussed earlier in this book, in a nutshell this can be achieved by (i) creating a digest (e.g., a hash) of the medical records, (ii) storing these digests in a blockchain, and (iii) forcing anyone who wants to access them to first verify the correctness of the digest. This is a typical application of blockchain: instead of storing the actual data in a blockchain, we use a blockchain to store a digest of the data, and, before providing access to the actual data, we force nodes to download these hashes and upload a proof of match between the digest and the data they have requested access to (in the case of medical records, for instance, to a hospital).

Creating reliable access records of medical data can support several potential novel applications. For instance, with such a mechanism we could monitor whether a private clinic has tried to sell our data to an advertiser. We could even be rewarded when others access our medical data. For instance, we could design a reward, paid off using an Ethereum ERC-20 token, that an individual receives any time their data are accessed (obviously in an anonymous form) by a research university as part of a specific research project.

9.4.3 Self-sovereign identity management

As individuals, we maintain several accounts that we created for different service providers over the Internet, such as retail Internet shops, content streaming services, or even government agencies providing their services online. Our accounts are identified by a username and password. More and more often, we also need to provide a mobile phone number or an email to support two-factor identification. Despite being used everywhere on the Internet, this system is not particularly convenient for us as users of digital services. We are required to remember a long list of usernames and passwords. We routinely waste quite a large amount of time trying to recover those when they slip out of our memory. Moreover, usernames and passwords can get stolen in bulk from service providers that do not protect the identify of their users adequately.

Is this the only way in which digital identity (or identity in general) of users can be managed? The answer is obviously no. Recently, the so-called 'self-sovereign identity' has emerged as a new paradigm for identity management in digital settings. In a nutshell, self-sovereign identity shifts the burden of the verification of the identity of a user from the user to the provider. In the traditional system based on usernames and passwords, the service providers hold the credentials (often called identity tokens) that define our identity, i.e., our usernames and passwords. We (the users) must provide these credentials to be authenticated by the providers and use their services. Conversely, in self-sovereign identity, the users hold the tokens that demonstrate their own identity. The providers verify the validity of these tokens to allow the users to access their services.

How does the self-sovereign identity paradigm work in practice in the case of digital identity? Instead of having a different identity token for each service provider, digital users can identify themselves using identity tokens provided by different public institutions or even private companies. Each service provider should then decide the number and/or type of such identity tokens that they deem sufficient to onboard and authenticate a new customer.

For instance, a local government agency of the city of King's Landing, where Mr. T. Lannister lives, issues to Mr. Lannister a digital identity token to demonstrate that he has lived there for the past 20 years. Mr. Lannister uses this token as a proof of identity to open a new a bank account with a national online bank. The bank in turn issues another identity token to Mr. Lannister. This token allows him to be identified when opening a new account with a content streaming service or an online public service to pay his electricity bills. Ms. A. Stark, an international student from overseas who is spending one year studying at King's Landing University, obtains an identity token from the university. This token proves that Ms. Stark is studying at this university for the next two semesters, entitling her to access many local and online services that would normally be available only to King's Landing citizens. Similarly to Mr. Lannister, Ms. Stark uses the token obtained from the university to open an online bank account. In practice, this means that the online bank trusts in the same way the identity token provided by the King's Landing local administration and the one provided by the local university to international exchange students.

Note that the self-sovereign identity paradigm has several advantages for the users. Most importantly, users need not maintain a different identity with each service provider and, at least in principle, need not share permanently with service providers any of their personal data to verify their identity. The identity tokens would be provided by users only when accessing a service and only to be verified by the service providers. To some extent, passports are a widespread means of identification that exploits some of the principles of self-sovereign identity. In fact, we do not hold access credentials specific to each single country in the world. Instead, passports (accompanied by a visa when necessary) are considered sufficient by foreign countries to let us identify ourselves and being admitted to visit a country. The way in which passports are created, however, clearly do not follow the self-sovereign principles. The issuing of passports is centrally controlled by the state. We cannot collect proofs of identity to obtain a passport from anybody else than the country in which we hold nationality.

The self-sovereign identity scenario clearly seems to match the underlying principles of blockchain. With self-sovereign identity, the digital identity becomes a distributed entity. As we have seen with the examples of King's Landing, the users can build their digital identity by collecting identity tokens from several independent organizations.

More in detail, we can analyze the fit of blockchain as a technology to support the self-sovereign identity (SSI) scenario using the tools that we presented earlier in this chapter (see Figure 9.8). Regarding Step 1 of the decision-making process:

- The SSI scenario is clearly multi-party. It involves several service providers and, most importantly, several potential providers of identity tokens.

- A trusted authority cannot be identified in the SSI scenario. The main idea underpinning SSI is that user identity is not certified by an authority, but users 'build' their identity collecting identity tokens from multiple providers (public and/ or private).
- The operation of an SSI scenario is naturally decentralized. As we discussed above, digital users collect identity tokens from different providers. These providers act independently, without any centralized coordination mechanism.
- Finally, the immutability scenario seems to be beneficial in the SSI scenario. Once an identity token is issued to a user, nobody should be allowed to destroy it and make it unusable. Identity tokens may be revoked by the providers, which may seem to be at odds with the immutability property of blockchain. However, this issue can be simply overcome by assigning an expiry date to the tokens. Like with ID cards or passports, identity tokens should be periodically re-issued to maintain their validity.

Based on the considerations made above, the outcome of Step 1 in the case of the SSI scenario is to proceed to the more technical appraisal of the suitability of blockchain of Step 2.

Without aiming at presenting any real technical solution (the interested readers may refer to [MGG+18] [PR21]), we could see that the output of the analysis in Step 2 is to consider a public blockchain for the SSI scenario.

The data to be managed in this scenario are likely to be small. They concern basic citizen registry data, or other minor information, such as id of accounts and other membership records. The SSI scenario does not require high performance. We are in fact unlikely to collect new identity tokens very frequently. Moreover, we are not likely to have to prove our identity very often. Even in scenarios where proving identity may be required often, for instance in payment scenarios, the number of times in

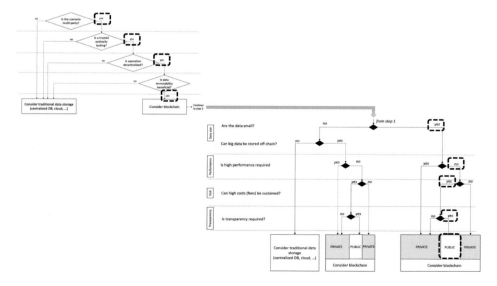

Figure 9.8 Blockchain for self-sovereign identity (SSI) management?

which identity must be proven can be reduced by assigning a validity period to each successful authentication (i.e., once our identity has been proven, we can be entitled to use a service for one day or one week without having to re-identify ourselves). Finally, the main idea of an identity management system is to be as much as possible 'universal'. The power of passports as a means of identification is that they are accepted worldwide. Similarly, a self-sovereign identity management should be accessible by any citizen of the world and by any institution or service that decides to use it. In this context, we could assume that the service providers may be willing to sustain the costs of the transaction fees for using a public blockchain. At the same time, using a public blockchain contributes to achieving the required level of transparency: all identity tokens should be available for access by anybody whenever needed.

Note that the SSI scenario discussed here is based on an ideal vision of a self-sovereign identity management system used worldwide and accessible to anybody. The concrete implementations of this scenario currently available (and that use blockchain) are usually developed in a local context. They aim at providing identity management services for local jurisdictions, e.g., a city or a province and focus on specific application services, like access to government online services [SKM+21].

9.5 Conclusions

In this chapter, we have presented a decision-making approach to guide the choice regarding whether to use blockchain in a given business scenario. Specifically, we have introduced two tools to support the decision, one focusing on the characteristics of the business scenario, such as whether it includes a central authority or welcomes the immutability of data, and one focusing on more technical aspects of the system to be implemented, such as the size of the data that must be managed by it or the level of performance required. We then presented three different classes of business scenarios and assessed their fit with blockchain technology using these two tools.

The next chapter focuses on blockchain and business models. That is, we increase the level of abstraction in assessing the suitability of blockchain for business, looking specifically at how blockchain can be used to modify an existing business model and how it can enable novel business models.

9.6 Questions and exercises

1 Discuss the application of the decision-making tools presented in this chapter to the case studies presented in Chapters 6 and 8.
2 Using the decision-making tools presented in this chapter, identify and discuss a business scenario, different from the ones already discussed in the chapter, in which the application of either a traditional database, a public blockchain, and private blockchain is suggested.
3 Extend the solution presented in Figure 9.5 to capture the case in which the data stored off-chain are also encrypted. Highlight, specifically, which keys (public or private) are used to encrypt/decrypt and where they are stored.
4 Consider more in detail the 'transparency' aspect discussed in this chapter. Specifically, consider the case in which the data can be encrypted or shared on a need-to-know basis among the nodes of a blockchain network and propose an

extension of the decision-making tool for Step 2 that considers these additional sub-aspects.

5 Consider the case of Powerledger briefly introduced in Section 9.2. Based on the information about Powerledger that you can find online, discuss the products that they offer and identify the business scenarios that they target. Then, using the aspects presented in this chapter, discuss why Powerledger (as a blockchain technology) fits the business scenarios that you have identified.

Note

1 Note that the decision aspects considered in the tools presented in this chapter are inspired by the discussion presented in [XWS19].

10 Blockchain and business models

Learning goals

10.A The reader can describe the notion of a (digitally enabled) business model and can discuss it in the broader context of electronic business.

10.B The reader can explain the importance of trustworthy information processing in the context of business models.

10.C The reader can explain several ways in which blockchain enables specific types of innovative business models and can classify business models.

10.D The reader can design drafts of new blockchain-enabled business models, which can be the basis for further detailed design work.

10.1 What is a business model?

In this section, we explain what a business model is. First, we have a look at the concept of a business model, observing that there are many definitions of the concept but that these all convey a similar underlying thought. Two variations can be identified, however: a variation that describes business models starting from a single business organization and a variation that describes business models starting from a business ecosystem that consists of multiple organizations. For both variations, we show how we can specify business models using specific techniques.

10.1.1 The business model concept

Briefly stated, a business model is a high-level model of how an organization brings its offerings to its market. There are many definitions of what exactly a business model is, partially dependent on the context of a specific definition. To illustrate the diversity of definitions, we present a few examples of definitions below.

1 A business model depicts the design of transaction content, structure, and governance so as to create value through the exploitation of new business opportunities [AZ01].
2 The business model tells a logical story explaining who your customers are, what they value, and how you will make money in providing them that value [Mag02].

DOI: 10.4324/9781003321187-13

3 A business model describes the rationale of how an organization creates, delivers, and captures value [OP10].

4 A business model is a setup of a number of collaborating parties to produce and deliver a concrete value-in-use to a specific customer segment [Gref15].

As we observe in the above definitions, business models can have an organization-centric character (inside-out perspective from the organization point of view) or an ecosystem-centric character (outside-in perspective). The definition 3 above is an example of an inside-out-oriented definition, the definition 4 is an example of an outside-in-oriented definition. It is not the purpose of this chapter to classify business model concepts, so we take this heterogenous domain as it is and focus on chosen specific business model concepts in the rest of this chapter.

Business models are strongly related to the goals of organizations. In a way, they all describe the reasons for the existence of business organizations, focusing more on the *why* and *what* questions then on the *how* question. To implement business models, however, the *how* question is obviously important. We will treat this question in Section 10.2 of this chapter. But first, we turn our attention to the ways to specify business models.

10.1.2 *Specifying business models inside-out*

When we specify a business model from the viewpoint of a single organization in a business ecosystem (or market), we take the inside-out perspective. We start from the characteristics of this organization and relate these to other organizations, such as providers and customers. The best-known and most popular technique to specify business models in this way is without much doubt the Business Model Canvas (BMC), which is described in a handbook for practical use [OP10]. The BMC technique is based on the research work in an earlier dissertation [Ost04] and complemented with a simple, intuitive graphical specification technique. The structure of the BMC is shown in Figure 10.1.

Central in the canvas is the *value proposition* of an organization. This value proposition is strongly related to the goal of the organization (as we have discussed in the first section of this chapter). To the left of the value proposition, we see the three elements

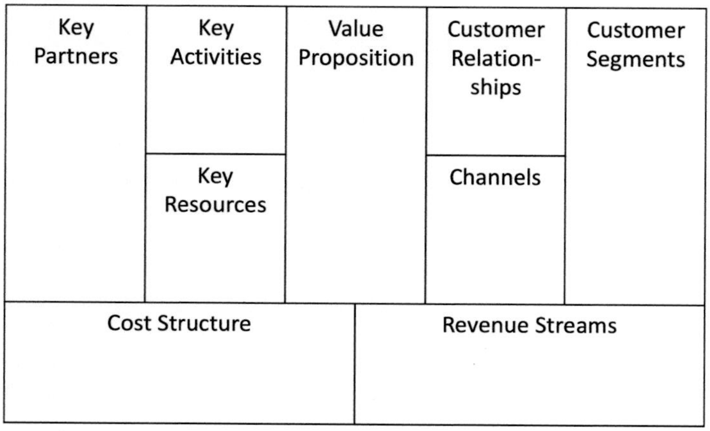

Key Partners	Key Activities	Value Proposition	Customer Relation-ships	Customer Segments
	Key Resources		Channels	
Cost Structure			Revenue Streams	

Figure 10.1 Business Model Canvas structure (adapted from [OP10]).

required to realize the value proposition. The *key activities* specify business activities to be executed. The *key resources* specify the resources needed to execute the key activities (which can include essential information technology infrastructure). The *key partners* are the external organizations that the organization at hand collaborates with to realize the value proposition. To the right of the value proposition, we see the three elements related to delivering the value proposition. The *customer segments* specify the customers to whom the value is to be delivered. The *customer relationships* specify the relational context in which the delivery takes place. The *channels* specify the conduits using which the value is delivered (either of a digital or physical nature). At the bottom of the BMC, we see the financial elements of a business model. The *cost structure* defines the costs associated with delivering the value proposition. The *revenue streams* describe the way the organization obtains its revenue from value delivery. Obviously, the revenue streams should balance the cost structure in a positive way to render a business model attractive.

We will see an application of the BMC in a blockchain context further in this chapter (in Section 10.3.3, to be precise).

10.1.3 Specifying business models outside-in

When we specify a business model from the viewpoint of an ecosystem of collaborating organizations, we take the outside-in perspective. We start with the relations between the individual organizations and only later focus on the internal details of the individual organizations in the collaboration. A typical technique in this class is the Business Model Radar (BMR), a business model specification technique that is part of the BASE/X business engineering framework, described for practitioners in a business modeling handbook [Gref15]. BASE/X is strongly inspired by service-dominant logic [VL04] and explicitly aims at agile, networked business. The BASE/X approach was initially developed in the CoProFind research project [GLv+13] [Luf14] and extensively used in the smart mobility business domain [TGG+19]. The graphical structure of the BMR is shown in Figure 10.2. Its circular shape represents a business ecosystem, in which several actors (organizations) collaborate in a peer-to-peer fashion. The BMR has a combination of a concentric and a radial structure.

In the concentric structure, the co-created *value-in-use* constitutes the center of the BMR. Following service-dominant thinking, it represents the value of a solution to a customer. It is neither a service delivering the value nor a product used to produce or transfer the value. The inner ring around the value-in-use contains the *actor value propositions*. Each actor value proposition represents the part of the central value-in-use contributed by a single actor. All actor value propositions add up to the central value-in-use. The middle ring contains the *actor coproduction activities*. An actor co-production activity defines the activities that an actor performs in the business for achieving the co-creation of value, i.e., its actor value proposition. The effects of this activity can be observed by the customer. The outer ring contains the *actor cost/benefits*. These define the financial and nonfinancial expenses/gains for each of the co-creation actors.

In the radial structure of the BMR, each 'pie slice' of the radar represents a *co-creation actor*, including the focal organization and the customer. The labels of the actors are either placed around the BMR or in a fourth outside ring (we use both formats in this chapter, they differ only slightly visually). The *focal organization* is the party that initiates the setup of the business model and participates actively in orchestrating the solution. The *customer* is always one of the parties contributing to the production of the value-in-use.

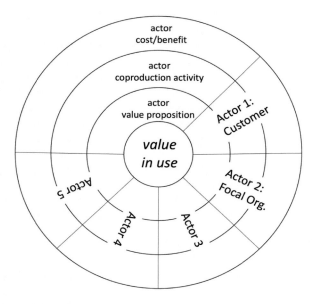

Figure 10.2 Business Model Radar structure (adapted from [Gref15]).

10.2   Business models in the digital age

As discussed in the previous section, business models describe the reasons for the existence of business organizations, focusing more on the *why* and *what* questions than on the *how* question. To implement business models, however, the *how* question is obviously important. The *how* question relates to two aspects. Firstly, it relates to business processes that operationalize business models: business process models describe the order in which activities are executed to reach a goal. Certainly in networked business, these processes can be complex [GT17]. Secondly, the *how* question relates to the resources used in the execution of these business processes – you might also label this as the *with what* question. These resources include (digital) technology that supports the processes. As this book is on the use of blockchain technology, we focus mostly on the second interpretation of the *how* question and place this in a digital context.

There are many business types and hence business models in which digital technology plays a role. Actually, it is quite hard to think of any modern business in which no computer technology is used at all. To better understand the spectrum of 'importance' of digital technology to business, it is good to distinguish between digitally supported business models and digitally enabled business models – we explain the two types below.

10.2.1 Digitally supported business models

A digitally supported business model is a model that can be executed better with the use of digital technology but that can also be executed without, be it with less favorable characteristics (for example, slower or at a higher cost). This means that the business model is not completely dependent on digital technology.

For example, the general business model of mainstream retail banking is nowadays supported by digital technology. The use of digital technology makes processes more efficient, for example by having mobile self-service applications for customers. Retail banking processes can, however, also be executed without this kind of digital technology, as we have done this for a long time when the technology was not yet available.

The level of innovation of digitally supported business models varies from case to case and often depends on the level of improvement that is achieved by the use of specific digital technology. If the level of improvement is that great that a business model is actually (economically) completely infeasible without the improvement, we actually have a digitally enabled business model.

In this book, we focus on blockchain as a digital technology to support business models. We discuss examples in Sections 10.3 and 10.4 of this chapter.

10.2.2 Digitally enabled business models

A digitally enabled business model is a model that is explicitly enabled by the use of digital technology, i.e., the essence of the model does not work at all without digital technology. Often, the model is enabled by a specific kind of technology and hence the model is dependent on this technology.

For example, the general business model of a webshop is enabled by the use of web and Internet technology – it literally cannot exist without this technology. The business model of on-demand electric scooter sharing is enabled by the use of mobile technology (to reserve scooters) and IoT technology (to track the location and use of scooters). One can say that the use of digitally enabled business models actually defines the domain of electronic business [Gref16].

Digitally enabled business models are often interesting when they are enabled by new types of digital technology, as this implies that they are innovative (but not necessarily always successful). In this book, we are specifically interested in blockchain as a new digital technology to enable business models, of course. We discuss an example in Section 10.5 of this chapter.

10.2.3 Types of e-business models and blockchain

We can distinguish between various classes of business models from an electronic business perspective. A high-level classification is the distinction between object provisioning models, intermediation models, and cooperation support models [Gref16], which aim at respectively purely transactional business, setting up collaborative business, and executing collaborative business. Below, we discuss these three classes in more detail, including the possible role of blockchain in supporting them, based on the concepts and examples presented in Chapter 9 and in Part 2 of this book.

In object provisioning e-business models, digital technology is used to provide objects to customers, where objects can be of a physical or digital nature. Business-to-consumer (B2C) webshops are a well-known example in this class, but far more complicated examples exist in business–to-business (B2B) supply chains. In business models in this class, blockchain can be used for several purposes. Firstly, blockchain can be used to record the execution of steps in ordering and delivery of objects, such that involved parties have a basis to agree on the status of the process. Consequently, disputes are avoided or can be transparently settled based on the information in the blockchain trace.

This may be overkill in simple B2C chains, but very relevant in complex B2B chains. Secondly, blockchain can be used for the distributed management of certification of objects that are provisioned through other channels. This means that explicit quality certificates of traded objects are stored in a way that is trusted by all involved parties. And obviously, blockchain can play a role in the provisioning of financial objects to pay for delivered objects. We discussed Bitcoin (Chapter 5) and Ethereum (Chapter 6) as public cryptocurrencies earlier in this book. In Chapter 6, we also presented how Ethereum ERC-20 tokens can be used to create private cryptocurrencies.

In intermediation e-business models, digital technology is used to create new collaborations between organizations, i.e., to bring parties together for collaboration without supporting the actual execution of the collaboration. These business models usually have some kind of a matchmaking character in the context of a specific business domain or market. Blockchain can be helpful in models in this class if trust has to be digitally established in a distributed setting to enable a new collaboration. This is certainly the case in business domains with dynamic relationships between organizations that do not share a prior, non-digital business context. Trust can be established for example by making profiles or certificates of parties available via blockchain in a reputable way. Here we see a similar mechanism as in the object provisioning class, but it is now applied to business partners instead of traded objects.

In cooperation support e-business models, digital technology is used to support the actual, operational collaboration between parties – either after intermediation or in existing collaboration settings. This means that digital technology helps the parties by exchanging business information and synchronizing their business activities. Blockchain is often used in cooperation support models as a means to create or enhance trust between partners in an operational collaboration by creating a situation of non-repudiation, i.e., a situation in which agreements made in the past cannot be denied by partners. This can be done for example by creating a shared trace of the execution of collaborative activities, by storing checkpoint data in a business process, or by storing information on business guaranteed between partners. The immutability of the blockchain ledger, introduced in Chapter 3, is the basis for this functionality.

Table 10.1 shows an overview of the discussed use of blockchain in business models belonging to the three discussed classes.

Table 10.1 Overview of business model classes with possible blockchain use modes

Business model class	*Goal of business model*	*Possible uses of blockchain*
Object provisioning	Provide traded objects to customers in a transactional way	Create non-disputable trace of object provisioning process Store quality certificate of a provided object Manage digital payment of provided objects
Intermediation	Bring e-business parties together to create new collaborations	Share partner profile in a reputable way Share partner certificate in a reputable way
Cooperation support	Support e-business parties in the execution of their collaboration with non-repudiation	Create non-disputable trace of collaboration process Store collaboration checkpoint data Store guarantees between partners

10.3   Blockchain as an efficiency booster

There are many business domains that have a heavy administrative aspect to guard the quality and safety of the processes in the domain. A typical example is the real estate trading domain (for example selling and buying houses), in which we see important administrative roles for notaries and land registry organizations. Typically, the formal processes performed by these roles are based on complex paper documents that have to be physically signed, or on direct electronic replacements of some of these documents (that can sometimes be digitally signed, depending on local laws). Obviously, these formal processes incur high costs for their execution, either in terms of time, in terms of money, or both. This is where digital technology can play a role to design digitally supported business models that allow for more efficient processes. We are talking about cooperation support models here (see Section 10.2.3), more precisely e-facilitator and e-collaborator business models [Gref16], which address efficiency in business collaborations. An e-facilitator is an organization that offers digital infrastructure for the collaboration between other organizations, without taking part in this collaboration itself. An e-collaborator deploys digital infrastructure for collaborations in which it is involved itself.

Given this context, in this section we take a look at blockchain as an efficiency booster in business ecosystems that require the handling of complex, certified dossiers related to physical objects that are traded. First, we take a look at the need for efficiency in the modern business world. Then, we discuss a business case from the world of trading high-tech, used spare parts that involves complex certified dossiers and the issues with respect to efficiency in this case. Next, we show how the use of blockchain can address these issues and hence can be the basis for a business model. We note that this can be seen as an application of non-fungible token technology. The implementation of non-fungible tokens as a special class of Ethereum smart contracts is discussed in Chapter 6.

10.3.1 The need for efficiency

We currently live in times of global markets. The transparency enabled by the internet has removed regional and national boundaries, enabling global trade on a formerly unprecedented scale. This opens up new possibilities for business, but also introduces new threats in the form of global competition. Depending on the kind of market, this can be a competition based on product or service quality if the prices can be variable, or competition on the process and hence price if the quality can be variable – or both, obviously.

In markets where the competition is mainly on process and price, efficiency becomes a main element of competitiveness. Digital technology can help in improving efficiency in various ways. Business process management technology [Kum18] can help in streamlining the execution of business processes. Business intelligence technology [GR16] can help in making better decisions for improving efficiency. IoT technology [Gre21] can help in efficiently tracking the whereabouts and status of physical objects in a digital way. And of course, these technologies can become more powerful if combined [GLT+18]. In this book, we are mainly interested in the role of blockchain technology. In Chapter 11, we show how blockchain technology can be combined with other technologies, such as IoT sensors, in an advanced business application context.

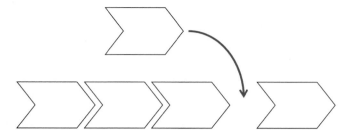

Figure 10.3 The principle of reintermediation (adapted from [Gref16]).

As we will see in this section, blockchain can be used to boost the efficiency of complex processes that require complex administration with a high level of trust through formal certification. From an e-business perspective, this can lead to a case of reintermediation: the insertion of a new node with additional functionality into an existing business network [Tur02] [Gref16], illustrated in Figure 10.3. The new node typically 'eats' some of the income of the other nodes. A well-known and relatively simple example of reintermediation in the business-to-consumer domain can be found in the many hotel booking platforms, which position themselves between hotels and travelers. In the business-to-business domain, we find more complex cases in which clear opportunities exist for the application of blockchain technology – we discuss this in this section.

10.3.2 Traditional certified spare-parts markets

Anybody who has ever had a serious problem with his or her vehicle – be it a bike or a car – knows that the availability of spare parts is essential to solve the problem. In normal consumer markets, it is generally not so hard to obtain an adequate spare part for your bike or car. This is different, however, in high-tech, strictly regulated markets such as the aviation market or the high-end medical devices market. We briefly discuss the case of the aviation market below, but other markets operate in a similar way. It is good to remember that we are talking here about markets for highly expensive, complex parts.

When there is a technical problem with a jetliner in the commercial aviation market that requires a repair, one cannot simply go to a shop around the corner to buy a necessary spare part. Any essential spare part has to comply with strict regulations concerning the characteristics of the part. In other words, all spare parts need to be officially certified to guarantee the safety of the airplane in which they are used. This holds for new spare parts, but even more for used spare parts.

For a new part, it must be completely clear for example by whom it was manufactured, where it was manufactured, when it was manufactured and for which context it has been certified. In a traditional setting, this means that a part is accompanied by a set of paper specification documents that state all of this and a set of paper documents that formally certify the correctness of the specification documents.

For a used part, all of this must be clear but additionally, the usage history of the part has to be clear and certified. For example, when a used landing gear is considered for replacing a broken landing gear in a jetliner, it must be clear how many take-off and landing cycles this used landing gear has already experienced in its history (to assess its wear), by which airline it has been used before (to assess the quality of the scheduled maintenance it has received so far) and which repairs it has undergone when and by whom (to assess the quality of any modifications to the part). This implies a set of documents that specify the history of the part and more paper-based certificates that guarantee the correctness of the specification of the history. The more a part has been used, the larger the dossier of the part gets – and the costlier it gets to process everything when a part is sold.

This document-centric certification process is an obstacle to an efficient used–parts market in global aviation. Sometimes, document logistics is far more complicated than parts logistics itself.

10.3.3 Blockchain-boosted certified spare-parts markets

Blockchain technology can be used to improve the efficiency of the aviation used–parts industry that we describe above. Using blockchain, we can replace paper-based documents and certificates that are created during the events in the lifetime of an airplane part by digital documents that are collected as transactions in the blockchain. The owner of a part registers all main events of a part in the blockchain, such that a complete history of the part is available when it is to be sold. The potential buyer of a spare part can inspect the complete historic specification of a spare part to assess whether it is usable for a given repair context. The trust management characteristics of blockchain are used in this case to assure the validity of all documents related to a spare part.

In Figure 10.4, we see a business model built around the concept of a certified spare-parts market, specified as a BMC (see Section 10.1.2 of this chapter). The business model is created for a company that positions itself as an intermediary in the used spare-parts market between sellers and buyers of used spare parts – a case of reintermediation as discussed in Section 10.3.1.

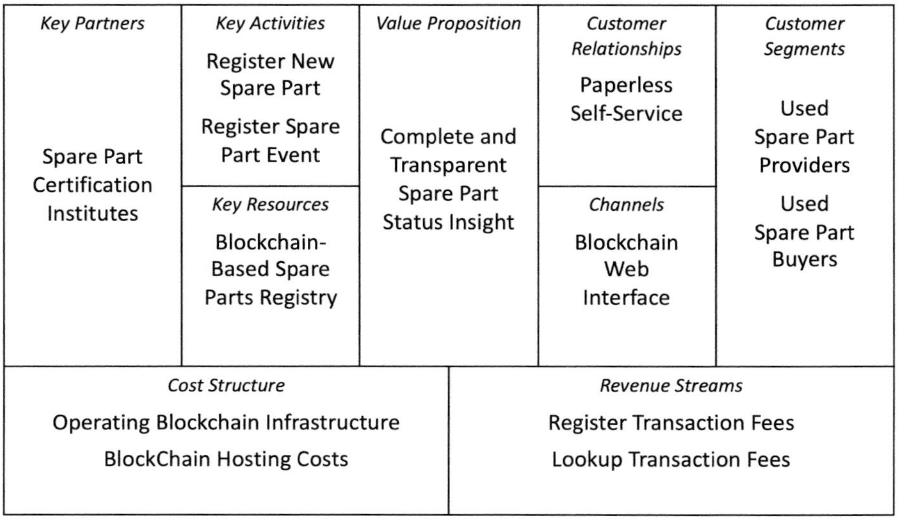

Key Partners	Key Activities	Value Proposition	Customer Relationships	Customer Segments
Spare Part Certification Institutes	Register New Spare Part / Register Spare Part Event	Complete and Transparent Spare Part Status Insight	Paperless Self-Service	Used Spare Part Providers
	Key Resources: Blockchain-Based Spare Parts Registry		Channels: Blockchain Web Interface	Used Spare Part Buyers

Cost Structure	Revenue Streams
Operating Blockchain Infrastructure / BlockChain Hosting Costs	Register Transaction Fees / Lookup Transaction Fees

Figure 10.4 Blockchain-boosted business model for certified spare parts history provider.

The business model of Figure 10.4 is generic: it is not specialized for a specific market like aviation or healthcare. The business model is built around the value proposition of complete and transparent insight into the status of spare parts. There are two customer segments: used spare part providers (sellers) and used spare part buyers. The customer relationships are defined around paperless self-service for both customer segments, using a web-based interface to a blockchain-based registry. A set of spare part certification institutes take the place of key partners in the business model. The key activities are registering new parts into the blockchain and registering any main life cycle event of a spare part (such as the part completing an amount of usage cycles, changing owner, receiving maintenance, or being repaired). The certification institutes are involved in these registration activities where necessary. The blockchain-based registry platform for spare parts is the key resource in this business model. Hosting and operating the platform is a main part of the cost structure. The revenue streams are formed by fees for registration transaction by part owners and lookup transaction by potential part buyers.

Depending on precise market characteristics, the business model can operate by being completely paperless, or can be extended with a paper document vault function, such that the intermediary stores the physical documents in a trusted way and the blockchain entries refer to this physical store where necessary. In this way, physical documents do not need to be transported between owners of parts. In either case, the application of blockchain can be used to boost the efficiency of a certified used spare-parts market, both in terms of the financial costs related with administration and certification processes, as with the time-wise costs of these processes. In this way, blockchain is the technological basis for a digitally enabled business model. This basis uses the technology of non-fungible tokens that we have discussed in the context of Ethereum in Chapter 6. More in detail, each spare part can be associated with a unique non-fungible token to which certification documents can be linked. At least part of the business logic to assign and verify the certifications can also be implemented as part of the non-fungible token smart contract.

10.4   Blockchain as a business trust enabler

In this section, we take a look at blockchain as a trust enabler from a business perspective. First, we look at the role of trust in business in general and in electronic business specifically. Then, we zoom in at a specific application domain to show how the use of blockchain technology can enable trust management mechanisms in complex business ecosystems. This involves cooperation support business models, typically of the e-facilitator type [Gref16] that we have already seen in the previous section.

We choose the domain of international, multi-modal logistics as this is a domain with complex business relationships that involve clear trust management aspects. We describe this domain first in its traditional form and then in an improved, blockchain-enabled form in which a trust provider is added to the network. The trust provider replaces other trust mechanisms, so the new business model is a digitally supported business model.

10.4.1 *The role of trust in (electronic) business*

As we have seen in Chapter 1 of this book, trust is an essential ingredient in more or less all business relations. Trust in business relations can be implicit or explicit. Trust is implicit when it has been built in an incremental way on the basis of a long-standing positive experience in collaboration. In other words, two organizations can 'learn' to trust each other. Trust is explicit when it is governed by clearly agreed mechanisms. In traditional business, these mechanisms often have the form of contracts or other forms of written agreements, which are typically certified by signatures of the involved parties, and which can be enforced using a legal system that forms the explicitly mentioned context of the contracts or agreements.

In modern electronic business (or e-business), organizations often engage in business relationships without implicit trust – for several reasons. One reason is the fact that business networks are increasingly becoming dynamic, meaning that organizations change partnerships more often. This means that there is no time to develop implicit trust. Another reason is the globalization of business, meaning that partners are found far away and possibly in different cultures and legal systems, thereby hindering the easy build-up of trust. This implies that in digital business, explicit trust management is often an essential ingredient.

Blockchain can be used in mechanisms for explicit trust management. We discuss several mechanisms in the next sections of this chapter. A special case of blockchain as a trust enabler is in the case of the outcome-based business, in which common agreements on reached outcomes are the basis for business settlements. We discuss this in the next chapter of this book.

10.4.2 Traditional multi-modal logistic markets

In the modern, global economy, large amounts of goods are shipped between countries or even between continents. To ship goods from their origin to their destination, we often require several modes of transportation. For example, electronic goods shipped from South Korea to Germany can be transported from factory to a deep-sea port in South Korea by truck, to a deep-sea port in the Netherlands by a container ship, to Germany by train and to final destination by truck. This means that the goods also need to be cross-docked at terminals between these modes of transportation. Often, the different modes of transportation and the cross-docking between them are operated by several independent companies. The entire process is called multi-modal logistics. To coordinate all transportation processes, typically a logistics service provider (LSP) is involved that handles the multi-modal logistics process for the shipper of the goods. A business model for such a multi-modal logistics service is shown in Figure 10.5 in the format of a BMR.

In the figure, we see that a goods shipper is the customer of the business model. The value-in-use of the business models is end-to-end (E2E) logistics (interpreted as a value, not as the physical process). The benefit of the customer (indicated by a plus-sign in the costs and benefits ring) is the relocation of goods (in the example from the factory in South Korea to a customer in Germany). The cost is a logistics fee (indicated by a minus sign) paid to the LSP. The LSP has this fee as the benefit and has two costs: its own operations and fees to be paid for transport and cross-docking to transport operators and terminal operators respectively.

Obviously, trust is an important aspect in the multi-modal logistics process. The goods may for example be a sea container full of smartphones, which constitutes a sizeable value. The trust is often implicit in the value proposition and hence in the benefit of the customer. All service providers have some checks and balances in their activities to guard the trust, for example by exchanging transport forms, but trust management is not an explicit element (as indicated by the parentheses in the model in Figure 10.5).

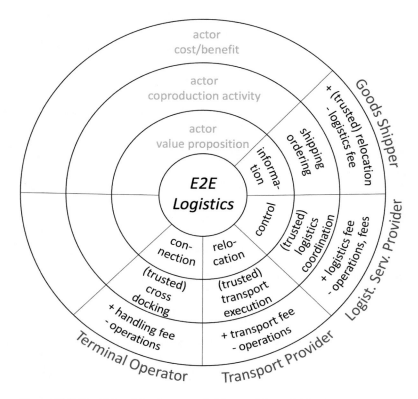

Figure 10.5 Traditional business model for multi-modal logistics.

Consequently, often there is no overall view and management of trust. This can lead to problems, for example when goods are misplaced or damaged and it is not clear which party is exactly responsible for this. Below, we will see how the use of blockchain can help in explicit trust management.

10.4.3 Blockchain-based, multi-modal logistics markets

In Figure 10.6, we see an adapted version of the business model in Figure 10.5. The most obvious difference is the addition of a party: the trust provider. By the addition of this party and its actor value proposition, the value-in-use of the business model can be adapted to trusted multi-modal logistics.

The trust provider provides explicit trust management by processing all major events of the multi-modal transportation process of a set of goods in a blockchain platform. The events are reported into the blockchain platform by all participants in the logistics process. For example, the LSP reports when a transportation order has been issued to a transport provider, a transport provider reports which goods exactly he has accepted for transport with a precise indication of time and location, etc. In doing so, all activities in the process become completely traceable and in case of any issues, the responsible party can be identified.

It can be argued whether the addition of the trust provider is a case of reintermediation (as discussed in the previous section). The trust provider does not explicitly

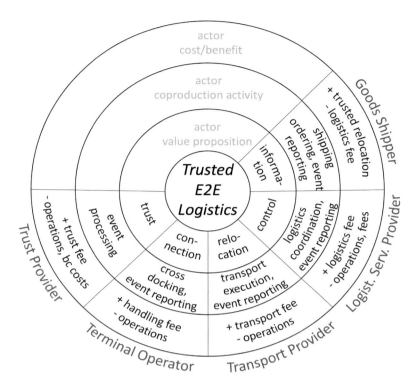

Figure 10.6 Blockchain-enabled business model for trusted multi-modal logistics.

position itself between the other organizations in the network, but rather replaces part of their paper-based functionality with a blockchain-based solution, which provides more structured functionality. From this perspective, we consider this a pure business network extension, rather than typical reintermediation.

10.5 Blockchain as a disintermediator

In this section, we discuss the possibilities for blockchain as a mechanism for disintermediation in a business network, i.e., how blockchain can possibly make organizations in a network redundant. This leads to new business models with an essentially different configuration, so to digitally enabled business models. These models go into the category of cooperation support models and in the subcategory of e-collaborator models [Gref16], which we have already seen in Section 10.3.

Below, we first discuss the concept of disintermediation a bit more precisely. Then we discuss the application of the concept, based on the application of blockchain, in the real estate business domain.

10.5.1 The concept of disintermediation

Disintermediation in e-business (see Figure 10.7) is the removal of a business organization from a business network because its functionality has become superfluous by the introduction of digital technology [EW99] [Tur02] [Gref16]. After the removal of the node, its income can be divided among the remaining nodes in the network. A very well-known example is that of the business-to-consumer web shop, which sits at the place of a wholesaler in a supply chain and removes the local, physical retailers (the traditional shops) from the chain.

Using the disintermediation principle, blockchain mechanisms can possibly cover the functionality of administrative, trust-building organizations in a business chain or network, such as a bank or a notary. In doing so, the costs of these organizations are removed from the network. Also, the network is no longer bound to the rules of these organizations (insofar these rules are not implied by legislation that the network is bound to, obviously, which can be an important issue as we will see further on).

In a sense, blockchain-based cryptocurrencies such as Bitcoin, as discussed in Chapter 5 of this book, create a disintermediation of the traditional banking system – even though some may argue that a new organization is introduced, actually creating a case of substitution [Gref16] instead of disintermediation. Substitution means that an existing link in a business chain is replaced by another link that has similar functionality, but can offer this functionality with better characteristics, for example, by being faster, cheaper, or more trustworthy.

10.5.2 The real estate business domain case

We have already mentioned the real estate domain briefly in Section 10.3 from the point of view of efficiency management. In this section, we look more extensively at the domain from the perspective of disintermediation, i.e., reshaping existing business chains.

In Figure 10.8, we see a high-level overview of a traditional real estate trading business chain. The chain is simplified for reasons of brevity and in some countries, the chain might be slightly different. The chain typically starts with advertising a house to be sold. Then, a real estate agent matches the seller with a buyer and prepares the transaction to pass the ownership of the house from seller to buyer. The actual transaction is executed by a notary who has the legal power to do so. The notary notifies the Land Registry office, which records ownership of real estate. Finally, the house buyer receives the documents that state his ownership.

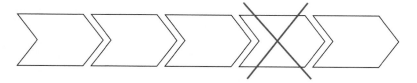

Figure 10.7 The principle of disintermediation (adapted from [Gref16]).

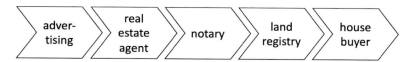

Figure 10.8 Traditional real estate business chain.

In many standard real estate sales transactions, the task of the notary is of quite a standard nature. Nevertheless, the provisioning of this task can be quite expensive. The main function of the notary is to make sure that all procedures in a transaction are executed correctly and to create formal trust in the execution of the sales transaction. Technically, it is possible to guard the correct execution of a real estate sales transaction by smart contracts and to create trust in the execution of that transaction by using blockchain mechanisms, as we have seen earlier in this book. From this technical perspective, it would be possible to disintermediate the notary from the business chain, as shown in Figure 10.9. Note that in many countries, if at all possible, this is not simple from a legal perspective – but this is not the main perspective of this book.

The disintermediation of the notary leads to a business chain as shown in Figure 10.10. Here we see that a blockchain registry is used to create a trusted relationship between parties, thereby fulfilling one of the main functions of the notary. Two smart contracts are used to ensure the correct execution of processes. The first smart contract is used to make sure that the ownership transaction between seller and buyer of the house proceeds correctly. The second smart contract supports the correct registration of the change of ownership toward the Land Registry office. The buyer of the house also has access to the blockchain registry, such that he or she can follow the process and extract relevant digital documents.

In Figure 10.11, we see the estate agent's business model for the new business chain in BMC format. Note that the customer is the house buyer, who also pays the house-buying transaction fee (in the original model with the notary, the house buyer pays the notary). This is the case in some situations – in some other situations, the house seller may be the customer and pay the fee, leading to a variation on the business model.

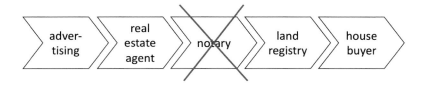

Figure 10.9 Disintermediation in a real estate business chain.

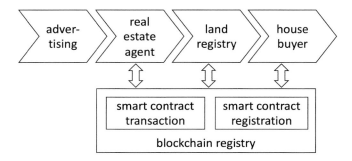

Figure 10.10 Blockchain-enabled real estate business chain.

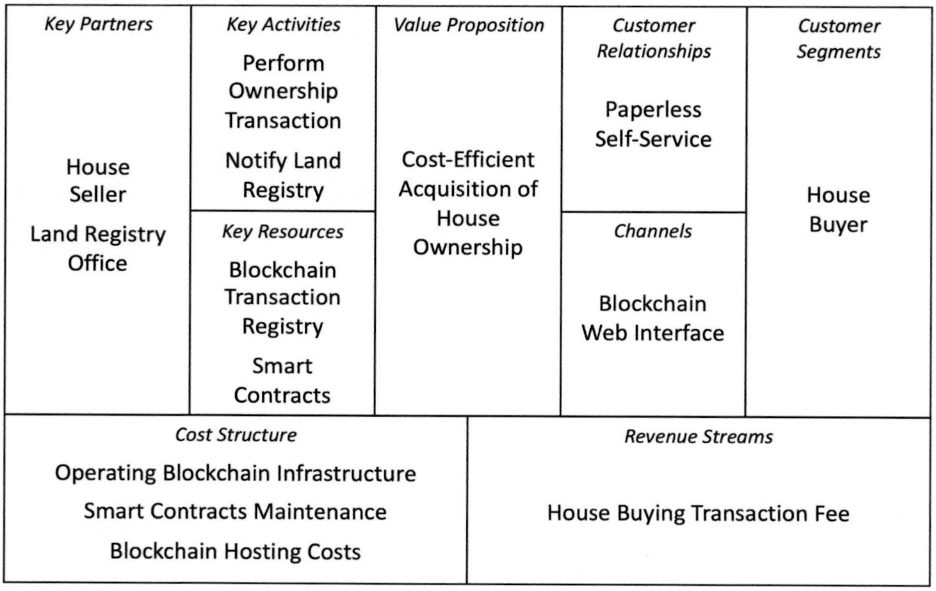

Key Partners	Key Activities	Value Proposition	Customer Relationships	Customer Segments
House Seller Land Registry Office	Perform Ownership Transaction Notify Land Registry **Key Resources** Blockchain Transaction Registry Smart Contracts	Cost-Efficient Acquisition of House Ownership	Paperless Self-Service **Channels** Blockchain Web Interface	House Buyer

Cost Structure	Revenue Streams
Operating Blockchain Infrastructure Smart Contracts Maintenance Blockchain Hosting Costs	House Buying Transaction Fee

Figure 10.11 BMC for blockchain-enabled real-estate transaction business model.

10.6 Designing blockchain-enabled business models

In this section, we discuss the design of blockchain-enabled business models. The starting point for a design is either the technology of blockchain, or a business problem or opportunity that can be addressed by using blockchain technology. In other words, we can either take a technology-push approach or a requirements-pull approach. In the overall introduction of blockchain into the business domain, it is the combination of a technology-push force and a requirements-pull force that generates what is called 'traction' or 'technology adoption' for the blockchain approach – this is illustrated in Figure 10.12.

We discuss the two approaches in the next two subsections. In business practice, a combination of both approaches may be used. And either of the two approaches can be used in the creation of new business opportunities – the starting point is different, so should be the market that is targeted.

10.6.1 Technology-push business model design

When you (try and) make a blockchain-based business model design from the technology-push perspective (the typical perspective of a computer scientist or a technology innovator in business), you start reasoning from the technical characteristics of blockchain technology in general or a specific blockchain implementation (depending on the scope of your design). This design approach is typically usable for explorative design or for design that is independent from specific application domains. But as we are talking about business model design, the design should always be performed such that it can be used for buy-in of business stakeholders: they are the target for business models, even if you start reasoning from technology.

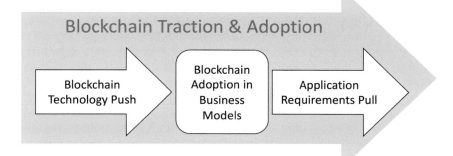

Figure 10.12 Technology-push and requirements pull (adapted from [Gref16]).

In using a technology-push approach, it is helpful to distinguish functional characteristics of blockchain from non-functional characteristics.

10.6.2 *Using functional characteristics of blockchain technology*

The functional characteristics determine *what* a blockchain platform can do in a business context. This means that you start with basic blockchain functionality as discussed in the previous chapters of this book. You can interpret the functionality in the context of general e-business drivers, like reach and richness [EW99] [Gref16].

The reach of an e-business scenario determines which customers can be reached. Many e-business models rely on extending reach (i.e., target more potential customers) in either the geographic, the temporal or the model (channel) dimension or a combination of these [Gref16]. For example, a web shop extends the geographical and temporal reach with respect to a physical shop because customers from far away can use the shop, even outside traditional shopping hours. A blockchain-enabled business model may for example extend the reach of trust because it relies on a digital trust provisioning mechanism rather than a physical one (like paper-based contracts). In situations where objects are traded in an asynchronous way (where typically one object is of a financial nature), this type of trust is very relevant when the parties participating in the trading are 'far apart', i.e., cannot rely on physical interaction. Here 'far apart' can indicate geographic distance, but also a difference in operating hours (which can obviously be caused by different time zones, but also by different business domains).

The richness of an e-business scenario determines how rich the interaction between a provider and a customer is in the scenario, measured for example by the number of interactions, the used media in the interactions or the customization of interactions toward customers [Gref16]. The richer a scenario is, the more opportunities a provider has to bind customers to its business. A blockchain-based business model may for example increase the richness of interaction because it allows more fine-grained interaction between parties (possibly governed by smart contracts) or because it allows transparent access to a complete history of events in a business collaboration, such that the parties in the collaboration can perform business analysis on this data.

10.6.3 *Using non-functional characteristics of blockchain technology*

The non-functional characteristics of blockchain technology determine the characteristics with which the functions of the technology are executed, or simply put 'how' it
functions from a performance point of view. Typical nonfunctional characteristics are
cost, speed, availability, and reliability of functions – the non-functional dimensions of
performance.

Non-functional characteristics can be used as a basis for business model design if
blockchain technology offers functions that perform significantly better from the perspective of a non-functional dimension than current solutions for the same functions. In
this case, a blockchain-based solution doesn't do other things than a competing solution
but does it better along the chosen dimensions. A typical example that we have seen
before in this chapter is the replacement of slow and costly paper-based procedures (like
physical contract and certificate handling) by faster and cheaper digital procedures.

10.6.4 *Requirements-pull business model design*

When you (try and) make a blockchain-based business model design from the
requirements-pull perspective (the typical perspective of a business scientist or a business
analyst), you start reasoning from problems or opportunities in an application domain
that can be addressed by the use of blockchain characteristics.

Obviously, it is important to identify problems or opportunities with enough relevance and urgency in a business domain (sometimes referred to as the 'big pains and
gains'). If the relevance is too small, too few people will be interested in your business
model. If the urgency is too small, people will be interested in your business model too
late (or it will stay on the list of possibly interesting things forever).

Designing a business model from a requirements-pull perspective can only be done
well with access to enough business domain knowledge. Without this, the 'pains and
gains' will not be adequately identified and understood. They need to be well understood to have an early impression whether there is a 'blockchain' aspect in them. To
gain this understanding, it is imperative to actively go and search the opinion of business
experts – this cannot be done within the walls of a technology innovation laboratory.

10.7 Conclusions

In this chapter, we have looked at business models in a blockchain context, i.e., at
business models for scenarios in which blockchain can be applied to support specific
functionality. By specifying a business model, we 'paint' the business reasons for the
application of blockchain in a structured way. In other words, we add the business-
oriented 'why' to the technical 'what' and 'how' of blockchain.

We have seen that there are different ways to specify business models. In the chapter,
we have discussed the business model canvas and the business model radar as two good
examples of specification techniques. The choice for a technique depends on the nature
of the business scenario and on the aspects that need to be emphasized (for example the
inside-out or the outside-in view).

We have distinguished between digitally supported business models and digitally
enabled business models. The latter type depends on the availability of digital technologies like blockchain. We have seen various ways in which blockchain can support

or enable a business scenario – the variations on what the business-oriented 'why' of blockchain is. In deciding about the use of blockchain (in designing the digital support for a business scenario and its business model), it is of paramount importance to answer this 'why' question explicitly. The better the answer, the better the investment in digital infrastructure like blockchain. Obviously, this question should be answered with the future of a business scenario in mind. The only thing that does not change in a typical e-business scenario, after all, is the fact that everything changes all the time.

10.8 Questions and exercises

1   Do you think that it is possible to model the business model radar (BMR) of Figure 10.6 in a business model canvas (BMC)? If yes, explain what might be the possible reasons of doing so (what does a BMC show better than a BMR?). If no, explain why this is not possible.
2   The business model of Figure 10.6 does not specify the aggregation level of goods that are considered by the model. The aggregation level can be a complete shipment (which can consist of multiple sea containers), a single sea container, a pallet in a sea container, or an individual product in a pallet. Which aggregation level would be most sensible under which circumstances and why?

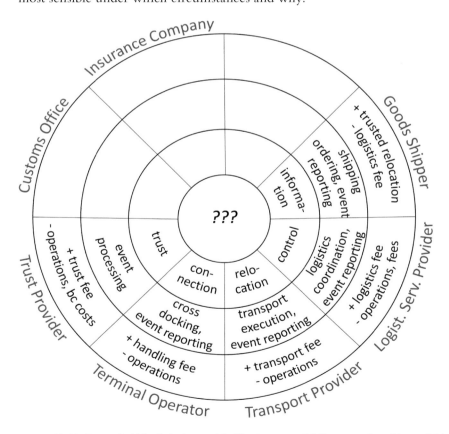

Figure 10.13 Extended blockchain-enabled business model for trusted multi-modal logistics.

3 As we have discussed with the business chain shown in Figure 10.10, there may (or will) be legal issues with this business chain, as the party that provides legality has been disintermediated. Discuss what would be necessary to make the new business chain legal. As this is not a book for a legal curriculum, try and use 'common sense' arguments.

4 In Figure 10.4, you see the BMC representation of a business model for the application of blockchain technology in the spare parts world. Transform this business model specification into the BMR format, as explained in Section 10.1.3. Tip: the BMR technique does not include resources (as it is completely value-oriented) – these are implicit in actor coproduction activities.

5 In Figure 10.6, you see the BMR of a blockchain-enabled, trusted multi-modal logistics service. Extend this business model radar with two additional parties (i.e., add two pie slides to the radar model, as illustrated in Figure 10.13): a customs office that checks goods upon crossing a border and an insurance company that insures goods during transportation against damage or loss. Consider whether this changes the central value-in-use of the business model and fill in the actor value propositions, actor coproduction activities and the cost and benefits of the two new actors. Pay special attention to the question whether the two added parties also have to report their events into the blockchain platform.

6 Create a business model specification in BMR format of the business chain shown in Figure 10.10. Consider explicitly which parties should be included in the model. Decide whether the seller of the house needs to be included as a party in the model. Also think whether the blockchain registry needs to be a separate party or is linked to the model in a different way.

11 Blockchain in outcome management

Learning goals

11.A The reader can describe the concept of outcome-based business and can explain the differences with respect to goods-based business and service-based business.

11.B The reader can analyze and design the main information flows required in outcome-based business scenarios.

11.C The reader can explain the necessity of explicit trust management in outcome-based business and can describe the role of blockchain in this context.

11.D The reader can explain that in complex business scenarios, blockchain can play an important enabling role to cater for the trusted data aspect, but typically other digital technologies are required as well to cater to other aspects.

11.E The reader can analyze and design business models in an outcome-based business context, as well translate these into blockchain-enabled scenarios.

11.1 The outcome economy concept

In the current economy, we see a major trend toward outcome thinking that is causing a shift of focus for many business organizations. In a traditional business setting, producers deliver products (or services) to their customers. The producers focus on optimizing the quality of their products to their standards and the customers are responsible for using these products to their best advantage. This often causes a mismatch between what is delivered to the customers and what they need to strengthen their own market position. In the new setting known as the outcome economy, customers expect producers to deliver their products such that they directly contribute to their success in their market. In other words, producers are expected to create value by delivering solutions to customers that in turn lead to quantifiable results for these customers [Acc15]: their outcomes.

To quantify results in an outcome management setting, i.e., measure and report the outcomes, advanced IT is required. Internet and Internet-of-Things (IoT) technologies [Gre21] are used to capture data in the customer context, Blockchain technology is used to store outcome data in a trusted way, and Business Intelligence (BI) technologies [GR16] are used to transform this data into actionable information in the provider context. In

DOI: 10.4324/9781003321187-14

other words, outcome management requires data-driven business management, which gets an increasingly real-time character in modern business settings.

From an e-business point of view, introducing outcome management in a business context can be considered a case of deconstruction and reconstruction of a market [EW99] [Gref16], as it completely changes interorganizational business relations.

The outcome economy concept has attracted substantial attention from industrial practice and academic research in recent years [NDY13] [Acc15] [CNK+16] [Bar16] [SPJ+20]. Examples of this shift from selling products (or services) to selling outcomes can be found in many domains. An illustrative example can be found in the aircraft engine industry, where business models are explored and the actual performance of engines is sold instead of the physical product [Bar16]. In the transport and logistics domain, business models are explored where the effects of data analytics services on transport efficiency are sold instead of the services themselves, e.g., to increase fuel economy of deep-sea vessels [Ato21]. These applications require real-time data capturing and advanced, trusted processing of this data – the latter not in the least because the data are the basis for billing the customer by the provider.

11.2 An outcome economy control model

This section presents the basic outcome economy control model. First, we present a traditional control model for a single organization used to control the quality of its output, either products or services. This traditional model is not outcome-based. Then, we extend this model to the level of a business chain or network to include the outcome management principle. In this chain-level model, a provider helps improving the outcome of its customers.

11.2.1 Organization-level business control model

In Figure 11.1, we see a very basic business control model [GWK+21]. A model like this is also known as a *cybernetic model* [Wik22]. Cybernetic control models are used in many engineering disciplines to describe and implement control systems with dynamic behavior. Control models have also found their way into software [Fra18]. We use control models to manage dynamic business outcome scenarios, using digital means (i.e., software plus also a bit of hardware for obtaining measurements).

In the figure, we see a business process that has an *input* and an *output*. A *sensor* is connected to the output channel to measure the quality of the output. The measurements of the sensor are used by a *regulator* to change the operating parameters of the business process in case the quality readings of the sensor are not according to standards. A regulator can be seen as a combination of an automated decision maker that determines when action has to be taken and an abstract actuator that makes sure that the action is executed (note that the physical actuation is encapsulated in the business process).

To make this abstract control model a bit more concrete, we discuss an example of milk production in a dairy farm, which is illustrated in Figure 11.2. The input is cattle feed (and some other ingredients) and the output is milk. The business process contains the activities for milk production, in which cows obviously play a major role. To check whether the produced milk conforms to the quality standards of the dairy farm, a sensor is attached to the output channel. Depending on the desired quality characteristics,

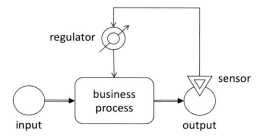

Figure 11.1 One-step, organization-level business control model.

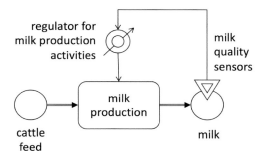

Figure 11.2 Application example of one-step business control model.

the sensor may measure for example the fat content of the produced milk. The measurements are sent to the regulator, which checks whether these are within the targeted bounds. If the milk does not confirm to quality requirements, the regulator instructs the business process to change parameters of the milk production process. In essence, the control loop is not so much different from the way you control the temperature in your house by manipulating your thermostat device.

11.2.2 *Chain-level business outcome control level*

In the previous subsection, we have looked at a control model for a single organization. In this model, a feedback loop is implemented to manage the quality of the output of an organization according to its own criteria. In this subsection, we extend this notion to chains of organizations with an inter-organizational control mechanism to enable business outcome management.

In Figure 11.3, we see a simple business chain of two organizations [GWK+21]. For reasons of brevity, we have kept the chain short, but the principle can be extended to chains of arbitrary length. In the chain, we see that the output of the first organization, the provider, is the input for the second organization, the customer. Following outcome thinking, there is a feedback loop from the output of the customer to the process of the provider. The sensor measures quality characteristics of the output of the customer in its environment and sends its data to the regulator of the business process of the provider. This way, the provider can adapt its process such that the quality of the customer's output is optimized. Obviously, both organizations can also have their local control loops to manage internal quality characteristics, as discussed in the previous subsection.

We illustrate this chain-level control model with an extension of the earlier milk production case, shown in Figure 11.4. In this case, the milk producer is the provider in the chain and the ice cream factory is the customer. Milk is the output of the provider and the input of the customer. To support the ice cream factory in achieving its best outcomes, the sensor measures quality characteristics of the ice cream that can be influenced by the milk producer, like the fat content of the ice cream, as this can be influenced by the fat content of the delivered milk. To support this feedback mechanism, the regulator can control characteristics of the milk production process, like the amount of skimming of the milk. In doing so, the dairy farm can sell 'perfect' milk for ice cream production and be remunerated based on the 'level of perfection' of the milk as demonstrated by the measured quality of the ice cream.

Obviously, the use of an outcome mechanism as shown in Figure 11.4 does not exclude the use of local quality control loops – in practice, a combination usually makes sense, as shown in Figure 11.5. Here we see (shown grayed in the figure) that a local control loop exists for managing the temperature of the produced ice cream. But we do not focus on these local control loops in this chapter.

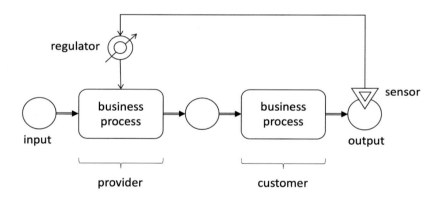

Figure 11.3 Multi-step, chain-level business outcome control model.

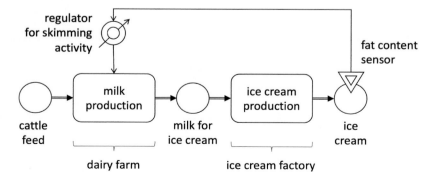

Figure 11.4 Outcome management for ice cream production.

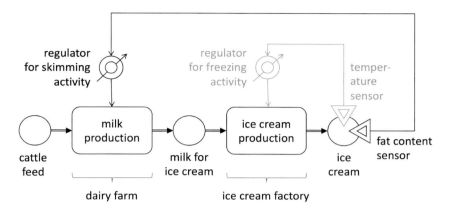

Figure 11.5 Example of combination of outcome management and local quality management.

11.3 Trust management in outcome-based business

In the previous sections of this chapter, we have discussed the concept and control model for outcome-based business. The control model is based on sharing information between organizations and this information should be trusted by all involved organizations. In this section, we explain how blockchain mechanisms can be used to create trust in this context. But before answering this 'how' question, we will focus on the 'why' question, explaining why this trust is so important in outcome-based business collaborations.

11.3.1 The need for trust

In an outcome management setting (as abstractly shown in Figure 11.3 and applied in Figure 11.4), a provider organization actively contributes to the realization of the outcome of a customer organization. The business relation between provider and customer is governed by this contribution, not by the mere provision of standard products or services. In other words, the customer is not so much interested in the provisioning of products or services, but for the positive effects that the use of these products or services creates in its market. In our ice cream example, the ice cream factory is interested in the way that the milk contributes to good ice cream, not for the milk itself – this is because its aim is to produce good ice cream, not to process milk.

Consequently, the remuneration of the provider by the customer should also be based on the provider's contribution to the outcome. As shown in Figure 11.6, this means that the provider bills the customer based on the measurements of outcomes in the customer's market environment: sensor outputs are used not only for control purposes but also for billing purposes. In the example of ice cream, the milk factory gets paid based on the amount and quality of the ice cream produced, so based on the combination of output counting and sensor measurements.

To have providers and customers agree on bills, they should first agree on the sensor readings during the period that is billed (note that output counting does not require any new technology, so we will ignore this in the following). In other words, the customer

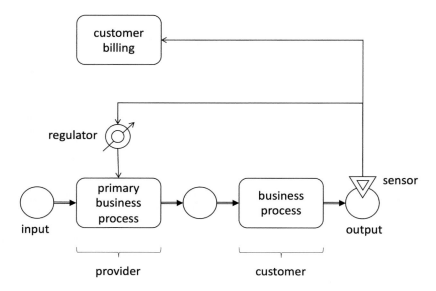

Figure 11.6 Chain-level business outcome control model with billing.

and provider should agree on the quantitative measurements that form the basis for calculating the remuneration. The sensor is, however, typically in the customer's environment and can therefore not be directly read by the provider. This calls for a solution to create a trusted environment for the acquisition, storage, and management of outcome measurements. In the next subsection, we show how blockchain technology can play an important role in this.

11.3.2 Trust management with blockchain

Based on the problem discussed in the previous subsection, we extend the scenario shown in Figure 11.6 with a trusted storage for outcome sensor measurements, which is shared between provider and customer in the scenario. This extended scenario is shown in Figure 11.7. In this figure, we see that a trusted data registry is used to store all outcome measurements that the sensor of the scenario produces. The data in this registry is the basis for the billing of the provider to the customer.

The trusted data registry is also used as a data source for the regulator in the scenario for several reasons. Firstly, this ensures that operational outcome management and outcome-based billing are based on exactly the same data, creating consistency in the business relationship between customer and provider. Secondly, it allows the regulator to take decisions based on mutually agreed time series, i.e., look back at shared business history to take optimal decisions. Thirdly, the data in the registry can be used in a situation where the customer and the provider have a dispute over outcome management decisions taken in the past.

As expected in the context of this book, the trusted data registry is based on blockchain technology as discussed in earlier chapters. We can apply the four business-side

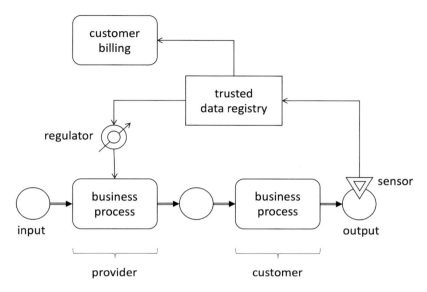

Figure 11.7 Trusted, chain–level business outcome control model with billing.

criteria of the decision model of Chapter 9 to validate whether blockchain is a good solution from a business point of view:

1   *Is an outcome management scenario a multiparty scenario?*
    Answer: Yes, since there are at least one provider and one customer (and often more customers, as we will see further down this chapter).
2   *Is there a trusted authority for business outcome management?*
    Answer: No, as this is a new business paradigm for which trusted third parties (TTPs) in general do not exist.
3   *Does the scenario involve centralized operations?*
    Answer: No, as the customer generates both outcomes and outcome data, and the provider processes the data and provides means for managing the outcomes, the operations are clearly distributed.
4   *Is immutability in data processing beneficial in outcome management?*
    Answer: Yes, as outcome data governs the financial relationship between the provider and customer, this data should be immutable.

So clearly, the answer is a yes for blockchain!

Obviously, using a blockchain–based trusted data registry comes at a cost (as also discussed in Chapter 9). This means that, firstly, there are infrastructure costs for setting up and managing the trusted data registry. Secondly, there are transactional costs to register sensor readings in the trusted data registry and – to a lesser extent – costs for accessing the registry to extract sensor readings. This means that such a registry has to be used in a wise way: it should be set up to offer the required data management functionality at a minimal cost. We address this topic in the next section of this chapter.

11.4 Data processing in outcome management

This section discusses data processing in outcome management scenarios in more detail. In doing so, it elaborates on the models that we have seen in the previous sections. We discuss several topics. First, we discuss the need for trusted preprocessing of sensor data. Next, we pay attention to various types of sensors and regulators in outcome scenarios, creating a basis for a typology of outcome scenarios from a system point of view. We also pay attention to federated data processing, which allows processing data from multiple customers in a single outcome management environment without endangering their business privacy.

11.4.1 Outcome data processing

In the scenario of Figure 11.7, we see that all sensor measurements are directly stored in the trusted data registry, which is based on blockchain technology. Consequently, each sensor reading created a blockchain transaction. As we have seen in earlier chapters of this book, transactions on a blockchain are not cheap, however, because of the involved computational effort. This means that directly storing measurements of a sensor that produces very frequent readings is not a good idea. In our ice cream example, the temperature sensor may produce a reading every second – and we certainly do not want to generate a blockchain transaction every second for this purpose.

To deal with this situation, we can use a blockchain specifically tailored for IoT applications, such as IOTA, which was presented in Section 8.6. Alternatively, we can extend the scenario of Figure 11.7 with a trusted data preprocessor, as shown in Figure 11.8. The aim of this preprocessor is to aggregate the output of a sensor such that we get trusted data at a frequency that is meaningful for the business relation between the customer and provider. For the ice cream case, this may for example be a frequency of

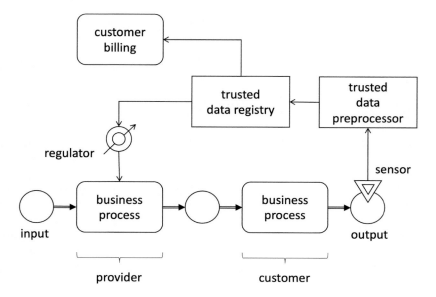

Figure 11.8 Trusted, chain–level business outcome control model with data preprocessing.

once per hour. The data preprocessor needs to be trusted in the same way as the sensor to create trust, for example via certification by a trusted third party.

The level and kind of aggregation of the trusted data preprocessor depend heavily on the business scenario at hand. In the ice cream case, the preprocessor may compute the average of all sensor readings during one hour of operation. In other scenarios, the aggregate function may be the minimum, maximum, or standard deviation of sensor readings, and the level of aggregation may be hugely different. We discuss a detailed case in our main case study on blockchain-based outcome management in Section 11.5 of this chapter.

The trusted data registry may use smart contracts (as discussed in Chapter 4 of this book) to compute the parameters that are used for customer billing. In this way, the remuneration of the provider is determined using immutable business logic implemented into the smart contracts by both parties. The rules in smart contracts can be based on the offline business contracts between the parties. In Section 11.5 we revisit this topic. However, while sharing the output data is fundamental for outcome management, using smart contracts is not strictly required. The provider and the customer can easily reproduce the same outcome measurements as long as they use the same outcome data as input for their calculations.

11.4.2 Types of sensors

Depending on the kind of outcome management scenario, we can have very different kinds of sensors to measure the outcomes. The choice of a sensor technology is called the embodiment of the sensor. The way the sensor function can be embodied depends heavily on the nature of the variables that describe the outcomes to be measured. From a systems point of view, these variables can be divided into three main classes, with corresponding sensor elements:

1 Variables the values of which are recorded in an existing information system of the customer. An example is the number of sales transactions, recorded in the enterprise resource planning (ERP) system of the customer. In this case, the sensor is a software interface to that information system of the customer.
2 Physical variables that can be measured directly in the customer's domain. Examples are the speed of a vehicle or the fat content of ice cream. In this case, the sensor is a physical measuring device in the field of operation of the customer with a software data interchange interface.
3 Non-physical variables that cannot be measured directly in a physical way. An example is the average satisfaction of the customers of the customer organization in the outcome management scenario. In this case, the variables are measured by and stored in a system external to the cybernetic feedback system, such as a social media system. To the cybernetic feedback system, such external systems are black boxes. Hence, the external system is the sensor.

Apart from the embodiment of the sensor, the data provisioning mechanism from sensor to regulator can be organized in two ways, either in a data-push or a data-pull fashion:

1 In the data-push fashion, the sensor element automatically provides the values to the regulator component on a periodic basis. In real-time feedback mechanisms, the period is short and the data takes the form of a continuous data stream.

Table 11.1 Overview of sensor types

	Data-push	Data-pull
Recorded data	(i) data provisioning software module	(ii) data query interface
Physical data	(iii) active IoT device or CPS	(iv) passive IoT device or CPS
External data	(v) external system with data stream subscription mechanism	(vi) external system with data query interface

2 In the data–pull fashion, the regulator element explicitly requests the values from the sensor element. In case of a real-time, continuous data stream, this may imply substantial overheads. In more 'sparse' circumstances, this can avoid unnecessary data transfer.

When we combine the two dimensions of the sensor feedback mechanism, we obtain the six classes of sensor elements shown in Table 11.1 [GWK+21]. We briefly discuss the six classes below.

Class i: data provisioning software module. Pushed recorded data is provided by a software module in an information system that retrieves the data from the data store of that system and sends it on its own initiative to the regulator element of our control framework. Data can be pushed on a periodic basis (such as once per minute) or on the basis of specific events (such as observed threshold values). The provisioning module can either be a standard module of the system or a plug-in inserted into the system for monitoring purposes.

Class ii: data query interface. Pulled recorded data is explicitly requested by the regulator element of our control framework. To enable this, the information system managing the recorded data needs to publish a query interface. The regulator element determines the moments that data is pulled and the exact nature of the data. In a typical outcome economy setting, the source system and the regulator belong to different organizations. This means that the query interface needs to subject to an access control mechanism with precisely defined access rights.

Class iii: active IoT device or CPS. Pushed physical data is provided by an active IoT device containing a measuring instrument or by a cyber-physical system (CPS), i.e., a digital system with physical components, that contains such an instrument. The measuring instrument is the device that performs the actual physical measurement. An example is a digital temperature sensor or a GPS location sensor. In this case, the sensor is 'wrapped' (encapsulated) by the IoT device or CPS that transmits the data resulting from measurements. The IoT device or CPS determines when data is sent and may perform data processing, such as averaging measurements.

Class iv: passive IoT device or CPS. Pulled physical data is provided by an IoT device or CPS like in Class iii, but in this class the IoT device or CPS is passive: it only provides data upon request by the regulator element. Like in Class ii, explicit access control is important in this class. An advanced CPS may have a query interface like the systems in Class ii. A simple IoT device typically has a simpler polling interface.

Class v: external system with data stream subscription mechanism. Pushed external data originates from active external systems that monitor the environment of the customer, which function as a sensor in the feedback loop. Examples of such systems are social media systems, traffic monitoring systems, and stock monitoring systems. Subscriptions are required for a data stream provided by these systems, where the subscription parameters specify the precise kind of data streamed. The streamed data is converted by the regulator element to perform for example sentiment analysis, transport quality analysis, and economic market impact (using the above-mentioned external system types).

Class vi: external system with data query interface. Pulled external data originates from active external systems that function as a sensor, like in Class v. To allow data pulling from the sensor, these systems provide external query interfaces. These query interfaces are often made available in the form of Web Services or public application programming interfaces (APIs). To use these web services or APIs, a subscription may be required.

Note that in the data-pull classes, the regulator does not receive the pulled data directly from the sensor, as this would violate the scenarios of Figures 11.7 and 11.8: the data would not reside in the mutually trusted data registry. Rather, the regulator commands the sensor to output data into the trusted data registry – possibly via a trusted data processor. This is illustrated in Figure 11.9.

Depending on the chosen sensor class and the specifics of the involved sensor, the functionality of the trusted data preprocessor can be determined. This functionality can involve data format transformation and data compression. Data format transformation is required if the format of the sensor data cannot be chosen, for example in class v where the data format is determined by the streaming mechanism and class vi where the format is determined by the remote query API. Data compression is required if the sensor produces greater volumes of data than the blockchain mechanism of the trusted data registry can handle, either for reasons of performance or cost (see the discussion in Chapter 8 of this book on handling data from the IoTs). If for example in a class iii scenario, raw IoT or CPS data (i.e., without aggregation by the sensor) is sent, the trusted data preprocessor typically needs to perform data aggregation or filtering to prevent overloading of the trusted data registry.

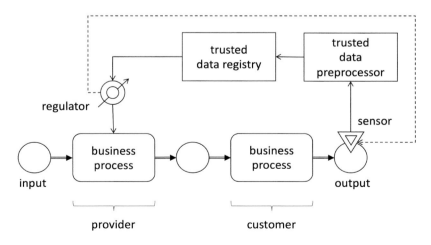

Figure 11.9 Regulator pulling preprocessed data from Class IV sensor.

11.4.3 Types of regulators

Similar to the embodiment of the sensor element in the cybernetic feedback mechanism (as discussed in the previous subsection), we can classify the types of embodiment of the regulator element. We focus on classifying the functionality of the data processing by the regulator, based on Gartner's ambition levels for data analytics [Gar12]. The lowest ambition level in this classification is formed by descriptive analytics, which uses data to merely describe what has happened in a situation under analysis. The second level of ambition is formed by diagnostic analytics, which not only analyses data to show what has happened, but also why it has happened (by searching for correlations or even causalities in the data). The third level is formed by predictive analytics, which uses data to predict what will happen in the situation under analysis (for example by extrapolating patterns in the data). The fourth and highest ambition level is that of prescriptive analytics, which uses data to construct a prescriptive model of the situation that tells the user what to do to reach specific objectives.

Following Gartner's four ambition levels from the low to the high ambition level, we have the following four classes of regulators for outcome management [GWK+21], summarized in Table 11.2:

Class a: descriptive regulator. A descriptive regulator interprets data from the sensor element in the customer environment and produces descriptions of this data, i.e., summarizes what happened in the market environment of the customer. Interpretation of this information is performed completely manually by the focal organization. A descriptive regulator typically requires rather simple analytics technology, so realization should not be problematic. The level of automation in the feedback mechanism is low in this case, however.

Class b: diagnostic regulator. A diagnostic regulator interprets data from the sensor element in the customer environment and produces diagnoses for the events that happened in the market environment of the customer in terms of the business process of the focal organization. To do so, it typically also requires measurements from the sensor element local to the customer. This provides the focal organization with input for reactively tuning its business process to optimize the outcome for its customer.

Class c: predictive regulator. A predictive regulator interprets data from the sensor element in the customer environment (and the local sensor of the focal organization) to generate predictions of the effects that changing the business process of the focal organization can have on the outcome of the customer organization. This enables the focal organization to tune its business processes proactively to optimize the outcome for its customer.

Class d: prescriptive regulator. A prescriptive regulator interprets data from the sensor element in the customer environment (and the local sensor of the focal organization) to generate models that prescribe the optimal parameters for the business process of the focal organization to optimize the outcome of its customer. Prescriptive analytics is the most advanced class of analytics, but it is considered in industry, e.g., for manufacturing [VHK19]. We propose its use in an outcome-based supply chain that requires a high level of automation. Using a prescriptive regulator means that human participation in data processing in the cybernetic feedback mechanism can be avoided in principle. If the prescriptive regulator can also

Table 11.2 Basic types of regulators

Type	Level of complexity	Level of automation
(a) Descriptive	Low	Low
(b) Diagnostic	Low–Medium	Medium
(c) Predictive	Medium–High	Medium
(d) Prescriptive	High	High

autonomously control the business process of the focal organization, we obtain a fully automated control loop. For example, this can be accomplished in manufacturing by linking it to a manufacturing process management system [EGV+18].

By selecting the right combination of sensor class and regulator class, we obtain a characterization of an outcome management scenario that can be used to select the right technology and systems to realize the blockchain-based, digital support for the scenario. Before we apply this in an elaborated business scenario, we need to deal with one more ingredient in the next subsection: the issue of multiple customers.

11.4.4 Federated data processing

So far in this chapter, we have discussed outcome management between a single provider and a single customer. In business practice, however, we may have a situation in which one provider serves multiple similar customers. In our ice cream example, a milk producer may serve one large ice cream factory, but also several small, artisanal ice cream factories. In the case that there are multiple similar customers, there is a good chance that these customers are competitors in the same market. This means that they will not be happy to send their outcome data to a registry that is also used by the other customers – after all, outcome data is very sensitive when it comes to competition! But if we would analyze the data on a per-small-customer basis, we may have too little data to get to the right outcome management decisions. For this reason, we have to extend the outcome management scenario such that we can use all data but the customers do not have to send sensitive outcome data to the trusted data registry.

   This extended scenario is illustrated in Figure 11.10. For reasons of simplicity, we show two customers (A and B), but the scenario can be trivially extended to an arbitrary number of customers. For data processing, we now use a so-called federated mechanism [GWK+21], using a federated regulator on the provider side and federated trusted data preprocessors on the customer side, which engage in federated learning [LB22] [LWW+21], a distributed type of data analytics.

   In distributed learning, part of the analytics functionality is moved from a central analytics module (in our outcome management case this is the regulator) to a set of decentral analytics modules (in our case these are the trusted data preprocessors). The decentral analytics modules perform part of the analytics functionality such that all sensitive detailed data elements are processed into more abstract data descriptors, which are subsequently sent to the central analytics module (in our scenario via the trusted data registry). The central analytics module knows how to combine these abstract data descriptors into new information. In learning about the data, it can send new versions of the decentral part of the analytics logic to the decentral modules, such that

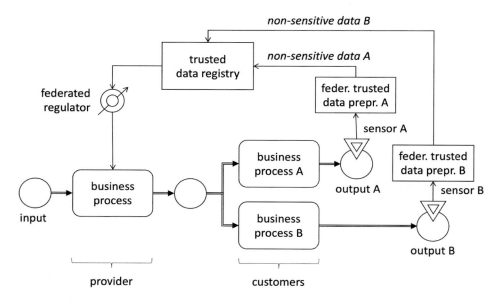

Figure 11.10 Federated data processing.

we get a distributed (federated) learning system. In this way, it is possible to perform data analytics across competing business organizations without violating their business privacy.

Now we have all the ingredients to describe a full-blown outcome management scenario around blockchain technology, we move to such a scenario in the next section.

11.5 A case study in sea container transport

This section is devoted to a case study to illustrate the theory that we have seen so far in this chapter. The case study is based on a business case developed by a large IT service provider for large sea container logistics operators [Ato21]. Below, we first outline the case from a business perspective. Then, we design the outcome management scenario with a single customer. Next, we discuss the technology embodiment of this scenario around a blockchain–based trusted data registry. Then, we extend the scenario to multiple customers using a federated learning mechanism. Finally, we place the technology of the developed scenario in the context of the reference architecture that we have discussed in Chapter 4 of this book.

11.5.1 Case outline

One of the main elements in international goods trading is the transport of these goods by sea containers. On long routes (often intercontinental), these sea containers are transported on large container vessels. To illustrate the 'size' of this business: in 2016, the Port of Rotterdam alone handled approximately 7.4 million sea containers [Por17]. A single large container ship can transport over 10,000 large (40 foot) sea containers.

A substantial part of the cost of this container transport is formed by the fuel costs of the container vessels. Reducing fuel consumption is therefore a promising way to reduce transportation costs (and in doing so, reduce the CO2 emissions of the transportation process). Reducing transportation costs improves the position of a shipping line on the global market. Reducing fuel consumption can be achieved by smart management of the engines of the container vessels – for example by carefully calculating the required engine power on specific parts of a trip in order to not waste any power. These calculations are made by advanced software, as too many variables are involved to arrive at optimal human estimates.

A large, international IT firm has created such software to offer this in an outcome-based scenario to shipping lines that operate large container vessels [Ato21]. This means that the IT firm does not get paid for the delivery of the software to the shipping line, but for the effect that the use of the software has on the reduction of fuel consumption of a fleet of vessels, i.e., for the fuel reduction outcome. We use this business case as the basis for the case scenario elaboration in the rest of this section, but have modified it in some respects for didactic purposes.

11.5.2 *Conceptual model with one customer*

In Figure 11.11, we see the conceptual model of the outcome-based fuel consumption management scenario. In the scenario, the IT firm acts as the provider in the role of business intelligence (BI) provider. The scenario contains a single shipping line as the customer. One shipping line can employ many container vessels, however. For reasons

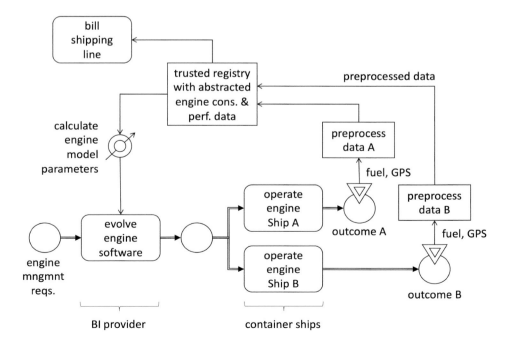

Figure 11.11 Conceptual model of container transport case.

of simplicity, we show two container vessels only: Ship A and Ship B – the extension to more container vessels is straightforward.

The scenario is built around a trusted data registry that contains abstracted engine fuel consumption and performance data of the ships involved in the scenario. This data registry needs to be trusted as it is the sole basis for the BI provider for billing the shipping line: only the outcomes are 'sold', not the BI software.

The main operation of the BI provider is to evolve the engine management software for the ships. The basis of the software is formed by the overall engine management requirements, which are input for the BI provider. The software is evolved either by improving the algorithms or the parameters used by the algorithms. New versions of the software or parameters are next forwarded to the involved ships to be deployed there. The effects of the use of the software on the ships are measured by sensors on board that measure fuel consumption and the position of the ship (the scenario has been simplified here for the sake of clarity).

These sensors are in principle IoT devices: hardware devices that make measurements of physical variables in the context of a physical ship: the current fuel consumption of the engine of a ship (for example, by a fuel flow sensor in the fuel line between the fuel tank and engine) and the current physical position of the ship (typically by a GPS sensor), such that the speed and direction of the ship can be calculated across measurements. As these sensors can make very frequent measurements, a preprocessor is needed to aggregate the measurements to a frequency that makes sense for the regulator in the scenario. The class of sensors in this scenario is Class iii: active IoT device or CPS (see Table 11.1). The sensors are of the IoT type, as they are not embedded in a complex CPS.

The trusted data registry should be able to store the sensor measurements sent (i.e., pushed) by a large fleet of container vessels. Transactions on the registry are frequent but small in data size. The data registry is accessible by both the BI provider and the shipping line, such that a transparent situation exists for outcome-based billing. It should guarantee a high level of trust in both directions.

The regulator element in the scenario calculates the engine model parameters. The parameters should be predictive: they should be the basis for better performance of the ships in the future. Hence, the class of the regulator in this scenario is Class c: predictive regulator. Using the predictions of the regulator, a new version of a prescriptive engine management software module is constructed in the main process of the BI provider. The frequency of this process is low, for example once a week.

Summarizing, this is an outcome management scenario as shown in Table 11.3.

Table 11.3 Summary of container transport fuel management scenario with one customer

Registry	Transactions		Trust		
	Frequency: high	Size: small	Level: high		Direction: both
	Class	Number	Frequency	Aggregation?	Federated?
Sensor	iii: active IoT	many	High (second)	Yes: averaging	No
Regulator	c: predictive		Low (week)		

11.5.3 Technical model with one customer

In Figure 11.12, we see the technical embodiment of the conceptual scenario of the container transport fuel management scenario in Figure 11.11, based on the characteristics of the scenario as discussed and partly summarized in Table 11.3.

For the trusted data registry, we obviously choose a blockchain solution. We are working with real-time data, which can lead to high frequencies of updates and large data volumes. Even though there is local data aggregation at the individual ships, working with a large fleet of ships can still lead to substantial data flows, which the blockchain platform should be able to handle. This leads to the challenges of combining the IoTs with blockchain technology that we discuss in Chapter 8 of this book.

The trusted data registry receives its data via satellite links from the ships. As satellite links are less dependable than 'wired' links, there may be problems with data transmission, which should be taken into account.

On the data provisioning side, the ships are equipped with physical sensors that have IoT-like characteristics. To reduce data streams (as discussed before), these sensors are coupled to systems that perform local data aggregation. Both the sensors and these data preprocessing units should be trusted by both parties involved in the scenario. For the shipping line, this is more obvious as these devices are on their ships. For the BI provider, this is less obvious. This means that a form of device certification may be in place.

On the data processing side (i.e., the regulator), we need a predictive data analytics engine that can analyze time series from multiple sources. Given the discussed satellite-based data feeds into the data registry, the analytics engine should be able to cope with missing data items in the time series.

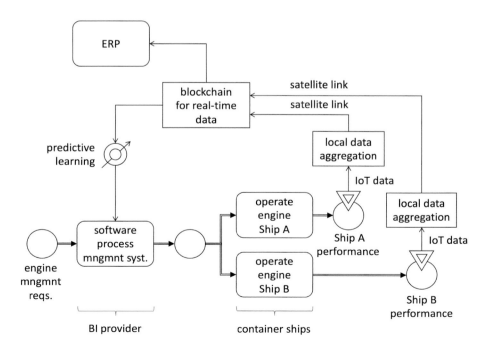

Figure 11.12 Technical model of container transport case with one customer.

Finally, the regulator sends instructions, based on the predictions it has made, to a software process management system. This system manages the evolution of the engine management software that the BI provider creates for the shipping line. These evolutions are parameterized by the instructions from the regulator.

11.5.4 Extending the model to multiple customers

In this subsection, we extend the scenario discussed above to one with multiple customers. We still have a scenario with possibly many ships that produce data, but now these ships are owned by multiple, competing shipping lines. As discussed in Section 11.4.4, this calls for a scenario with a federated learning mechanism to enable data privacy of the individual shipping lines. Even given the data abstraction coming with federated learning, the trust characteristics of the data registry should be even more strict to not introduce any risks with respect to data leaks. As shown in Table 11.4, the summary of the multi-customer scenario stays the same as the single-customer scenario (shown in Table 11.3) except for these two elements.

For reasons of brevity, we omit the conceptual model of the multi-customer scenario, as it is the combination of Figures 11.10 and 11.11. The technical model of the multi-customer scenario is shown in Figure 11.13 (as an extension of Figure 11.12). We see in this model that the data analytics is distributed following the federated learning mechanism. Obviously, this makes the local preprocessors linked to the sensors on the ships more sophisticated, as they perform part of the data analytics.

There is one important additional technical consideration, though that might be overlooked. In the federated learning scenario, the BI provider will generate new versions of the algorithms used in the decentral data preprocessors as part of the overall learning process, and hence needs to distribute new versions of the data preprocessing software to all of the ships involved in the scenario (which may be many). In practice, it may be hard to precisely synchronize updating all the ships at exactly the same time, implying that at some moment data may be generated by different versions of the preprocessing software, leading to confusion in the central predictive federated learning unit. This calls for one of two solutions. The first is using distributed software version control, making sure that decentral new versions are activated in a fully synchronized way, possibly pausing the data feed for a short while. The second is tagging data feed records that are sent to the blockchain-based data registry with the software version that produced them. This allows to either filter the output of the registry at a specific moment in time, or to make the central learning unit smarter to take source version information into account in its analytics functionality.

Table 11.4 Summary of container transport fuel management scenario with multiple customers

Registry	Transactions		Trust		
	Frequency: very high	Size: small	Level: very high		Direction: both
	Class	Number	Frequency	Aggregation?	Federated?
Sensor	iii: active IoT	many	High (second)	Yes: averaging	Yes
Regulator	c: predictive		Low (week)		

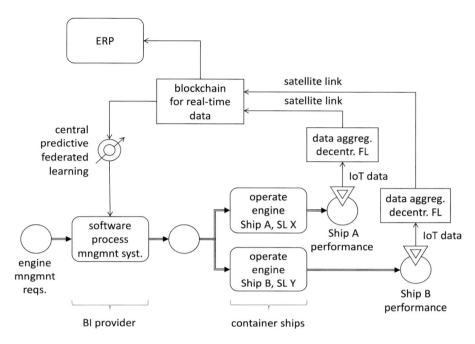

Figure 11.13 Technical model of container transport case with multiple customers.

11.5.5 Placing the technology in the reference architecture

When we place the technology shown in Figure 11.13 in the reference architecture for blockchain applications that we discuss in Chapter 4 of this book, we get the technology setup shown in Figure 11.14. The solid arrows in the figure denote data flows, the dashed arrow denotes the transfer of new software versions.

In the data layer at the bottom of the figure, we see the modules that generate and preprocess the data in the individual ships. As there are typically multiple ships, we have shown multiple boxes of each type. The decentral federated learning modules each send their outputs to the smart contracts module in the blockchain layer in the middle of the figure. As discussed before, this is done in a data–push mode (see Table 11.4).

The smart contracts module in the blockchain layer (see Chapter 4 of this book) processes the incoming data from the data layer. It contains the rules to check whether the data conforms to the business relation between the BI provider and the shipping lines (as typically stipulated in bilateral, offline contracts between the BI provider and each of the shipping lines). The smart contracts module stores all approved data in the ledger. When the BI provider is entitled to bill a shipping line, the smart contracts module informs the business layer of the BI provider with the appropriate data. As we mentioned in Section 11.4.1., smart contracts can also be used to implement at least part of the outcome measurement business logic. We do not consider this explicitly in Figure 11.14. In other words, the smart contracts in the figure are used only to validate and store the data injected from the data layer.

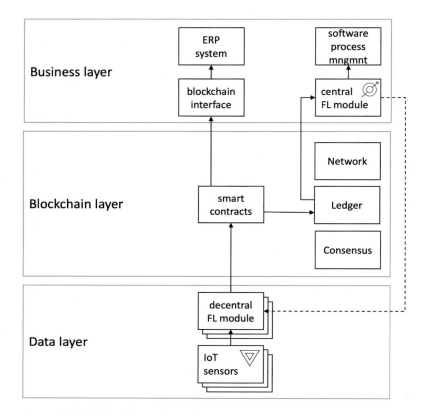

Figure 11.14 Technology of container case study in blockchain reference architecture.

The business layer contains two parts of the BI provider logic: the outcome management part (on the right-hand side in the figure) and the billing part (on the left-hand side in the figure).

In the outcome management part, the central federated learning module (i.e., the regulator of out control model) pulls data from the blockchain ledger. Using this data it updates its outcome prediction model and sends this to the software process management system. This system takes care that new versions of the software for the ships are created when necessary and sends these new versions to the individual ships (as shown by the dashed line in the figure). Note that this dashed line 'completes the control loop', which is essential for any cybernetic control system [Wik22]. For reasons of brevity, we omit the details of the software transport and installation mechanism here.

In the billing part, messages from the smart contracts arrive at a blockchain interface. We have included this interface because we assume that the ERP system does not include a blockchain interface. The blockchain interface formats the received data such that the ERP can process it and sends it to the ERP system. There, it is used as the basis for billing each of the shipping lines when the business outcomes of the shipping lines allow this.

11.6 Business model design for outcome management

In this section, we revisit the concept of the business model as we have seen in Chapter 10 of this book and apply it to outcome-based business scenarios. By working with business models, we can elaborate on the business-wise viability of outcome management scenarios. We do this by analyzing the contributions of the parties participating in a scenario (do they need to be in the scenario?) as well as their costs and benefits (do they want to be in the scenario?).

In this section, we first look at choosing a business model specification technique and using it in the right way. Next, we discuss an example from the sea container transport case that we have seen earlier in this chapter.

11.6.1 Choosing a business model specification technique

In the previous chapter, we have seen that there are different business model specification techniques. In particular, we have discussed the business model canvas and the business model radar techniques as examples of available techniques. The canvas technique is more appropriate for an inside-out description of a business model, whereas the radar technique is more appropriate for an outside-in description of a business model. When we specify blockchain-based, outcome management business models, we can obviously use these techniques as well.

When we view a blockchain-based, outcome management business model strongly from the BI provider perspective, we can use the business model canvas technique. In this case, the BI provider is the focal company of the canvas. The blockchain platform provider becomes a key partner in the business model. Possibly, there are other key partners. The customer of the outcome scenario obviously becomes the customer in the business model canvas.

When we view an outcome management business model from the ecosystem perspective, we better use the business model radar technique. In this case, the BI provider becomes the orchestrator of the business model, the outcome customer becomes the customer of the business model and the blockchain platform provider becomes an additional party. Possibly, there are one or more other additional parties. In the next subsection, we show an example of the use of the business model radar technique based on the case study in the previous section of this chapter.

11.6.2 An example business model for the sea container case

In Figure 11.15, we see a business model radar of the sea container case study of the previous section. The business model radar is for the variation with a single customer. Note that we show 'a' business model radar and not 'the' business model radar, as there are more ways to design it.

In our design shown in the figure, we have taken reduced fuel usage as the outcome to optimize the scenario that the business model describes. This outcome is used as the value-in-use of the radar. We see four parties in the business model radar.

The customer party on the radar is the shipping line. Its actor value proposition is formed by the outcome data. Its coproduction activities consist of running the local data infrastructure onboard the sea vessels and the provisioning of data. Its benefit is formed by reduced fuel costs. Its cost is the share of the benefit that it has to pay to the

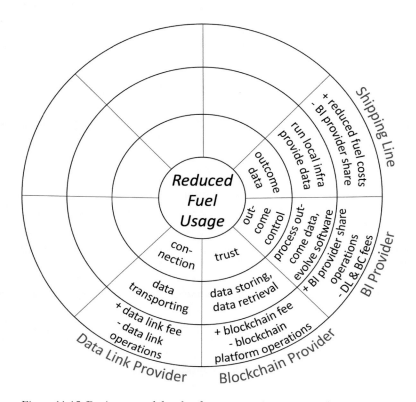

Figure 11.15 Business model radar for sea container case with one customer.

BI provider. We have not included the costs of ruining the local data infrastructure as we assume that these costs are negligible in the business model.

The orchestrate of the party in the radar is the BI provider. Its actor value proposition is outcome control. Its coproduction activities consist of processing the outcome data and evolving the outcome management software. The BI provider receives a share of the financial benefits of the customer as its benefit. Its costs are formed by operations costs and the fees it has to pay to the data link provider and the blockchain provider.

The blockchain provider brings trust as its actor value contribution. The data link provider brings connection as a value. Both these providers are paid by the BI provider.

This means that the BI provider is the central party in the ecosystem with respect to financial flows. This is a design choice for which there are alternatives. For example, all three providers on the radar might get compensated directly by the customer. The choice that we have made is based on the idea that the BI provider offers a complete solution to the customer and hence manages the financial flows in the ecosystem.

11.7 Conclusions

In this chapter, we have seen outcome management scenarios as complex, cybernetic business scenarios in which blockchain forms a backbone for trusted data management.

Trusted data management is essential in outcome management scenarios, as data forms the only basis for the financial transactions between the customer and the outcome management provider in the scenario. Smart contracts, as a part of a blockchain mechanism, can be used to further increase trust in data processing related to customer outcome management and provider remuneration.

We have discussed a case study in container transport that shows a complex application scenario for blockchain technology. Plotting the scenario onto our reference architecture for blockchain shows how a scenario structure maps to a technology structure.

The case study also shows that in real-world outcome management scenarios, we need to combine blockchain technology with other digital technologies. Blockchain provides the trust aspect but there are more digitally supported aspects that require other technologies. In the container transport scenario, these are data analytics and federated learning technologies, internet-of-things (IoT) technologies and (wireless) data transport technologies. When designing full-blown scenarios in which trust in data is essential, blockchain is an important technology, but cannot be used to address all aspects.

Finally, we have seen how the business model techniques discussed in the previous section can be used to model the business aspect of outcome management scenarios.

11.8 Questions and exercises

1 In this chapter, we have discussed a case study from the logistics business domains. Can you think of other business domains in which blockchain-based outcome management is applicable? (Hint: there are many!) The criterion is that the domain contains clear, quantifiable customer outcomes and an explicit trust relation required to enable outcome-based billing from provider to customer.

2 In Section 11.5, a case study for outcome management in a sea container transport by large sea vessels is described. Would it be possible to design a similar scenario for transport of sea containers by trucks (one of the modes of transport to get a container from a sea vessel to the ultimate destination), with trucking companies as customers. If not, why not? If yes, what are the main differences with the sea vessel scenario?

3 What kind of rules would be included in the smart contracts shown in Figure 11.14? Note that the smart contracts have dual purposes!

4 In Section 11.4, the conceptual model for the container shipping scenario with multiple customers has been omitted. Construct this model and check it for consistency with the technical model in Figure 11.13.

5 Extend the business model radar of Figure 11.15 to the case with multiple customers (and hence a federated learning mechanism), as discussed in Section 11.4 Consider whether it is necessary to extend the slice structure of the radar (i.e., whether the set of participating parties changes).

6 Try and create the business model canvas version of the business model radar in Figure 11.15. Use the hints in Section 11.6.1 and the examples of the application of the business model canvas in Chapter 10 as starting points for guidance and inspiration.

7 Use the technical decision model of Chapter 9 to determine whether the case study of Section 11.5 should use a public or private blockchain infrastructure. Discuss whether it makes a difference whether there is one customer or there are many customers.

References

[Acc15]   Accenture (2015). *Digital Business Era: Stretch Your Boundaries. Accenture Technology Vision 2015.* Dublin: Accenture.

[AZ01]   Amit, R., & Zott, C. (2001). Value creation in eBusiness. *Strategic Management Journal, 6–7*(22), 493–520. https://doi.org/10.1002/smj.187.

[ABB+18]   Androulaki, E., Barger, A., Bortnikov, V., Cachin, C., Christidis, K., De Caro, A., … & Yellick, J. (2018). Hyperledger fabric: A distributed operating system for permissioned blockchains. *Proceedings of the Thirteenth EuroSys Conference,* 1–15. https://doi.org/10.1145/3190508.3190538.

[Ant17]   Antonopoulos, A. M. (2017). *Mastering Bitcoin [AsciiDoc].* Mastering Bitcoin. https://github.com/bitcoinbook/bitcoinbook (Original work published 2013).

[AW18]   Antonopoulos, A. M., & Wood, G. (2018). *Mastering Ethereum: Building Smart Contracts and Dapps.* Sebastopol, CA: O'Reilly Media.

[AHL+16]   Arasteh, H., Hosseinnezhad, V., Loia, V., Tommasetti, A., Troisi, O., Shafie-khah, M., & Siano, P. (2016). Iot-Based Smart Cities: A Survey. *In Proceedings of the 2016 IEEE 16th International Conference on Environment and Electrical Engineering (EEEIC)* (pp. 1–6).

[ASC69]   *ASCII Format for Network Interchange* (Request for Comments RFC 20) (1969). Internet Engineering Task Force. https://doi.org/10.17487/RFC0020.

[Ato21]   Atos (2021). *Smart Connected Vessels: Commercial Model.* Atos Codex IoT Services CT-200402. Bezons: Atos.

[AIM10]   Atzori, L., Iera, A., & Morabito, G. (2010). The internet of things: A survey. *Computer Networks,* 54(15), 2787–2805.

[Bac02]   Back, A. (2002). HashCash – A denial of service counter-measure. http://www.hashcash.org/papers/hashcash.pdf.

[Bar16]   Barkai, J. (2016). *The Outcome Economy: How the Industrial Internet of Things Is Transforming Every Business.* Createspace Independent Publishing Platform.

[BWW+07]   Behrens, T. E., Woolrich, M. W., Walton, M. E., & Rushworth, M. F. (2007). Learning the value of information in an uncertain world. *Nature Neuroscience, 10*(9), 1214–1221.

[BL17]   Bernstein, D. J., & Lange, T. (2017). Post-quantum cryptography. *Nature, 549*(7671), Article 7671. https://doi.org/10.1038/nature23461.

[Bro09]   Brown, D. R. L. (2009). *SEC1: Elliptic Curve Cryptography, Certicom Research.* https://www.secg.org/sec1-v2.pdf.

[Bro18]   Brown, R. G. (2018). *The Corda Platform: An Introduction.* https://www.corda.net/wp-content/uploads/2021/11/corda-platform-whitepaper.pdf.

[CCM21]   Comuzzi, M., Cappiello, C., & Meroni, G. (2021). An Empirical Evaluation of Smart Contract-Based Data Quality Assessment in Ethereum. In J. González Enríquez, S. Debois, P. Fettke, P. Plebani, I. van de Weerd, & I. Weber (Eds.), *Business Process*

Management: Blockchain and Robotic Process Automation Forum (pp. 51–66). Springer International Publishing. https://doi.org/10.1007/978-3-030-85867-4_5.

[CNK+16]   Connerty, M., Navales, E., Kenney, C., & Bhatia, T. (2016). Manufacturing companies need to sell outcomes, not products. *Harvard Business Review.* https://hbr.org/2016/06/manufacturing-companies-need-to-sell-outcomes-not-products.

[Dai98]   Dai, W. (1998). *B-Money.* http://www.weidai.com/bmoney.txt.

[Dav72]   Davidson, P. (1972). Money and the real world. *The Economic Journal, 82*(325), 101–115.

[DF19]   De Michele, R., & Furini, M. (2019). IoT Healthcare: Benefits, Issues and Challenges. In *Proceedings of the 5th EAI international conference on smart objects and technologies for social good* (pp. 160–164).

[DLM+18]   Dumas, M., La Rosa, M., Mendling, J., & Reijers, H. A. (2018). *Fundamentals of Business Process Management,* Second Edition. Heidelberg: Springer.

[EGV+18]   Erasmus, J., Grefen, P., Vanderfeesten, I., & Traganos, K. (2018). Smart hybrid manufacturing control using cloud computing and the internet-of-things. *Machines, 6,* 62.

[EW99]   Evans, P., & Wurster, T. (1999). *Blown to Bits: How the New Economics of Information Transforms Strategy.* Boston, MA: Harvard Business School Press.

[Fra18]   Frank, S. (2018). *Control Theory Tutorial: Basic Concepts Illustrated by Software Examples.* Cham: Springer.

[Gar12]   Gartner (2012). *Magic Quadrant for BI Platforms – Analytics Value Escalator.* Gartner.

[Gre21]   Greengard, S. (2021). *The Internet of Things.* Cambridge: MIT Press.

[Gref15]   Grefen, P. (2015). *Service-Dominant Business Engineering with BASE/X: Business Modeling Handbook.* Eindhoven: Independently Published.

[Gref16]   Grefen, P. (2016). *Beyond e-Business: Towards Networked Structures.* Abingdon: Routledge.

[Gref16a]   Grefen, P (2016). *Business Information System Architecture* (Fall 2016 Edition). Eindhoven: Eindhoven University of Technology.

[GLT+18]   Grefen, P., Ludwig, H., Tata, S., Dijkman, R., Baracaldo, N., Wilbik, A., & D'Hondt T. (2018). Complex Collaborative Physical Process Management: A Position on the Trinity of BPM, IoT and DA. In *Collaborative Networks of Cognitive Systems* (pp. 244–253). Berlin: Springer. https://doi.org/10.1007/978-3-319-99127-6_21.

[GLv+13]   Grefen, P., Lüftenegger, E., van der Linden, E., & Weisleder, C. (2013). *BASE/X: Business Agility through Cross-Organizational Service Engineering.* Beta Working Paper 414. Eindhoven: Beta Research School.

[GT17]   Grefen, P., & Türetken, O. (2017). Advanced business process management in networked e-business scenarios. *International Journal of E-Business Research, 13*(4), 70–104. https://doi.org/10.4018/IJEBR.2017100105.

[GWK+21]   Grefen, P., Wilbik, A., Kuitems F., & Blanken, M. (2021). Outcome-Based Business Design in IoT-Enabled Digital Supply Chain Transformation. In *Procs. IEEE International Conference on Internet of Things and Intelligence Systems* (pp. 28–34). https://doi.org/10.1109/IoTaIS53735.2021.9628770.

[GR16]   Grossmann, W., & Rinderle-Ma, S. (2016). *Fundamentals of Business Intelligence.* Berlin: Springer.

[HKG+20]   Hasselgren, A., Kralevska, K., Gligoroski, D., Pedersen, S. A., & Faxvaag, A. (2020). Blockchain in healthcare and health sciences—A scoping review. *International Journal of Medical Informatics, 134,* 104040. https://doi.org/10.1016/j.ijmedinf.2019.104040.

[Haw22]   Hawkins, J. (n.d.). *One Year On, El Salvador's Bitcoin Experiment Has Proven a Spectacular Failure.* The Conversation. Retrieved 3 October 2022, from http://theconversation.com/one-year-on-el-salvadors-bitcoin-experiment-has-proven-a-spectacular-failure-190229.

[Her21]   Hernandez,J.(2021,September7).ElSalvadorJustBecametheFirstCountrytoAccept Bitcoin as Legal Tender. *NPR*. https://www.npr.org/2021/09/07/1034838909/ bitcoin-el-salvador-legal-tender-official-currency-cryptocurrency.

[IOT22]   *IOTA Industry Marketplace*. (2022, 07). Retrieved from IOTA Industry Marketplace: https://industrymarketplace.net/.

[IOT22a]   *IOTA Mobility*. (2022, April). Retrieved from IOTA Foundation: https://www.iota.org/solutions/mobility-and-automotive.

[Jen22]   Jenkinson, G. (2022). NFT market worth $231B by 2030? Report projects big growth for sector. https://cointelegraph.com/news/nft-market-worth-231b-by-2030-report-projects-big-growth-for-sector.

[KT16]   Kohli, R., & Tan, S. S.-L. (2016). Electronic health records: How can is researchers contribute to transforming healthcare? *MIS Quarterly*, *40*(3), 553–574.

[KV22]   Kshetri, N., & Voas, J. (2022). Blockchain's carbon and environmental footprints. *Computer*, *55*(8), 89–94.

[Kum18]   Kumar, A. (2018). *Business Process Management*. Abingdon: Routledge.

[KR19]   Kumar, A. & Rosenbach, E. (2019). The truth about the Dark Web. https://www.imf.org/en/Publications/fandd/issues/2019/09/the-truth-about-the-dark-web-kumar.

[LWW+21]   Li, Q., Wen, Z., Wu, Z., Hu, S., Wang, N., Li, Y.,…, & He, B. (2021). A survey on federated learning systems: vision, hype and reality for data privacy and protection. *IEEE Transactions on Knowledge and Data Engineering*, *35*(4), 3347–3366.

[LR11]   Lidula, N. W. A., & Rajapakse, A. D. (2011). Microgrids research: A review of experimental microgrids and test systems. *Renewable and Sustainable Energy Reviews*, *15*(1), 186–202. https://doi.org/10.1016/j.rser.2010.09.041.

[LB22]   Ludwig, H., & Baracaldo, N., eds. (2022). *Federated Learning: A Comprehensive Overview of Methods and Applications*. Cham: Springer Nature.

[Luf14]   Lüftenegger, E. (2014). *Service-Dominant Business Design*. Eindhoven: Eindhoven University of Technology.

[Mag02]   Magretta, J. (2002). Why business models matter. *Harvard Business Review*, *80*(5), 86–92.

[Mer19]   Meroni, G. (2019). *Artifact-Driven Business Process Monitoring*. Cham: Springer.

[MPV19]   Meroni, G., Plebani, P., & Vona, F. (2019). Trusted Artifact-Driven Process Monitoring of Multi-Party Business Processes with Blockchain. In C. Di Ciccio, R. Gabryelczyk, L. García-Bañuelos, T. Hernaus, R. Hull, M. Indihar Štemberger, A. Kő, & M. Staples (Eds.), *Business Process Management: Blockchain and Central and Eastern Europe Forum* (pp. 55–70). Springer International Publishing. https://doi.org/10.1007/978-3-030-30429-4_5.

[MSD+12]   Miorandi, D., Sicari, S., De Pellegrini, F., & Chlamtac, I. (2012). Internet of things: Vision, applications and research challenges. *Ad Hoc Networks*, *10*(7), 1497–1516.

[MGG+18]   Mühle, A., Grüner, A., Gayvoronskaya, T., & Meinel, C. (2018). A survey on essential components of a self-sovereign identity. *Computer Science Review*, *30*, 80–86. https://doi.org/10.1016/j.cosrev.2018.10.002.

[Nak08]   Nakamoto, S. (2008). Bitcoin: A peer-to-peer electronic cash system. https://bitcoin.org/bitcoin.pdf.

[NXW+22]   Newman, J. I., Xue, H., Watanabe, N. M., Yan, G., & McLeod, C. M. (2022). Gaming gone viral: An analysis of the emerging esports narrative economy. *Communication & Sport*, *10*(2), 241–270.

[NDY13]   Ng, I., Xin Ding, D., & Yip, N. (2013). Outcome-based contracts as new business model: The role of partnership and value-driven relational assets. *Industrial Marketing Management*, *42*, 730–743.

[Nie19]   Nielsen, L. (2019). *Personas—User Focused Design*. Springer. https://doi. org/10.1007/978-1-4471-7427-1.

[Ost04]   Osterwalder, A. (2004). *The Business Model Ontology: A Proposition in a Design Science Approach*. Lausanne: HEC.

[OP10]   Osterwalder, A., & Pigneur, Y. (2010). *Business Model Generation*. Hoboken, NJ: John Wiley & Sons.

[PMC+20]   Popov, S., Moog, H., Camargo, D., Capossele, A., Dimitrov, V., Gal, A.,… & Attias, V. (2020). *The Coordicide*. IOTA Foundation. http://files.iota.org/ papers/20200120_Coordicide_WP.pdf, accessed in July 2022

[Por17]   Port of Rotterdam (2017) *Facts & Figures, A Wealth of Information, Make It Happen*. Rotterdam: Port of Rotterdam.

[Pre10]   Preneel, B. (2010). The First 30 Years of Cryptographic Hash Functions and the NIST SHA-3 Competition. In J. Pieprzyk (Ed.), *Topics in Cryptology—CT-RSA 2010* (pp. 1–14). Springer. https://doi.org/10.1007/978-3-642-11925-5_1.

[PR21]   Preukschat, A., & Reed, D. (2021). *Self-Sovereign Identity*. Shelter Island, NY: Manning Publications.

[RIA01]   Ragab, A. H. M., Ismail, N. A., & Allah, O. S. F. (2001). An efficient message digest algorithm (MD) for data security. *Proceedings of IEEE Region 10 International Conference on Electrical and Electronic Technology. TENCON 2001 (Cat. No.01CH37239)*, *1*, 191–197. https://doi.org/10.1109/TENCON.2001. 949578.

[RTK+16]   Rasouli, M. R., Trienekens, J. J. M., Kusters, R. J., & Grefen, P. W. P. J. (2016). Information governance requirements in dynamic business networking. *Industrial Management & Data Systems*, *116*(7), 1356–1379. https://doi.org/10.1108/ IMDS-06-2015-0260.

[RP00]   Rieffel, E., & Wolfgang, P. (2000). *An Introduction to Quantum Computing for Non-Physicists | ACM Computing Surveys*. https://dl.acm.org/doi/abs/10.1145/ 367701.367709.

[Riv92]   Rivest, R. L. (1992). *The MD5 Message-Digest Algorithm* (Request for Comments RFC 1321). Internet Engineering Task Force. https://doi.org/10.17487/ RFC1321.

[RSA78]   Rivest, R. L., Shamir, A., & Adleman, L. (1978). A method for obtaining digital signatures and public-key cryptosystems. *Communications of the ACM*, *21*(2), 120–126.

[RTH+18]   Rossberg, A., Titzer, B. L., Haas, A., Schuff, D. L., Gohman, D., Wagner, L.,…& Holman, M. (2018). Bringing the web up to speed with WebAssembly. *Communications of the ACM*, *61*(12), 107–115.

[Sal20]   Salam, A. (2020). *Internet of Things for Sustainable Community Development*. Heidelberg: Springer.

[SAB07]   Schuster, E. W., Allen, S. J., & Brock, D. L. (2007). *Global RFID: The Value of the EPC Global Network for Supply Chain Management*. Heidelberg: Springer.

[SBF+20]   Sedlmeir, J., Buhl, H. U., Fridgen, G., & Keller, R. (2020). The energy consumption of blockchain technology: Beyond Myth. *Business & Information Systems Engineering*, *62*(6), 599–608. https://doi.org/10.1007/s12599-020-00656-x.

[SG96]   Shaw, M., & Garlan, D. (1996). *Software Architecture: Perspectives on an Emerging Discipline*. Prentice Hall.

[SM20]   Silvano, W. F., & Marcelino, R. (2020). Iota tangle: A cryptocurrency to communicate internet-of-things. *Future Generation Computer Systems*, *112*, 307–319.

[SPJ+20]   Sjödin, D., Parida, V., Jovanovic, M., & Visnjic, I. (2020). Value creation and value capture alignment in business model innovation: A process view on outcome-based business models. *Journal of Product Innovation Management*, *37*(2), 158–183.

[SMJ21]   Song, J.-G., Moon, S.-J., & Jang, J.-W. (2021). A scalable implementation of anonymous voting over Ethereum blockchain. *Sensors*, *21*(12), Article 12. https://doi.org/10.3390/s21123958.

[SYZ+21]   Song, Y., Yu, R. F., Zhou, L., Yang, X., & He, Z. (2021). Applications of the Internet of Things (IoT) in smart logistics: A comprehensive survey. *IEEE Internet of Things Journal*, *8*(6), 4250–4274.

[SKM+21]   Stockburger, L., Kokosioulis, G., Mukkamala, A., Mukkamala, R. R., & Avital, M. (2021). Blockchain-enabled decentralized identity management: The case of self-sovereign identity in public transportation. *Blockchain: Research and Applications*, *2*(2), 100014. https://doi.org/10.1016/j.bcra.2021.100014.

[Sza94]   Szabo, N. (1994). *Smart Contracts*. https://www.fon.hum.uva.nl/rob/Courses/InformationInSpeech/CDROM/Literature/LOTwinterschool2006/szabo.best.vwh.net/smart.contracts.html.

[Sza05]   Szabo, N. (2005). *BitGold*. https://nakamotoinstitute.org/bit-gold/.

[Tru18]   Truby, J. (2018). Decarbonizing Bitcoin: Law and policy choices for reducing the energy consumption of Blockchain technologies and digital currencies. *Energy Research & Social Science*, *44*, 399–410.

[Tur02]   Turban, E., et al. (2002). *Electronic Commerce: A Managerial Perspective*. Upper Saddle River, NJ: Prentice Hall.

[TGG+19]   Turetken, O., Grefen, P., Gilsing, R., & Adali, O. (2019). Service-dominant business model design for digital innovation in smart mobility. *Business & Information Systems Engineering*, *61*(1), 9–29. https://doi.org/10.1007/s12599-018-0565-x.

[VC14]   Van Gorp, P., & Comuzzi, M. (2014). Lifelong personal health data and application software via virtual machines in the cloud. *IEEE Journal of Biomedical and Health Informatics*, *18*(1), 36–45. https://doi.org/10.1109/JBHI.2013.2257821.

[VL04]   Vargo, S., & Lusch, R. (2004). Evolving to a new dominant logic for marketing. *Journal of Marketing*, *68*, 1–17. https://doi.org/10.1509/jmkg.68.1.1.24036.

[VHK19]   Vater, J., Harscheidt, L., & Knoll, A. (2019, March). Smart Manufacturing with Prescriptive Analytics. In In *2019 8th International Conference on Industrial Technology and Management (ICITM)* (pp. 224–228).

[Wik22]   Wikipedia (2022) *Cybernetics* [online]. https://en.wikipedia.org/wiki/Cybernetics (Accessed: September 7, 2022).

[XHL+18]   Xu, Q., He, Z., Li, Z., & Xiao, M. (2018). Building an Ethereum-Based Decentralized Smart Home System. In: *2018 IEEE 24th International Conference on Parallel and Distributed Systems (ICPADS)* (pp. 1004–1009). https://doi.org/10.1109/PADSW.2018.8644880.

[XWS19]   Xu, X., Weber, I., & Staples, M. (2019). *Architecture for Blockchain Applications* (pp. 1–307). Cham: Springer.

[ZGH+21]   Zheng, G., Gao, L., Huang, L., & Guan, J. (2021). *Ethereum Smart Contract Development in Solidity*. Cham: Springer.

[ZXK+17]   Zhong, R. Y., Xu, X., Klotz, E., & Newman, S. T. (2017). Intelligent manufacturing in the context of industry 4.0: A review. *Engineering*, *3*(5), 616–630.

Index